AF608166

THE CATHOLIC UNIVERSITY OF AMERICA
CANON LAW STUDIES
Number 68

THE PAULINE PRIVILEGE

AN HISTORICAL SYNOPSIS AND COMMENTARY

A DISSERTATION

Submitted to the Faculty of Canon Law of the Catholic University of America in Partial Fulfillment of the Requirements for the Degree of

DOCTOR OF BOTH LAWS

BY

DONALD J. GREGORY, S.T.B., J.U.L.
Priest of the Archdiocese of St. Paul

THE CATHOLIC UNIVERSITY OF AMERICA
WASHINGTON, D. C.
MCMXXXI

Nihil Obstat:

VALENTINUS T. SCHAAF, O.F.M., J.C.D.,

Censor Deputatus.

Washingtonii, D. C., die XXX Aprilis, 1931.

Imprimatur:

JACOBUS C. BYRNE,

Administrator Archdioecesis Sancti Pauli.

Sancti Pauli, die I Maii, 1931.

WASHINGTON TYPOGRAPHERS, INC.
WASHINGTON, D. C.

To the Memory of

the

MOST REVEREND AUSTIN DOWLING, D.D.,

Late Archbishop of St. Paul

TABLE OF CONTENTS

PRINCIPAL ABBREVIATIONS

AAS—*Acta Apostolicae Sedis.*
AER—*The American Ecclesiastical Review.*
AkKR—*Archiv für katholisches Kirchenrecht.*
ASS—*Acta Sanctae Sedis.*
CIC—*Codex Iuris Canonici.*
Coll.—*Collectanea S. Congregationis de Propaganda Fide.*
Eph. Th. Lov.—*Ephemerides Theologicae Lovanienses.*
Fontes—*Codicis Iuris Canonici Fontes.*
HPR—*The Homiletic and Pastoral Review.*
Jus Pont.—*Jus Pontificium.*
LQS—*Theologisch-praktische Quartalschrift* (commonly known as *Linzer Quartalschrift*).
Mansi—Mansi, J. D., *Sacrorum Conciliorum Nova et Amplissima Collectio.*
MPL—Migne, J. P., *Patrologiae Cursus Completus—Series Latina.*
MPG—Migne, J. P., *Patrologiae Cursus Completus—Series Graeca.*
NRT—*Nouvelle Revue Théologique.*
Periodica—*Periodica de Re Canonica et Morali Utili praesertim Religiosis et Missionariis.*
S. C. C.—*Sacra Congregatio Concilii.*
S. C. S. Off.—*Sacra Congregatio Sancti Officii.*
ZKT—*Zeitschrift für katholische Theologie.*

FOREWORD

Among the more practical problems of ecclesiastical jurisprudence with which pastors of souls and diocesan officials of the present day are engaged, the Pauline Privilege enjoys perhaps a rank of eminent degree. Especially is this true of the United States of America, where an ascendant non-Catholic population and a Civil Law which permits of divorce upon the slightest provocation, frequently fancied or even fabricated, tend to promote the utility of the Privilege. All ecclesiastical authorities are cognizant of the institution's fundamentals, but it is in the investigation of its finer features that this dissertation devises a sufficient guaranty for its existence.

In the initial stages of the work there has been provided an historical background of minor proportions, more properly, a bare resumé, for no claim is made to perfection in this section. For the most that has been attempted with the sources at hand is an endeavor to ascertain the course of development of the institution and to determine the various factors that influenced the legislation of the past.

In that section concerning the present discipline of the Code, no divagation from the channels of pure and safe doctrine has been suffered; rather, the mind of Holy Church and the common interpretation of approved authors have been the guiding influences in the formation of the text. Controversies have been avoided wherever possible and problems interwoven with the Privilege disregarded, e.g., the power of the Sovereign Pontiff to dissolve *matrimonium legitimum consummatum*, or the validity of Baptism when received in an heretical denomination. And although a doctrine suitable for the Universal Church has been submitted, especial attention has been afforded to a few problems which particularly affect the capacity of the Privilege in the United States.

The writer takes this occasion to express his sincere gratitude to the members of the Faculty of Canon Law for their untiring and able assistance in the preparation of this dissertation; to the librarians of the University Library for their many courtesies; to all, and especially to Miss Helen D. McNulty, who have so generously aided him in the final revision of the text for the press.

INTRODUCTION

§1. *The Indissolubility of the Matrimonial Bond*

If consideration is made of the Law of Nature after the fall and of the Law of Moses, it may easily be seen that marriage had fallen from its original state of honor and purity. For under the Law of Nature we read that the Patriarchs, acting under Divine dispensation, took to themselves many wives at the same time,[1] while according to the Law of Moses it was permissible, should cause exist, to repudiate one's wife by giving her a bill of divorce.[2] Practically all idea of the permanent union of one man and one woman seems to have been lost not only to the pagans but also to the chosen people. And because of the false concepts regarding the indissolubility of marriage prevalent among these peoples, it was imperative that with the coming of Christ a definite stand should be taken with regard to this question.

Thus it was that our Divine Lord on many occasions[3] expressed Himself regarding the indissolubility of the marriage bond, summing up all His doctrine in the precise statement, "What therefore God hath joined together, let no man put asunder."[4] This teaching was equally binding on both man and woman,[5] and it embraced those marriages entered into in infidelity as well as those contracted by Christians.[6] As a consequence of this Divine mandate, and with few exceptions,[7]

---

[1] Genesis, 16:3; cf. "Divorce," *Cath. Encycl.*, IX, 699.

[2] Deuteronomy, 24:1.

[3] Matthew, 5:32; Mark, 10:11-12; Luke, 16:18.

[4] Matthew, 19:6; Mark, 10:9.

[5] "From the fact that the human soul is a moral entity essentially the same whether it energizes a male or a female body, it follows that in either case it is subject to the same moral law."—Fletcher, *Christian Feminism*, p. 11; cf. Leibell, *Readings in Ethics*, p. 792.

[6] Pirhing, *Jus Canonicum*, lib. IV, tit. XIX, n. 36; Schmalzgrueber, *Jus Ecclesiasticum Universum*, lib. IV, tit. XIX, n. 18.

[7] *Matrimonium ratum* may be dissolved by a Papal rescript or by solemn religious profession—Canon 1119. *Matrimonium legitimum* may be dissolved by virtue of the Privilegium Fidei—Canons 1120-1127.

there can only be an absolute violation of matrimony where a second marriage is attempted while one of the parties to a previous union still lives.[8]

§2. *The Marriage of Christians*

When God instituted marriage[9] He also endowed the purely natural contract with the attributes of unity and indissolubility.[10] Christ declared this when He said: "Have ye not read, that he who made man from the beginning, 'made them male and female'? And He said: 'For this cause shall a man leave father and mother, and shall cleave to his wife, and they shall be in one flesh.' " [11] It was from this text that Christ deduced His doctrine and promulgated anew the original Divine law of monogamic and indissoluble marriage.[12] If the Israelites of old had for a time been permitted to forget the severity of the matrimonial bond, it was only because of the hardness of their hearts.[13] No longer was this to be allowed, for the Mosaic bill of divorce was abrogated forever.[14] In the new dispensation Christ had raised marriage to the dignity of a Sacrament,[15] thus making the marriage contract and the Sacrament inseparable;[16] so that in virtue of this legislative act of Christ, whenever the matrimonial consent is given between spouses who are members of the mystical body of Christ through Baptism, there is also effected the Sacrament.[17]

---

[8] Canon 1069, §1; Tournely, *De Matrimonio*, p. 220.

[9] Genesis, 1:27-28; 2:18, 21-24.

[10] Genesis, 2:24; cf. Wernz, *Jus Decretalium*, IV, n. 359.

[11] Matthew, 19:4-5.

[12] Council of Trent, Sess. XXIV, *de matrimonio*, Can. 2; Tournely, *De Matrim.*, p. 220; Pesch, *Theol. Dogmat.*, VII, n. 763; Frassen, *Theol. Dogmat.*, Tract. III, disp. 3, art. 1, n. 4.

[13] Mark, 10:4-5; Schmalzgrueber, *Jus Eccles. Univ.*, lib. IV, tit. XIX, nn. 7-8.

[14] Matthew, 19:9; Schmalzgrueber, *Jus Eccles. Univ.*, lib. IV, tit. XIX, n. 16; c. 8, X, *de divortiis*, IV, 19.

[15] Leo XIII, const. "*Arcanum*," 10 Feb., 1880,—*Fontes*, n. 580; Council of Trent, Sess. XXIV, *de matrimonio*, Can. 1.

[16] Council of Trent, Sess. VII, *de sac. in genere*, Can. 1; Pius IX, "*Syllabus*," a. 1864, ad n. 66,—*Fontes*, n. 543; Leo XIII, const. "*Arcanum*"; Canon 1012, §2.

[17] S. Poenit., instr., 15 Jan., 1866, ad 3,—*Coll.* n. 1280; S. C. S. Off., instr. (ad Praef. Mission. Martinicae, etc.), 6 July, 1817,—*Fontes*, n. 855.

This indissolubility of Christian marriage is further strengthened once the union has been consummated,[18]—a union likened to that existing between Christ and His Church which cannot be broken.[19] This, in short, was the doctrine of Christ[20] and of His Apostles;[21] it has been the steadfast teaching of the Church,[22] as evidenced in the works of the Ecclesiastical Writers and of the Fathers,[23] in the decrees of Councils,[24] in the pronouncements of the Popes,[25] and in the teaching of theologians and canonists.[26]

§3. *The Marriage of Infidels*

If there is no diriment impediment of the natural or of the Divine positive law present,[27] matrimonial consent given between two infidels constitutes a true and indissoluble marriage.[28] And this attribute of indissolubility remains as long as the parties are constant in infidelity. They cannot break the bond by

---

18 Canon 1118.

19 Billuart, *Cursus Theologiae*, XIX, dissert. 5, art. 2, p. 419; Hurter, *Theol. Dogmat.*, III, n. 746.

20 Matthew, 19:6 sq.

21 Romans, 7:2-3; I Cor., 7:10.

22 Cf. Roskovany, *De Indissolubilitate Matrimonii*, p. 4 sq.

23 Tertullian, *De Exhort. Castit.*, c. V; St. Ambrose, lib. I, *De Abraham*, c. VII, n. 59; St. Augustine, *De Bono Conjugali*, c. XVIII, n. 21; c. XXIV, n. 32; St. John Chrysostom, homily XX, *Ep. ad Ephes.*, n. IV.

24 Cf. Nampon, *Catholic Doctrine as Defined by the Council of Trent*, p. 576.

25 Eugene IV, *"Instructio pro Armenis"*; const. *"Exultate Deo,"* 22 Nov., 1439,—*Fontes*, n. 52; Pius IX, ep. *"La lettera,"* 9 Sept., 1852,—*Fontes*, n. 514; Leo XIII, const. *"Arcanum,"* 10 Feb., 1880,—*Fontes*, n. 580.

26 Cf. Petrovits, *The New Church Law on Matrimony*, n. 544.

27 Since they are not members through Baptism of the mystical body of Christ, infidels are not subject to ecclesiastical laws. Cf. Pirhing, *Jus Canon.*, lib. IV, tit. XIX, n. 39; lib. IV, tit. I, n. 146.

28 Matthew, 19:6; I Cor., 7:13; Perrone, *De Matrimonio Christiano*, II, 315; De Coninck, *De Sacramentis et Censuris*, XXVI, dub. 5, n. 55; Pontius, *De Sacramento Matrimonii*, VII, c. 48, n. 1; De Justis, *De Disp. Matrim.*, II, c. 15, n. 25; Benedictus XIV, *De Synodo Dioecesana*, VI, n. 4; Raymundus de Peneforte, *Summa*, IV, 10; Sanchez, *De Sacramento Matrimonii*, VII, disp. 73; Pirhing, *Jus Canon.*, lib. IV, tit. XIX, n. 37; Hurter, *Theol. Dogmat.*, III, n. 760; Lancelloti, *Institutiones Juris Canonici*, lib. II, *de divortiis*, p. 90, *rub.* a; S. C. S. Off., instr. (ad Vic. Ap. Oceaniae Central.), 18 Dec., 1872,—*Fontes*, n. 1024.

mutual agreement, for the marriage consent is not the cause of the indissolubility;[29] the union cannot be severed by a bill of divorce, because that has been abolished under the Christian dispensation;[30] the Roman Pontiff cannot interfere, as infidels are outside of his jurisdiction;[31] nor can the Civil Law dissolve such a marriage, for this power, contrary to Divine Law, was never granted to the State.[32] However, if one member of this infidel union becomes converted to the Christian religion, then under specific circumstances there may be had a perfect separation with the privilege of entering a new marriage.[33] It is with the consideration of these conditions, otherwise known as the Pauline Privilege, that this work is concerned.

---

[29] Schmalzgrueber, *Jus Eccles. Univ.*, lib. IV, tit. XIX, n. 18; Creusen, "Baptême Douteaux et Mariage Indissoluble," *NRT*, LII (1925), 235.

[30] Matthew, 19:9; c. 8, X, *de divortiis*, IV, 19; Schmalzgrueber, *Jus Eccles. Univ.*, lib. IV, tit. XIX, n. 16.

[31] Canon 87; Pirhing, *Jus Canon.*, lib. IV, tit. I, n. 146; Biederlack, "Ueber das sog. Paulinische Privilegium," *ZKT*, VII (1883), 318.

[32] Schmalzgrueber, *Jus Eccles. Univ.*, lib. IV, tit. XIX, n. 18; Grandclaude, *Jus Canonicum*, lib. IV, tit. XIX, p. 171; Creusen, "Baptême Douteaux et Mariage Indissoluble," *NRT*, LII (1925), 235.

[33] I Cor., 7:12-16; c. 8, X, *de divortiis*, IV, 19; Pontius, *De Sacramento Matrimonii*, VII, c. 48, n. 1; Cornely, *Comment. in I Ep. ad Cor.*, p. 182 sq.

PART I
PRELIMINARY DISCUSSION

CHAPTER I

THE FOUNDATION OF THE PAULINE PRIVILEGE IN SACRED SCRIPTURE

ART. I. THE TEXT IN FIRST CORINTHIANS

St. Paul spoke on this subject in his First Epistle to the Corinthians, which was written for the purpose of directing the faithful at Corinth in the many problems that arose in the infant church located there. As it was to a large extent Paul's reply to a letter of inquiry from the Corinthian faithful,[1] it was necessarily of a highly practical nature. And not the least of the topics touched therein was the method of treating marriages contracted in infidelity, where one spouse had later become a convert to Christianity.

The Jews regarded all contact with pagans as a positive defilement,[2] and this reasoning, together with the moral degradation of pagan Corinth, probably induced the Christian converts of that city to question the propriety of continuing marital relations with a heathen husband or wife. Therefore, it is suitable and even necessary that the Pauline passage which constitutes the answer to this problem be quoted in detail.

> For to the rest I speak, not the Lord. If any brother hath a wife that believeth not, and she consent to dwell with him, let him not put her away. And if any woman hath a husband that believeth not and he consent to dwell with her, let her not put away her husband. For the unbelieving husband is sanctified by the believing wife: and the unbelieving wife is sanctified by the believing husband: otherwise your children should be unclean; but now they are holy. *But if the unbeliever depart, let him depart. For a brother or sister is not under servitude in such cases. But God hath called us in peace.* For how

[1] I Cor., 7:1; cf. M'Clymont, *The New Testament and Its Writers*, p. 104.

[2] Acts, 10:14-15, 28; 11:3 sq.; Gigot, *Christ's Teaching Concerning Divorce in the New Testament*, p. 134, note.

> knowest thou, O wife, whether thou shalt save thy husband? Or how knowest thou, O man, whether thou shalt save thy wife? [3]

Art. II. Exegesis of the Text

In this passage there are several elements discernible, the precise intent of which must be determined accurately. The first element consists in the short introductory statement: "For to the rest I speak, not the Lord," which establishes St. Paul's exact purpose in penning the passage. He knows of no pronouncement of Christ on such mixed marriages, and hence, what he has to say of such unions is his own teaching. Yet, because he writes, "I speak, not the Lord," it is not to be concluded that what follows is not a divine command or counsel. The Apostle is not engaged in distinguishing between divine and human precepts or counsels, but between divine precepts as introduced by Christ and divine rules or advices as promulgated by himself. In both cases the doctrine has the sanction of divine authority, for in writing this letter St. Paul exercised the plenitude of the Apostolic authority which he had received from the Lord and under the inspiration of the Holy Ghost.[4]

The second element extends to the end of verse 14, and deals with the case of a mixed marriage wherein the infidel spouse is willing to continue marital relations with the converted party. Here the Apostle decides that in such a case the Christian should continue in the union.[5]

The last element, comprising verses 15 and 16, considers a precisely different kind of marriage that has become a mixed union and in which the pagan consort prefers to sever matrimonial relations with his Christian partner. St. Paul again

---

[3] I Cor., 7:12-16.

[4] MacRory, *The Epistles of St. Paul to the Corinthians*, pp. 94-95; Vermeersch, *De Casu Apostoli seu Fidei Privilegio*, n. 2.

[5] Some exegetes construe this as a positive command that there be no separation; others consider it as mere advice in which the Apostle does not absolutely insist that the Christian party must continue the common life, but that, where possible, he would recommend it. Cf. Cornely, *Comment. in I Ep. ad Cor.*, p. 181.

justifies his decision that, if the unbeliever depart, let him depart.[6]

Retaining this division of the entire passage, there must be determined: (1) to which class of Christians these words were addressed; (2) the validity of their marriages; (3) the nature of the dissolution of the matrimonial bond in this instance, in virtue of the Pauline Privilege.

§1. *The Apostle Speaks of Marriage Contracted in Infidelity*

It is evident that the class to which St. Paul is here speaking is not the same as that mentioned previously in verses 8 and 9, or in 10 and 11.[7] For in verses 8 and 9 he addresses the "unmarried" and the "widows," whereas the group being questioned in verses 12 to 16 is actually bound by the matrimonial tie. And in verses 10 and 11 St. Paul is referring to a marriage in which both parties are Christians. Consequently, in verses 12 to 16 the Apostle strictly considers those who are parties to a mixed union, effected by the conversion of one spouse.[8] This has been the interpretation of the text throughout the ages of Christianity,[9] as witnessed by St. Augustine[10] and reliable exegetes.[11] Furthermore, there is a confirmation of

---

[6] St. Thomas, *Comment. in Omnes Epistolas D. Pauli A.*, I, 321.

[7] Verse 8: "But I say to the unmarried, and to the widows: it is good for them if they so continue, even as I. 9: But if they do not contain themselves, let them marry. For it is better to marry than to be burnt. 10: But to them that are married, not I, but the Lord commandeth, that the wife depart not from her husband. 11: And if she depart, that she remain unmarried, or be reconciled to her husband. And let not the husband put away his wife."

[8] Tertullian, lib. II, *Ad Uxorem*, c. 2—*MPL*, I, 1290; Cornelius a Lapide, *Commentarius in Omnes Divi Pauli Ep.*, p. 193; Gigot, *Christ's Teaching Concerning Divorce*, p. 124; Cornely, *Comment. in I Ep. ad Cor.*, p. 179.

[9] Fahrner, *Geschichte des Unauflöslichkeitsprinzips*, p. 147, says that Tertullian was the first among the Ecclesiastical Writers or the Fathers to speak of the Pauline Privilege. Cf. Tertullian, lib. II, *Ad Uxorem*, c. 2—*MPL*, I, 1290.

[10] Lib. I, *De Sermone Domini in Monte*, c. 16—*MPL*, XXXIV, 1252.

[11] Bernardini, *Opera Omnia*, IV, p. 241; Tirini, *Comment. in I Ep. ad Cor.*, p. 570; Meyer, *Commentary on the New Testament*, p. 202; Calmet, *Comment. Litteralis in Omnes Libros Novi Testamenti*, III, p. 614; Cornely, *Comment. in I Ep. ad Cor.*, p. 179.

this interpretation in the constant practice of the Church, for never does she declare as dissolved a marriage entered into by a Catholic and an infidel when the necessary requirements have been met and the proper dispensation obtained.[12]

§2. *The Validity of Infidel Marriage*

The teaching of the Church has already been touched upon[13] that provided there is no diriment impediment of the natural or Divine positive laws present, the marriage of two infidels, though not a Sacrament, is nevertheless a true and valid marriage.[14] This doctrine is implicitly contained in the words of St. Paul himself, for he gave his approval to the continuation of such a union—a thing impossible of sanction if he considered such cohabitation as intrinsically evil concubinage.

§3. *The Nature of the Dissolution Granted by St. Paul*

But with the conversion to Christianity of one member of this infidel union, then, under certain conditions, there may be had a perfect separation and the right to enter a new marriage.[15] This was a necessary concession granted to the Christian consort lately converted, for in like circumstances the Jewish Law was most strict. During the early days of the Church there were constant occurrences of mixed marriages caused by the conversion of one of the parties, and whenever this happened the Jewish Law was most severe in demanding that the spouse remaining true to Judaism divorce his Christian consort.[16] For according to their system of religion, to continue in such an "unholy" union would be a defilement for the Jewish party.[17]

---

[12] Cf. *infra*, page 55.

[13] Cf. *supra*, pages XIV; S. C. S. Off., 18 June, 1856.—*Fontes*, n. 936.

[14] Tournely, *De Matrim.*, p. 127; Pirhing, *Jus Canon.*, lib. IV, tit. I, n. 146; Hurter, *Theol. Dogmat.*, III, n. 760; Perrone, *De Matrim.*, II, p. 279; *Praelectiones*, IX, *de matrimonio*, C. 2, §2, 4.

[15] Pontius, *De Matrim.*, VII, c. 48, n. 1; c. 8, X, *de divortiis*, IV, 19; Cornely, *Comment. in I Ep. ad Cor.*, p. 182.

[16] Mielziner, *The Jewish Law of Marriage and Divorce*, p. 122; Edersheim, *Sketches of Jewish Life in the Days of Christ*, p. 158; Gigot, *Christ's Teaching Concerning Divorce*, p. 133.

[17] Acts, 10:14-15, 28; 11:3 sq.; Gigot, *op. cit.*, p. 134.

With this article of the Jewish Law in mind, there would be but few converts to Christianity if such conversion could only work hardship on the neophyte. Or, having sought the truth, converts of weak will might lapse back into Judaism when they found themselves deserted by their Jewish partners. Therefore, it was imperative that some consideration be shown to the Christian convert, and with this idea at heart St. Paul mapped out in a very few words the course to be followed—*"If the unbeliever depart, let him depart."*

There can be no doubt but that the Apostle referred to a complete dissolution of the matrimonial bond, and not merely to an imperfect divorce or separation from bed and board.[18] He justifies his action in the words, "For a brother or sister is not under servitude in such cases." But what greater servitude can be thought of than to bind a convert to a spouse who may be a detriment to the practice of the True Faith? [19] And having the Rabbinic legislation before him, it was the intention of St. Paul to grant a privilege to the convert. If, in the words "Let him depart," the Apostle meant only to authorize a separation and not the right to remarry, he would be granting little or nothing; for separation had already become a fact by the departure of the unbeliever. And in declaring the faithful party not to be subject to servitude, St. Paul may reasonably be understood to refer to that species of slavery which would arise from the necessity of remaining unmarried while forced to live apart from the former partner.[20]

Hence, the opinion of the Fathers,[21] the teaching of the Popes,[22] the common view of exegetes, theologians and canonists,[23] and the practice of the Church[24] have always agreed that

---

[18] Van Steenkiste, *Comment. in Omnes S. Pauli Epist.*, I, p. 284.

[19] Corluy, *Spicilegium*, p. 490; Hurter, *Theol. Dogmat.*, III, n. 759, note 2.

[20] MacRory, *The Epistles of St. Paul to the Corinthians*, p. 98.

[21] St. Ambrose, *"In Ep. I ad Cor.,"*—De Journel, *Enchiridion Patristicum*, n. 1307; St. John Chrysostom, *"In Ep. I ad Cor.,"*—*ibid.*, n. 1190.

[22] Innocent III, ep. *"Quanto te magis,"* 1 May, 1199,—c. 7, X, *de divortiis*, IV, 19; ep. *"Guademus in Domino,"* a. 1201,—c. 8, X, *de divortiis*, IV, 19; cf. Denziger, *Enchiridion*, nn. 405, 408.

[23] Cornelius a Lapide, *Comment. in Omnes Divi Pauli Epist.*, p. 193; Tirini, *Comment. in I Ep. ad Cor.*, p. 570; Cornely, *Comment.*, p. 186;

in this passage St. Paul authorized not only a complete dissolution of the matrimonial bond, but the right of remarriage as well.

Art. III. Definition of the Privilege

The Pauline Privilege, also known as the *Casus Apostoli* or the *Privilegium Fidei*, is a canonical institution embracing a special concession granted by St. Paul in consequence of a power divinely conceded to him,[25] by virtue of which a marriage validly contracted and even consummated in infidelity may be dissolved if one of the parties receives Baptism[26] and the one remaining in infidelity departs. But only when the convert enters a new marriage is the former bond dissolved.[27]

Van Steenkiste, *Comment. in Omnes S. Pauli Epist.*, I, p. 284; Pesch, *Theol. Dogmat.*, VII, n. 763; Billuart, *Cursus Theol.*, XIX, dissert. 5, art. 2; Wirceburgensis, *Theol. Dogmat.*, X, p. 521; Benedictus XIV, *De Synodo Dioeces.*, VI, c. 4; XIII, c. 21; Sanchez, *De Matrim.*, VII, disp. 73, 74; Raymundus de Peneforte, *Summa*, IV, 10; Reiffenstuel, *Jus Canonicum Universum*, lib. III, tit. XXXIV, n. 4; and all modern canonists.

[24] S. C. S. Off., (Cochinchin.), 1 Aug., 1759, ad 1,—*Fontes*, n. 810.

[25] "Catholica enim doctrina docemus, auctoritatem humanam, etiam ecclesiasticam, in vinculum veri matrimonii nihil posse, ita ut omnis potestas quam in hac re Ecclesia, etiam per S. Pontificem, exercet, a positiva Dei voluntate et concessione proficiscatur. Ecclesia ministerialem tantum in hac re provinciam gerit."—Vermeersch, *De Casu Apostoli*, n. 2; cf. MacRory, *The Epistles of St. Paul to the Corinthians*, pp. 94-95; *infra*, page ——.

[26] Pichler, *Epitome Juris Canonici*, lib. III, tit. XXXIII, n. 2; Zitelli, *De Dispensationibus Matrimonialibus*, p. 121; Vecchiotti, *De Sacramento Matrimonii*, p. 406; Rupprecht, *Notae Historicae in Universu Jus Canonicum*, lib. IV, tit. I, n. 20; Benedictus XIV, *De Synodo Dioeces.*, VI, c. 4, n. 3. Whether, however, the Privilege is so joined to the Sacrament of Baptism that it belongs to Christian adherents of a non-Catholic denomination when they profess the faith by the reception of Baptism, is a question disputed by authors. This problem will be discussed at greater length in a later chapter. Cf. *infra*, page 50.

[27] Benedictus XIV, ep. "*Postremo Mense,*" 28 Feb., 1747, ad 58,—*Fontes*, n. 377; const. "*Apostolici ministerii,*" 16 Sept., 1747, ad 4,—*Fontes*, n. 381; S. C. C., *Florentina*, 27 July, 1726, and, 29 Mar., 1727, —*Fontes*, nn. 3321, 3324; Feije, *De Imped. et Disp. Matrim.*, n. 498; "Divorce," *Cath. Encycl.*, V, 60.

PART II
HISTORICAL RESUMÉ

CHAPTER II

HISTORICAL DEVELOPMENT OF THE PAULINE PRIVILEGE

The problem relative to marriages between the faithful and infidels, and the particular question concerning the conditions of a marriage contracted between two infidels, when only one of them was converted to Christianity, had been quite essential in the life of the first Christian communities. And the question had preserved its practical influence throughout the conquering march of Christianity in the first four centuries. These first centuries, and those immediately following, saw the triumphant progress of the Gospel, its adoption by the barbarian hordes that swept down from the North and out of the East, and, during the Carolingian period, its final happy intrenchment in the minds and hearts of most nations of the West.

About the year 1000 almost all traces of paganism had been obliterated. Jewish communities, which had thrived in their promised land of Spain, were now everywhere isolated as "foreign colonies within the State," with the result that the continual mixture between Christians and Jews was practised no more. Such combinations could have made our institution most practical, and the fact that it did not become but a mere relic of the past may be laid to the rare conversions of the Jews, which now and then necessitated the application of the Pauline Privilege.

The period between the years 1000 and 1400 is important in the history of the Privilege. For although it appeared to be more removed from real life and was less susceptible to practical application, nevertheless, during the Golden Age of Canon Law it saw its fixation in a form that was to become definite.

In the epoch which immediately followed the great geographical discoveries, the Privilege found a vast field of application in the newly opened mission countries. The 16th and 17th centuries, a period less brilliant and lacking much in interest for the evolution of the majority of canonical institutions, were for the Privilege much more important in many aspects than the Golden Age of Canon Law. And this was generally true as well for the doctrinal questions connected theoretically and practically with the Privilege, relative to the value of marriages contracted in infidelity and to the power of the Church with regard to such marriages.

Continuing in the 18th and 19th centuries, Pontifical Constitutions and Instructions of the Roman Congregations were forthcoming in order to regulate the circumstances under stress of which a convert from paganism might break the matrimonial bond contracted in infidelity. And these same Roman documents reasserted the opinions of theologians on the controvertible questions attached to the institution.

Hence, for the sake of convenience in discussing the historical evolution of the Pauline Privilege, the following conspectus has been divided into three periods: (1) From the grant of the Privilege by St. Paul down to the time of Gratian; (2) from Gratian to the Council of Trent; (3) from the Council of Trent to the codification of ecclesiastical law now in force. This, then, shall be the plan followed in the consideration of the legislative development of the Pauline Privilege down through the centuries.

Art. I. Prior to the Decree of Gratian

§1. *In Roman Law*

When the political history of the first three centuries is fully considered, surprise should not be expressed at finding so few direct and explicit references to the Pauline Privilege. Religion was purely an incorporation of the State, so that when Christianity reared its head, spoke its truths and attacked the religion of the State as false, it was looked upon as a form of treason and its advocates were punished with death.[1] Consequently, until the time of Constantine it was most dangerous to be

[1] Funk, *Manual of Church History*, I, pp. 39-42.

publicly known as a Christian, and although conversions followed rapidly they were generally kept a secret in order that the convert might not be subjected to persecution.

With regard to marriage and divorce, the legislation of the Roman Law of this period was very lax.[2] Divorce originally could be effected by the mutual consent of both parties,[3] but the dissolubility of marriage so increased by degrees that either party might terminate marriage by addressing to his consort a formal *libellus repudii.*[4]

But with the advent of the Christian Emperors, marriage laws were gradually enforced with the view of making the matrimonial relations more binding and in accord with the principles of the Church.[5] Thus, for example, when Christianity was free to teach its doctrines openly and without fear, legislation was enacted by the Church[6] and by the State[7] which prohibited marriages between Christians and Jews.

So although there was matrimonial legislation which touched upon other canonical questions, none may be discovered of any which directly or indirectly involved the application of the Pauline Privilege. Among the possible grounds of divorce enumerated by Justinian[8] there is mentioned the possibility of a

---

[2] Sherman, *Roman Law in the Modern World,* II, n. 485.

[3] Digest, 24, 2, 1; cf. Westermarck, *The History of Human Marriage,* III, p. 321, note 4.

[4] Digest, 24, 1, 39; 24, 2, 9; cf. Buckland, *A Text-book of Roman Law,* p. 117; Sohm-Ledlie, *Institutes of Roman Law,* n. 84; Leage, *Roman Private Law,* p. 97; Cogliolo, *Manuale del Diritto Romano,* n. VIII, *de Verborum Significatione,* v. "Divortium."

[5] Cf. Novels 117, 10-12; 134, 11; Howard, *History of Matrimonial Institutions,* II, pp. 28-33; Brunnemann, *Commentarius in Codicem Justinianeum,* I, p. 473, n. 9.

[6] Cf. Schenk, *The Matrimonial Impediments of Mixed Religion and Disparity of Cult,* pp. 17-25.

[7] "Ne quis Christianam mulierem in matrimonium Judaeus accipiat: neque Judaeae Christianus coniugium fortiatur. nam si quis aliquid huiusmodi admiserit, adulterii vicem commissi huiusmodi crimen obtinebit: libertate in accusandum publicis quoque vocibus relaxata."—Code, I, 9, 6; cf. Code Theod., III, 7, 2; XVI, 8, 6; Gothofredus, *Corpus Iuris Civilis Romani cum Notis Integris,* II, p. 61, note 1; Gothofredus, *Codex Theodosianus cum Perpetuis Commentariis,* I, p. 320; Bartolus, *Commentaria Omnium Iuris,* VII, p. 25.

[8] Code, V, 17; Novel 117, 10-12.

woman being granted a divorce upon the unjust departure of her husband. But the conversion of the wife to Christianity is not adduced as the motive of desertion, nor is anything said about the man's refusal to be converted.[9]

The silence of Roman Law on the Privilege can easily be understood when it is kept in mind that the Church herself but rarely mentioned the institution during these early centuries. Another explanation of this failure of the law might be offered by the following theory: in ecclesiastical law there is the diriment impediment of consanguinity, upon which ground the validity of a marriage bearing all the conditions of the Pauline Privilege might be attacked quite apart from the application of the Privilege. By analogy, since Justinian law forbade and dissolved a union entered into between a Jew and a Christian, or between two Jews when one became a Christian, *perhaps* the Roman legislator considered this impediment sufficient to break the bond without borrowing further from ecclesiastical law. Such an explanation is admittedly only partial, and it appears of little consequence in as much as the law of Rome said nothing about those marriages entered into between Christians and infidels other than Jews.

§2. *In the Works of Ecclesiastical Writers and of the Fathers*

But very few evidences of the Pauline Privilege are to be found in the writings of the early Church.[10] Tertullian, the first writer to discuss the question,[11] declares that the words of St. Paul do not permit the intermarriage of Christians and infidels, and, he adds: "Caeterum manifestum est scripturam istam eos fideles designare, qui in matrimonio gentili inventi a Dei gratia fuerint." [12] He insists the Scriptures prove that the converted party need not believe that he must separate from his

---

[9] Brunnemann, *Comment. in Codic. Justin.*, I, p. 473, nn. 9-10, evidently harbors no doubt but that Justinian truly had the Pauline Privilege in mind, in as much as the latter revised the list of divorce causes in order that it might agree with the counsels of the Gospel.

[10] Cf. Wernz-Vidal, *Jus Canonicum*, V, n. 631, note 57.

[11] Fahrner, *Geschichte des Unauflöslichkeitsprinzips*, p. 147.

[12] Lib. II, *Ad Uxorem*, cap. 2—*MPL*, I, 1290.

unbelieving wife, for, he writes: "In pace nos vocari a Domino, et posse infidelem a fideli per usum matrimonii lucrufieri."

In a letter spuriously ascribed to Pope Eutychianus,[13] a surprising element is discovered in the problem, apart from the two already mentioned by Tertullian. In speaking of a marriage contracted between two infidels, the author says that if the infidel husband had sent away his wife before he received Baptism, he may, if he so desires, take her back after he receives the Sacrament.[14] And, moreover, if she refuses to accept Christianity, the converted husband may refuse to continue married life with her. As to how far this is to be understood in the sense of a complete separation, it is difficult to determine. But the letter is most important in that it allows some form of separation to the faithful party. Therefore, there have been discovered so far three elements in the evolution of the institution: (1) The marriage must have been contracted in infidelity; (2) one of the spouses must have been baptized; (3) the Christian partner was allowed some form of a separation in case the infidel consort refused to accept the faith.

St. Ambrose strictly insists on the illiceity of divorce, speaks of the evils that subsequently fall upon the children,[15] and in treating of verse 12 in our passage of St. Paul[16] he says that matrimony contracted among the unbaptized is not of Divine institution, nor has it the requisite of indissolubiltiy. He does

---

[13] Authors admit that this is a counterfeit, but they offer no suggestions to prove the probable authorship and date of composition. Cf. c. 2, 3, C. XXVIII, q. 1, where it is attributed to Pope Eutychianus; but this is false according to Mansi, I, p. 1126; Jaffe, n. CX; Hardouin, I, p. 1126. Jemolo, in *Studi Sassaresi*, II (1923), p. 267, declares that this letter was entirely unknown to the writers of the 4th and early 5th centuries, but that it was to be found in the penitential works of the 8th century. Cf. *Poenitentiales Theodori*, n. 264 (ed. Hildenbrand); Burchardus, *Decretum*, IX, n. 59; Ivo, *Decretales*, VIII, n. 195.

[14] "Si quis gentilis gentilem uxorem dimisserit ante baptismum; post baptismum in potestate eius erit, eam habere, vel non habere."—*Decretum Euticiani Papae*, ad 5,—Mansi, I, p. 1126. Hardouin, I, p. 1126, says that this is taken from the "*Poenitentiales Theodori*," XXVIII, q. 1, "*Si quis gentilis.*"

[15] *Commentaria in Evangelium Lucam*, c. 16 · *Corp. Script. Eccl. Latin.*, XXXII, 392.

[16] *In I Ep. ad Cor.*,—*Enchiridion Patristicum*, n. 1307.

not declare whether in the case contemplated by St. Paul it is lawful to pass to a second marriage, and when treating of the time of dissolution of the matrimonial bond, he taught that although Baptism cleanses from all sin it does not dissolve a marriage.[17]

St. Augustine also holds this, for he considers it adultery to enter a second marriage after such a separation.[18] However, he did permit an imperfect separation in that he allowed the Christian spouse to leave the infidel if the latter refused to cohabit peacefully, if he demanded sinful actions of his Christian partner, or if he attempted to induce the Christian party to return to his former error.[19]

From a consideration of these conditions placed by St. Augustine, it would seem that some form of interpellation or some method of interrogation must have been used to determine whether any or all of these conditions were present. Although the saintly Bishop of Hippo would grant the convert permission to leave the infidel, nevertheless, he cautioned the former to give the latter an opportunity of embracing the Christian religion,[20] which happy termination could best be brought about by the good example of the Christian party.[21] Throughout the whole discussion St. Augustine takes the attitude that the words of St. Paul do not constitute a command, but that they are merely counsel or advice [22] which imposed no obligation on the convert; and he follows the lead of the Apostle in declaring: "Sed quia ita licitum est, ut non expediat." [23] If, however, the Christian party did desire to discontinue marital rela-

---

[17] Lib. I, *De Officiis*, cap. ult., n. 50—*MPL*, XVI, 97; cf. c. 4, D. XXVI.

[18] Lib. I, *De Adult. Conjug.*, c. 18—*MPL*, XL, 462.

[19] Lib. I, *De Adult. Conjug.*, c. 18—*MPL*, XL, 462; cf. c. 9, C. XXVIII, q. 1; *De Fide et Operibus*, c. 16—*Corp. Script. Eccl. Latin.*, XLI, 72; cf. c. 4, C. XXVIII, q. 1.

[20] Lib. I, *De Adult. Conjug.*, cc. 13, 14, 18—*Corp. Script. Eccl. Latin.*, XLI, 361-362, 366; cf. c. 7, 9, C. XXVIII, q. 1.

[21] *De Bono Conjugali*, c. 11—*Corp. Script. Eccl. Latin.*, XLI, 205.

[22] Lib. I, *De Sermone Domini in Monte*, c. 16—*MPL*, XXXIV, 1252; cf. c. 5, C. XXVIII, q. 1.

[23] Lib. I, *De Adult. Conjug.*, c. 18—*Corp. Script. Eccl. Latin.*, XLI, 366; cf. c. 9, C. XXVIII, q. 1.

tions, he might do so; but any attempt at a second marriage was to be looked upon as adultery.

About this same time there appeared a commentary of all the Epistles of St. Paul (with the exception of that to the Hebrews), which, since the 16th century, has been known as the Ambrosiaster.[24] During the Middle Ages this commentary was commonly, but erroneously, ascribed to St. Ambrose,[25] and even now it is generally included among the collections of his works.[26] This letter gave the first clear application of the Pauline Privilege and, if up to this time there was only doubt as to the exact nature of the dissolution, the Ambrosiaster in unmistakable language decreed that the matrimonial bond was completely broken, and it granted the right of remarriage.[27]

In addition to defining the exact nature of the separation, the letter is important in that it specifies one of the conditions

---

[24] From a study of the letter it can be demonstrated definitely that its origin dates back to about the year 370 A. D., to the pontificate of Pope Damasus, and not long after the reign of the Emperor Julian. Thus, in *I Timothy*, 3:14, we read: "Ut cum totus mundus Dei sit, Ecclesia tamen domus eius dicatur, cuius *hodie* rector est Damasus"; and again, in *II Thess.*, 2:7: "Usque ad Dioclaetianum, et *novissime* Julianum, qui arte quadam et subtilitate coeptam persecutionem implere non potest." Cf. Tixeront, *A Hand-book of Patrology*, p. 240; Souter, *A Study of Ambrosiaster* (Cambridge Texts and Studies, VII, 4); Wittig, *Der Ambrosiaster Hilarius*, p. 33; Schanz, *Römische Literaturgeschichte*, VII, IV, p. 354.

Smisniewicz, *Die Lehre von den Ehehindernissen bei Petrus Lombardus*, etc., p. 127, insists that the Ambrosiaster and the Pseudo-Isidorian Decretals are the work of one and the same author, and that they were forged about the year 850. But he presents no evidence to support his theory.

[25] Cf. "Ambrosiaster," *Cath. Encycl.*, I, 406; Wernz-Vidal, *Jus Canon.*, V, n. 631, note 57. The letter was falsely or incorrectly quoted by Gratian as having been written by St. Gregory. "Haec non sunt inventa apud B. Gregorium, sed apud B. Ambrosium ad C. VII:1 Corinthiorum eadem fere leguntur plenius atque aptius exposita."—*Notationes Correctorum* ad c. 2, C. XXVIII, q. 2.

[26] Migne, *Patrologiae Cursus Completum—Series Latina*, XVII, 45-508; Ballerini, *S. Ambrosii Opera Omnia*, 6 vols., Milan, 1875.

[27] "Si infidelis discedit odio Christianae fidei, discedat. Non est enim frater aut soror subjectus servituti in huiusmodi. Non est enim peccatum dimissio propter Deum, si alii se copulaverit. Contumelia quippe Creatoris solvit jus matrimonii circa eum, qui relinquitur. Infidelis autem discedens et in Deum peccat, et in matrimonium, nec est ei fides servanda coniugii, qui propterea discessit, ne audiret Christum esse Deum Christianorum coniugiorum."—c. 2, C. XXVIII, q. 2.

necessary that the concession be applied; for the author says: "Si infidelis discredit *odio Christianae fidei,* discedat. *Contumelia quippe Creatoris solvit jus matrimonii.*" From this it would appear that malice toward the Faith was the only ground on which the dissolution might be effected. But it has already been seen that St. Augustine, about this same time, permitted the convert to leave for several other reasons.

It is not to be thought that the Ambrosiaster favored or permitted the right of remarriage to be exercised promiscuously, but it granted this concession to the Christian party only in case the infidel had departed or refused to continue a peaceful cohabitation.[28] In the event that the latter was willing to support a peaceful marital life, the teaching of St. Augustine was at hand to solve the difficulty; namely, that the convert was under no obligation to dismiss an infidel spouse who consented to continue happily in the union.

Prior to this time the opinion was prevalent that it was either a duty, or at least advisable, to continue living with the infidel. For the idea of the indissolubility of the matrimonial bond, when one spouse had converted, was paramount in the minds of all, and only when the infidel refused to cohabit peacefully might the convert leave. But now the Ambrosiaster expresses a view radically different from any that has gone before, for it emphasizes the right of remarriage and the complete breaking of the first bond.

In the East, St. John Chrysostom seemed to be familiar with the application of the Pauline Privilege, for he attempted to resolve the antinomy between the unlimited permission, which was almost an exhortation, given to the husband to expel an adulterous wife, and the Pauline precept given to the Christian husband not to expel his infidel wife. Here the Saint is in harmony with the advice of St. Paul, for, he says: "Uxorem habens infidelem vocatus es? Mane cum illa; ne propter fidem ejicias uxorem." [29] But, on the other hand, if the infidel should order his Christian wife to offer sacrifice to idols, or to be his associate in such impiety as an alternative to

---

[28] Jemolo, "Il Privilegio Paolino," *Studi Sassaresi,* II (1923), 258.

[29] *In Ep. I ad Cor.,* homily 19—*MPG,* LXI, 156.

departing, then it is better to break the matrimonial bond rather than to fail in the duties of the true Christian religion.[30] St. John's use of the term *disrumpi* would seem to insinuate the complete severance of the tie, and as such it is understood as the absolute dissolution of a matrimonial bond contracted in infidelity.[31]

Although he does not mention the Pauline Privilege by name, Cassiodorus indirectly refers to it when he says that a convert to Christianity should strive to win his infidel partner from the false religion to which she adheres.[32] But the author is less definite in what he proposes next, for he adds that if the infidel refuses to accept Christianity, her consort should *condemn* her "quoniam cum obstinatis et perditis nulla potest esse concordia." [33]

§3. *In the Decrees of Councils*

In Canon 63 of the Fourth Council of Toledo,[34] (a. 633), there is a more direct reference to the Privilege; [35] although the legislation enacted there was only that of a particular Council dealing with conditions peculiar to Spain, and as such it had no immediate bearing on the Church Universal.[36] The Council ruled that converts from Judaism should refuse to continue cohabitation with a partner remaining true to the Jewish religion, unless the latter would likewise consent to accept the Faith. This would appear to be most stringent as law, but it

---

30 "Si autem infidelis discedit, discedat. Hic enim nulla est fornicatio. Quid sibi vult autem illud: 'Infidelis si discedit'? Verbi gratia si te iubet sacrificare aut sociam impietatis esse propter connubium, vel discedere: *melius est disrumpi connubium, quam piam religionem."*—*In Ep. I ad Cor.*, homily 19—*MPG*, LXI, 155.

31 Cf. Wernz-Vidal, *Jus Canon.*, V, n. 631, note 57.

32 *In Ep. I ad Cor.*, VII:12—*MPL*, LXX, 1333.

33 *Loc. cit.*

34 Mansi, X, 634; cf. c. 10, C. XXVIII, q. 1.

35 Wernz-Vidal, *Jus Canon.*, V, n. 631, note 57, does not seem to think that this Council was referring to the *Casus Apostoli* at all, but rather that it had in mind the impediment of Disparity of Cult. Cf. Rosset, *De Sacramento Matrimonii*, nn. 607, 611.

36 Cf. Estius, *In Quatuor Libros Sententiarum Commentaria*, lib. IV, dist. 39, pars 3; Soto, *Sententiarum*, lib. II, dist. 39, art. 2, q. 1.

was legislation suited to the conditions existing in Spain at that time. For the Jews were very pertinacious in their error and there was always the possibility of a convert lapsing back into it. For another reason this Council is important in the history of our institution, in that it was the first to regulate for the children born of such a union. According to Canon 63, these children were to follow the Christian religion no matter whether the converted party happened to be the mother or the father.[37]

Toward the end of the same century another Council, this time in the East, apparently [38] mentioned the Privilege, the pseudo-Council of Trullo, (a. 692). The West never recognized the one hundred and two disciplinary canons of this particular Council, for they were merely reaffirmations of earlier canons and they exhibited an inimical attitude toward all churches not in accord with Constantinople, especially the Western Churches.[39] To whatever kind of marriages Canon 72 of this Council referred,[40] the application contained therein became the constant practice of the Oriental Church.

§4. *In the Penitential Writers and Works of the 8th to 11th Centuries*

The Penitential Books of the 8th and 9th centuries permit a separation in a marriage which has all the conditions of the

---

[37] "Filii autem, qui ex talibus nati sunt, fidem atque condicionem matris (i.e., a Christian mother, as is evident from what precedes) sequantur. Similiter illi, qui procreati sunt de infidelibus mulieribus et fidelibus viris, Christianam sequantur religionem, non Iudaicam superstitionem."—Mansi, X, 634.

[38] De Becker, *De Sponsalibus et Matrimonio,* p. 259, is of the opinion that this Council was speaking in Canon 72 more of mixed marriages with the impediment of mixed religion, than of the application of the Pauline Privilege. Cf. Wernz-Vidal, *Jus Canon.,* V, n. 631, note 57.

[39] Cf. "Trullo," *Cath. Encycl.,* IV, 311.

[40] "Non licere virum orthodoxum cum muliere haeretica conjugi, neque vero orthodoxam cum viro haeretico copulari. Sed et si quid eiusmodi ab ullo ex omnibus factum apparuerit, irritas nuptias existimare et nefarium conjugium dissolvi. Si quis autem ea, quae a nobis decreta sunt, transgressus fuerit, segregetur."—Mansi, XI, 975; cf. De Becker, *De Spons. et Matrim.,* p. 259.

Casus Apostoli, and furthermore, they allow the convert to remarry.[41] If this latter privilege is not stated in such express terms in the Penitentials, it may nevertheless be concluded from the general trend of thought which they exhibit.[42]

For example, Theodore of Canterbury,[43] (a. 668), in quoting the letter falsely attributed to Pope Eutychianus, says that not only was the Christian free if the infidel departed, but if the latter refused to accept Christianity, the converted spouse should dismiss her. Here there is a recurrence of the opinion that Baptism was the cause of the dissolution of the matrimonial bond.

The approval of Hincmar of Rheims is to be respected when he also declares that the bond of marriage is dissolved by the reception of Baptism,[44] for he was foremost in the ranks of those who ardently defended the indissolubility of the matrimonial alliance. Basing his arguments on the Ambrosiaster, Hincmar would permit the Christian husband to separate from his infidel wife even though she consented to live peacefully with him. He says that St. Paul merely *advised* the convert not to do this, and since it is not his *duty* to remain with his infidel wife, he may be permitted to enter a second marriage if the infidel leaves because of hatred for the Faith. In this case the original bond is broken and the convert is absolutely free to remarry.[45] Hincmar's opinion regarding the indissolubility of marriage is logical in his system of thought, for he insists that only in a Christian marriage is the Sacrament received, and it is this sacramentality which forms the foundation for indissolubility. But a marriage entered into in infidelity is not a Sacrament because it is *ex Dei decretum*.[46]

In opposition to the theories of Theodore and Hincmar that Baptism is the cause of dissolving the bond, there were decl-

---

[41] Cf. Jemolo, "Il Privilegio Paolino," *Studi Sassaresi*, II (1923), 269.

[42] Cf. Fahrner, *Geschichte des Unauflöslichkeitsprinzips*, p. 149.

[43] *Poenitentiales Theodori*, II, c. 12, n. 18—Mansi, XI, 53; cf. Ott, "Card. C. Tarquini ueber das Paulinische Privileg," *AkKR*, L (1883), 229-230.

[44] Sirmond, *Hincmari Archiep. Remens.*, II, p. 667.

[45] Hincmar, *De Divortio Lotharii*,—*MPL*, CXXV, 642.

[46] Hincmar, *op. cit.*,—*MPL*, CXXV, 642.

sions laid down by two Councils. The Council of Meaux, (a. 845), declared in Canon 1: *"Crimina enim in baptismo soluuntur, non coniugia,"* [47] and the Council of Tribur, (a. 895), repeats this same thought in its 39th Canon.[48] Fahrner says [49] that this argument is based on a pseudo-Roman Synod, and that it is really an opinion of Pope St. Innocent I (d. 417) favoring the theory that such marriages of infidels, when one party is baptized, are indissoluble.[50]

The authors of this period added no new element in the evolution of the Privilege, but they were content in the main to accept and teach the doctrine as expounded by the Fathers of the Church. St. Augustine particularly seemed to be the guiding star of the age, and his teaching that infidelity was nothing less than spiritual fornication, for which cause a Christian husband might dismiss his pagan wife, was generally advocated. Thus, Sedulius Scotus was content to quote St. Augustine copiously, and like the holy Bishop he says that although a man may dismiss his wife for the cause of fornication, i.e., infidelity, nevertheless he must not forget that the words of St. Paul were given only in the form of advice. Consequently, a Christian husband is free to continue marital relations with his infidel wife.[51]

Venerable Bede, on the other hand, gave as his opinion that a Christian husband should dismiss a pagan wife and, while counseling this action, he would not permit the husband to enter another marriage.[52]

Rhabanus Maurus follows Scotus closely in advising that, although the convert may leave the infidel, it is better not to do so because of the possibility of conversion following on the

---

[47] C. 1, C. XXVIII, q. 2; c. 3, D. XXVI.

[48] Mansi, XVIII, 151.

[49] *Geschichte des Unauflöslichkeitsprinzips*, p. 150, note 5.

[50] Innocentius I, ep. *"Magna me gratulatio,"* 13 Dec., 414, ad 2.—Mansi, III, 1059; cf. c. 3, D. XXVI.

[51] "Fornicatio est etiam ipsa infidelitas. Dicimus autem permisit causa fornicationis uxorem dimitti; sed quia permisit, non jussit, dedit locum Apostolo monendi, ut qui voluerit non dimittat uxorem infidelem, quia sic fortasse possit fidelis fieri."—Sedulius Scotus, *In Ep. I ad Cor.*, c. 7—*MPL*, CIII, 141.

[52] *In Marci Evangelium Expositio*, III, c. 10—*MPL*, XCII, 230.

heels of good example.[53] In this opinion he disagrees with Bede, and even continues drastically by declaring that a Christian husband could dismiss an apostate Christian wife and then enter a new marriage. But he would not grant a like concession to a Christian wife under identical circumstances.[54] The Third Council of Aix-la-Chapelle, (a. 862), gathered to consider the case of Lothar and Tetberga, quoted this opinion of Maurus in its 8th Canon,[55] but it was later reproved and condemned by the Holy See.

Both Hincmar of Rheims and Atto of Vercelli attacked this line of reasoning, for not only were they staunch defenders of the marriage bond, but they were also absolute in their doctrine on the equality of man and woman. The former says: "Quia una est lex viri et feminae, ut supra Scripturarum et Catholicorum Patrum sententiis demonstravimus"; [56] and Atto is equally explicit when he states: " Et vir uxorem non dimittat.' His verbis ostenditur quod uterque lege una contingitur. Ac per hoc non sunt illi audiendi qui dicunt potiorem sexum et minorem, caput et membrum, una lege constringi non debere." [57]

In the *Decretum* of Ivo of Chartres there are three Chapters dedicated to a discussion of the Pauline Privilege. The counterfeit letter of Pope Eutychianus constitutes the first two Chapters, and the third quotes Canon 1 of the Council of Meaux.[58] Ivo's *Panormia* repeats the same texts,[59] but from

---

[53] Rhabanus Maurus, *In Ep. I ad Cor.*, c. 7—*MPL*, CXII, 65.

[54] Regardless of the fact that in granting his Privilege St. Paul intended that it be applied equally to man and woman, the idea prevailed among authors that the man alone might benefit by it. This inequality of the sexes in the application of the Privilege was first sponsored by the false letter of Pope Eutychianus, and it has generally enjoyed the favor of writers until almost the 13th century.

[55] Mansi, XV, 613, 616; Hardouin, XV, 617.

[56] Hincmar, *Epistolae*, n. XXII—*MPL*, CXXVI, 145; cf. *De Divortio Lotharii*,—*MPL*, CXXV, 642, 686, 732; *De Praedestinatione*, XXV, n. 188—*MPL*, CXXV, 252.

[57] Atto, *Expositio in Ep. I ad Cor.*, c. 7—*MPL*, CXXXIV, 352.

[58] Cf. Jemolo, "Il Privilegio Paolino," *Studi Sassaresi*, II (1923), 292.

[59] *Panormia*, lib. VI, cc. 97-98, 100—*MPL*, CLXI, 1266; throughout this entire work Ivo quotes St. Augustine freely.

the first work there may be gathered the following rules as expounded by Ivo for the application of the Privilege.[60] (1) The husband who marries and also abandons his wife in infidelity may take her back after his Baptism, if he so desires. (2) In case one spouse is converted, the matrimonial bond still remains, as Baptism does not break it; and although continued cohabitation with the infidel party is not a duty, yet it is best to do so. (3) If, however, the infidel tries to lead the convert into sin, then the latter may break the relationship and is free to enter a second marriage.[61]

Art. II. From Gratian to the Council of Trent

Until the 12th century the limits of the power of the converted consort to abandon the infidel or not, were still fashioned according to the Augustinian formulation of St. Paul's advice. Namely, that it was permissible and even necessary to dismiss an infidel spouse who would not cohabit *sine contumelia Creatoris* or if there was any danger of perversion, but that it was much better not to depart from one who was willing to continue in a peaceful marital life. Regardless of this interpretation of the Pauline passage, taught by St. Augustine "ex professo," all authors were agreed in admitting that the converted party could enter a second marriage for the only reason that the infidel consort refused to accept Christianity. It was Gratian who finally established in his teaching the principle which very soon became and remained the dominating rule in the application of the Pauline Privilege.

§1. *In Gratian and His Contemporaries*

The fundamental ideas common to all the writers in regard to the Privilege have been seen up to the advent of Gratian and his *Decretum*, but all of these opinions lacked more or less the quality of clear-cut doctrine. Gratian's stand was to become more decisive in his treatment of many points connected with

[60] *Decretum*, lib. VIII—*MPL*, CLXI, 625; cf. c. 3, D. XXVI.

[61] Cf. Fahrner, *Geschichte des Unauflöslichkeitsprinzips*, p. 151.

the problem. He has dedicated to the Privilege, though not entirely isolated it from its accompanying questions, Cause XXVIII of the *Decretum*, wherein he makes extensive use of the collections of Ivo of Chartres.

In Question 1 of this Cause he directly refers to the Privilege in Canons 2 to 5 and 7 to 10. In Canons 2 and 3 he quotes the spurious letter of Pope Eutychianus, and Canons 4 and 5 are excerpts from St. Augustine's *De Fide et Operibus* and *In Sermone Domini in Monte* respectively.[62] Because of his severe adherence to Ivo of Chartres, Gratian falsely ascribes Canon 7 to St. Ambrose, when as a matter of fact it properly belongs to St. Augustine and is found in his *Epistola ad Hilarium Syracusanum*, epistola 89.[63] Canons 8 and 9 were adopted from St. Augustine's *De Adulteriis Conjugiis;* Canon 8 from Chapters 13 and 14 of the work, and Canon 9 from Chapter 18 and following. Canon 10 includes a direct quotation of Canon 63 of the Fourth Council of Toledo.[64]

Continuing in Question 2 of the same Cause, Canon 1 is a reiteration of Canon 1 of the Council of Meaux; [65] but Canon 2 gives the view of St. Ambrose stated in his *Epistola I ad Cor.*, c. VII, as opposed to the above opinion quoted in the Council of Meaux.[66]

Gratian first treats of the nature of a marriage contracted in infidelity, and insists that it is a true marriage. Moreover, if it has been entered into according to the rules laid down by the civil law of the State, it is a *legitimum coniugium*. He contrasts the indissolubility of such a union with that of two Christians, deciding that matrimony between infidels is not a *coniugium ratum* because it lacks the sacramental character which is the basis of indissolubility.[67]

---

[62] *De Fide et Operibus*, c. 16; *In Sermone Domini in Monte*, lib. I, c. 16; cf. *supra*, page 16.

[63] "Deceptus ab Ivone Gratianus canonem 7, causa XXVIII, quaestio 1, sub Ambrosii nomine laudavit, quando tamen tribuendus erat Augustino in Epistola ad Hilarium Syracusanum."—Berardi, *Gratiani Canones Genuini*, III, 103; cf. *Notationes Correctorum* ad c. 7, C. XXVIII, q. 1.

[64] Cf. *supra*, page 19.

[65] Cf. *supra*, page 22.

[66] Gratian wrongly ascribes this to Gregory; cf. *supra*, page 17, note 25.

[67] *Dictum* ad c. 17, C. XXVIII, q. 1.

In addition to considering the solubility of such a marriage, Gratian also puts the question whether married persons can also avail themselves of the Privilege when they both married as infidels, but later on were converted to Christianity. In this case he decides that through the conversion of both parties the marriage becomes sacramental and indissoluble, and as such it cannot be broken any more than the marriage of two Christians.[68]

In consideration of a third possibility, he then asks whether the Privilege can be used in the case where two Christians married, and later one party apostatized and left the faithful partner. This problem he decides by saying that the deserted Christian spouse need not follow the apostate, but neither may he marry again. The Privilege cannot be used in this contingency "quia ratum coniugium fuerit inter eos, quod nullo modo solvi potest." [69]

After admitting the Pauline separation founded on the Scriptural passage,[70] Gratian quotes the two seemingly contradictory texts from the Council of Meaux [71] and the Ambrosiaster.[72] There is no doubt but that Gratian agreed in general with the principles determined by his predecessors, but he sought to give a more definite explanation of these ideas. So having in mind the distinction between the case in which the infidel consents to continue a peaceful cohabitation and that in which he departs, the author indicates his stand by reconciling the above texts. He says [73] that a distinction must be made between separation from an infidel who wishes to continue the marriage and the refusal of the convert to follow the infidel who has already departed. In the first case the convert is free to leave the infidel, but as long as the latter lives, the convert may not remarry. In the second case the convert is under no obligation

---

[68] *Loc. cit.*

[69] *Dictum* ad c. 2, C. XXVIII, q. 2.

[70] *Proemium* ad C. XXVIII, q. 2.

[71] "Crimina enim in baptismo solvuntur, non coniugia."—c. 1, C. XXVIII, q. 2.

[72] "Contumelia quippe Creatoris solvit ius matrimonii circa eum, qui relinquitur."—c. 2, C. XXVIII, q. 2.

[73] *Dictum* ad c. 2, C. XXVIII, q. 2.

to follow the infidel who has deserted and he is allowed to contract a new marriage. Gratian does not indicate in just which cases the conclusion may be reached that there has been a departure of the infidel; but he leans toward the opinion of Ambrosiaster, as shown by the Rubric to c. 2, C. XXVIII, q. 2: "Licet fideli uxorem aliam ducere, quam Christianae fidei odio infidelis dimittit."

Peter Lombard is in full agreement with Gratian in all points regarding the Privilege. Like the author of the famous *Decretum,* he distinguishes between the various possible marriages to which there was question of applying the Privilege; between a mixed marriage that is such because of the impediment of Disparity of Cult, and one that has become such by the conversion of one spouse.[74] And he is opposed to the opinion that would allow the use of the concession in the case of Christian marriages when one spouse has apostatized.[75] He follows the lead of St. Augustine in saying that the continuation of the marriage contracted in infidelity depends entirely upon the will of the converted party. But in the same breath he adds that if the infidel consents to continue in a happy married state, the Christian spouse ought not dismiss the infidel "propter liberam benevolentiam." Although he allowed this choice of continuing the conjugal life to the convert, it cannot safely be concluded that he permitted the convert to contract another marriage purely because he dismissed his unbelieving wife of his own volition. On the contrary, and in imitation of St. Augustine again,[76] he would deny such permission even though the unbeliever were guilty of wrong other than *contumelia Creatoris.*[77]

Lombard also cites authorities for both sides of the question [78] whether or not the convert may enter a new marriage.

---

[74] *Sententiarum,* lib. IV, dist. 39, c. 2, n. 356.

[75] *Op. cit.,* lib. IV, dist. 39, c. 4, n. 360.

[76] *De Fide et Operibus,* c. 16—*Corp. Script. Eccl. Latin.,* XLI, 72; *De Sermone Domini in Monte,* lib. I, c. 16—*MPL,* XXXIV, 1252.

[77] *Sententiarum,* lib. IV, dist. 39, c. 4, n. 358.

[78] The Ambrosiaster upholding the affirmative (c. 2, C. XXVIII, q. 2), and Canon 1 of the Council of Meaux supporting the negative (c. 1, C. XXVIII, q. 2).

and then he states his own solution.[79] The convert who takes advantage of the permission given by God to leave the infidel, but who does not follow the advice of St. Paul to remain, cannot pass on to a new marriage *propter legem benevolentiae.* But the convert who does not transgress the Pauline counsel, for the reason that the infidel is the guilty party and has already abandoned his spouse, is allowed to contract a second marriage.

Lombard, as well as Gratian before him, was preoccupied with the task of reconciling two contradictory texts, with the result that both authors formulated a rule which gave juridical sanction to a moral precept. With the doubt remaining as to when the infidel was considered as having departed, this rule certainly added to the institution no semblance of clearness or logical rigidity. Indeed, both Gratian and Lombard considered only the behavior of the converted party. They judge in his regard that which is licit and that which is illicit, and Lombard speaks of the observance by him of the "lex benevolentiae." From their doctrine it would appear that the prohibition to remarry, when the convert had dismissed his unbelieving spouse, would be nothing more than the sanction attached to the violation of the precept of charity. Hence, it would seem to be a safe presumption that the general rule was freedom to remarry, and that the prohibition was the exception.[80]

But this is not true, for the traditional view [81] which both Gratian and Lombard accepted must be retained, and consideration must be made not for the convert but for the infidel. For it was upon the action of the latter that the matrimonial bond stood or was broken. Consequently, the perseverance of the matrimonial tie is to be held as the general rule, and the exception is seen in the breaking of the bond in the case of a particular manifestation of anti-Christian spirit by the unbeliever.

The Decretists contributed their share to the development of the Pauline Privilege in that they all dwelt on the institution

[79] *Sententiarum*, lib. IV, dist. 39, c. 4, n. 359; cf. Biederlack, "Ueber das sog. Paulinische Privilegium," *ZKT*, VII (1883), 311.

[80] Cf. Jemolo, "Il Privilegio Paolino," *Studi Sassaresi*, II (1923), 297.

[81] Cf. Ambrosiaster, *supra*, page 17; c. 2, C. XXVIII, q. 2.

more or less at length. But their assistance was comparatively unimportant, for they added minor considerations but failed to prove progressive in clarifying the fundamental principles of the Privilege. For the most part the writers of this time are in perfect agreement on these basic points, and generally they follow closely the teaching of Gratian and Peter Lombard.[82]

The rule proposed by Gratian, that the Christian may pass to a new marriage only if the infidel partner refuses to cohabit *sine contumelia Creatoris*, is not explained by any of the Decretists. Many of them concern themselves in allaying the contradiction between the advice found in the statement of St. Paul and the precept expressed in Canon 63 of the Fourth Council of Toledo. Thus, Paucapalea,[83] Roland [84] and Rufinus [85] resolved the contradiction by considering the Canon of the Council as a particular law applicable to the Jews alone, and in addition, they say the fact that St. Paul had reasons which did not exist at the time of the Council must be borne in mind.

The position of Jews, whose partners in marriage converted to Christianity, was also a source of worry to Gandulphus. This writer took a singular stand when he decided that such a Jewish consort "sive consentiat cohabitare, sive non, infidelis dimitti potest, et licebit fideli ducere uxorem, vel virum, si mulier fuerit infidelis." [86]

This doctrine was supported and even extended by another author, Robert Flamesbury, who added to the statement of Gandulphus his own dictum that: "In solis Iudaeis aliter est, quia quidquid sit, neuter reliquum potest retinere, nisi ambo convertantur. Solutum est ergo matrimonium, licet quidam

---

[82] Cf. Fahrner, *Geschichte des Unauflöslichkeitsprinzips*, p. 155.

[83] *Die Summa des Paucapalea über das Decretum Gratiani* (ed. Schulte), p. 117.

[84] *Die Summa Magistri Rolandi nachmals Papstes Alexander III* (ed. Thaner), p. 135.

[85] *Die Summa Decretorum des Magister Rufinus* (ed. Singer), pp. 452-458.

[86] *Die Glosse zum Dekret Gratians* (ed. Schulte), p. 52; cf. c. 10, C. XXVIII, q. 1; IV Council of Toledo, *can. 59*,—Mansi X, 634; Gillmann, "Zum Problem vom Privilegium Paulinum," *AkKR*, CIV (1924), 243-249.

dicant, quod non, et male, ut videtur, quia sic cogeretur quis invitus continere." [87]

But so strict an indictment and dissolution of the bond could not sustain itself; it was attacked by Tancred [88] and opposed by the decree *Interrogatum* of Pope Clement III.[89] For in this decree the Pontiff grants to the Jewish and Saracen converts an express permission to continue marital relations with their infidel partners, even though the marriage had been contracted originally in direct violation of the ecclesiastical laws concerning consanguinity.

During this period consideration was still being given to the question concerning the time of dissolution of the matrimonial bond, and authors were still at odds in trying to determine a solution of the problem. Regardless of the fact that St. Paul evidently settled this question in the very grant of the Privilege,[90] John of Faenza quoted two opinions that were prevalent in his day; that of Gratian, denying that Baptism was the only requisite, and that of Hugh of St. Victor, who favored the affirmative.[91] The fact that John of Faenza does not argue against this latter opinion that Baptism alone breaks the bond would seem to indicate that such a leaning was still in vogue in his day.

Another step in the evolution of the institution was the teaching of Bernard of Pavia, a doctrine which exercised great influence on the development of the legislation in the course of the following centuries. In general, Bernard followed the theories of his predecessors, but aside from them he proposed a new case. If, he said, the infidel wife who formerly repu-

---

[87] *Summa de Matrimonio et Usuris ex Roberti Poenitentiali* (ed. Schulte), p. XVII.

[88] *Tancredi Summa de Matrimonio* (ed. Wunderlich), p. 45.

[89] Clement III, ep. *"Interrogatum,"* a. 1188,—Mansi, XXII, 553; Hardouin, XXII, 562.

[90] St. Paul could not have advised the Christians, as he did in I Cor., 7:12, to continue marital relations with their infidel partners if the matrimonial bond were dissolved by the Baptism of one party. For, were this true, he would have been granting Apostolic sanction to innumerable cases of unmitigated concubinage.

[91] Schulte, "Die Rechtshandschriften der Stiftsbibliotheken von Gottweig," *Weiner Sitzungsber.*, LVII (1867), 587.

diated her Christian husband now becomes a Christian herself, the question arises whether or not the husband is obliged to resume cohabitation. Bernard gave a two-fold answer to this possibility: if the Christian husband had already utilized his right and married again, then he is not only *free* to remain in that second alliance, but he is *bound* to do so. But if he has not taken advantage of the concession to remarry anew, then he is obliged to return to his recently converted wife.[92]

§2. *In Pontifical Decrees*

Contrary to all tradition regarding the application of the Pauline Privilege to Christian marriages,[93] there appeared about this time a very peculiar decision, commonly attributed to Pope Celestine III.[94] The case was stated thus: the matrimonial contract was validly entered into between two Christians, but later the husband of this union abandoned his wife out of hatred and apostatized from the Faith. In the course of time he entered and consummated a second marriage with a pagan, and the Catholic wife also contracted and consummated a new marriage, with ecclesiastical approbation. From the nature of the response given by Celestine to this case when it was brought to his notice, it would appear that he believed a Christian marriage could be dissolved in virtue of the Pauline Privilege if one

---

[92] *Bernardi Papiensis Summa Decretalium* (ed. Laspeyres), p. 291-292.

[93] Cf. *supra*, page 5.

[94] Gasparri, *De Matrimonio*, n. 1328; Esmein, *Le Mariage en Droit Canonique*, II, p. 80. "Scilicet Caelestinus, dictum cuius habuisti olim in decretali *De Conversione Infidelium*, cap. *'Laudabilem,'* et male dixit Caelestinus." *Glossa Ordinaria* ad v. *"Praedecessor"* in c. 7, X, *de divortiis*, IV, 19. But Giraldi, in his glossa on the *"Quanto"* of Innocent III, says that the opinion previously ascribed to Celestine III regarding the Pauline Privilege was falsely imputed to him by the *Glossa* as a definition contained in his *Decretals;* whereas, as a matter of fact, it was not a definition, but a mere opinion expressed by Celestine before he had made an examination of the question. Hence, Innocent III says: "Quidam Praedecessor noster sensisse aliter *videatur*," and not, "Praedecessor suum aliter *definivisse*." Cf. Giraldi, *Expositio Juris Pontificii*, II, pars I, n. 735. Furthermore, in his decretal *"Laudabilem,"* Celestine says: "Idem si quidem iuris erit in sequenti casu, *quem proponere studuisti*, etc." Cf. c. 1, X, *de conversione infidelium*, III, 33.

of the parties apostatized out of hatred for the Faith.[95] For he decided that the Christian wife's second marriage was valid, declaring: "Non enim videtur nobis, quodsi prior maritus redeat ad unitatem ecclesiasticam eadem a secundo debeat recedere et resignari priori, maxime quum ab eo visa fuerit ecclesiae iudicio discessisse et teste Gregorio [96] contumelia Creatoris solvat ius matrimonii circa eum qui relinquitur odio fidei Christianae." [97]

If this is to be looked upon in the light of a pontifical decision issued by Celestine, it was of short life and inconsequential as a principle to be invoked in the future. For his successor in the See of Peter, Innocent III, in a letter to Bishop Hugo of Ferrara, corrected any false impression that might have arisen. In this epistle [98] Innocent considered two cases: the first, that of a marriage contracted in infidelity, which later has become a mixed union by the conversion of one party; the second, that of a Christian marriage wherein one spouse has apostatized and lapsed back into infidelity. As a solution to the first case, Innocent decreed: "Si enim alter infidelium conjugum ad fidem catholicam convertatur, altero vel nullo modo, vel saltem non sine blasphemia divini nominis, vel ut eum pertrahat ad mortale peccatum, ei cohabitare volente; qui relinquitur, ad secunda, si voluerit, vota transibit." This is an application perfectly in accord with the spirit expressed in Ambrosiaster.[99] Concerning the second hypothesis, Innocent said that although the *contumelia Creatoris* appears greater here because of the sacramental character of the marriage, nevertheless, "non credimus, quod in hoc casu is, qui relinquitur, vivente altero possit ad secundas nuptias convolare." The different solution of the

---

[95] The fact that a Pope renders a wrong decision in a particular case in no way argues against the dogma of Papal Infallibility. Cf. Gasparri, *De Matrim.*, n. 1328.

[96] This principle is still being attributed to St. Gregory, whereas it rightly belongs to Ambrosiaster.

[97] Celestine III, ep. "*Laudabilem,*" a. 1191,—c. 1, X, *de conversione infidelium,* III, 33; cf. Mansi, XXII, 638; Jaffe, n. 17649.

[98] Innocent III, ep. "*Quanto te magis,*" 1 May, 1199,—c. 7, X, *de divortiis,* IV, 19; cf. Denziger, *Enchiridion,* n. 406.

[99] Cf. c. 2, C. XXVIII, q. 2.

two cases has its explanation in this, that there is true marriage among infidels, but not ratified; while marriage among Christians is both true and ratified because it is a Sacrament of the Faith, which is never lost once it has been acquired.

About two years later Innocent addressed a letter to the Bishop of Tiberias,[100] in which he answered the same question regarding all infidels that had been answered concerning Jews and Saracens by Clement III.[101] Namely, whether those who had contracted marriage in infidelity in direct violation of the ecclesiastical laws on consanguinity could continue marital relations with an infidel after they themselves had received Baptism. The Pontiff answered the question in the affirmative, and in doing so he established a rule for handling those cases in which the Christian spouse had practiced polygamy before his conversion. Although Innocent was not quite clear in stating which wife the converted husband might retain, he is strict on the doctrine of monogamy and seems to favor the first legitimate wife, even if she had been abandoned in infidelity. If this first wife consented to live in peace with the convert, then he is to be obliged to take her back.[102] This attitude was decidedly a change from that contained in the spurious letter of Pope Eutychianus.[103] The general principles of this epistle were also expressed by Innocent in a third letter, this to Bishop Albert of Livonia; [104] and all three documents were eventually included among the Decretals of Gregory IX.

Pope Urban III has been accused by some authors of a charge similar to that placed against Celestine III.[105] The Bishop of Florence asked the Pope if a Christian wife who had dismissed her husband without due ecclesiastical procedure because he had fallen into heresy, could, on his repentance and return to the Faith, be compelled to receive him back. Urban made a dis-

---

[100] Innocent III, ep. *"Gaudemus in Domino,"*—c. 8, X, *de divortiis*, IV, 19; cf. Denziger, *Enchiridion*, n. 407.

[101] Clement III, ep. *"Interrogatum"*; cf. *supra*, page 30.

[102] Cf. Sanchez, *De Matrim.*, VII, disp. 73, n. 4.

[103] Cf. *supra*, page 15.

[104] Innocent III, ep. *"Deus, qui ecclesiam suam,"*—c. 9, X, *de divortiis*, IV, 19.

[105] Cf. Fahrner, *Geschichte des Unauflöslichkeitsprinzips*, p. 165.

tinction in his answer,[106] namely, that if she had dismissed him with the hope of moving him to repentance she should be obliged, if need be, to return to him. But if his dismissal had had the consent of the lawful ecclesiastical superiors and there was no hope of their married life being resumed, then she should not be compelled to return to him. From this answer it is impossible to determine if Urban had in mind a perfect dissolution of the matrimonial bond, or only a permanent separation from bed and board. But the latter supposition is more in accord with the circumstances of the case quoted, and furthermore, no mention is made in the letter of the wife having entered a second marriage.

§3. *In the Works of the Commentators*

The Commentators in their turn developed only some of the points of the institute, but they said little or nothing about the practical application of the Privilege. A complete explanation was still lacking to the question, why a marriage between two infidels is broken when one of the two is converted and the other refuses to live peacefully with the convert. From the 13th to the 16th centuries, authors were habitually setting aside all major questions the while their attention was taken up in the consideration of minor problems connected with the institute. Thus, for example, the idea of the *contumelia Creatoris,* originally large, was amplified more and more; so that finally there is to be found in the works of Raymond de Peneforte,[107] Tancred,[108] and the Abbas Antiquus[109] an interpretation embracing three distinct cases. These three hypotheses were: (1) Wherein the infidel party absolutely refuses to cohabit; (2) Wherein the infidel consents to continue cohabitation, but *cum contumelia Creatoris;* (3) Wherein the infidel party attempts to lead the convert into mortal sin,[110]

---

[106] Urban III, ep. "*De illa vero,*"—c. 6, X, *de divortiis,* IV, 19.

[107] *Summa,* lib. IV, tit. 10.

[108] *Tancredi Summa de Matrimonio* (ed. Wunderlich), p. 45.

[109] *In Libros Decretalium aurei Commentarii,* p. 131.

[110] "Tunc censetur fidelis ab infideli pertrahi ad peccatum, quando fidelis, attenta propria eius fragilitate, periculo lapsus in peccatum exponitur sive

and especially that of apostasy. In later years this identical interpretation was adopted by a great number of authors.[111]

Hostiensis likewise accepted this view, and applied it to the question regarding the time of dissolution of the first bond. In the company of Panormitanus[112] and others, Hostiensis declared: "Notabis enim, quod hic solvitur matrimonium non per sententiam sed *ipso iure propter contumeliam Creatoris.*"[113] And farther along in his work he quotes the theory of those who hold that the second valid marriage of the convert is the efficient cause of the dissolution, and he disagrees with it. These authors, who agreed with Hostiensis, were misled in their teaching because they based their decision on a false interpretation of Ambrosiaster's principle: "Contumelia Creatoris solvit ius matrimonii circa eum, qui relinquitur." On the other hand, most writers interpret this as an indication of a just cause for the dissolution of the bond through a new marriage on the part of the Christian.

The decision advocated by Pope Innocent III in his letter "*Gaudemus,*" that the matrimonial bond is dissolved *only* by a second valid marriage, was much more common. According to Innocent: "Quod si conversum ad fidem, et illa conversa sequitur, antequam propter causas praedictas legitimam ille ducat uxorem, eam recipere compelleretur." But the Pontiff could not in conscience have ordered such a procedure if the bond of the first marriage were severed by the *contumelia*

---

levi suasione, sive violenta, aut importuna suggestione."—Pirhing, *Jus Canon.*, lib. IV, tit. XIX, n. 35; cf. Sanchez, *De Matrim.*, VII, disp. 74, n. 6; De Becker, *De Spons. et Matrim.*, pp. 415-418.

[111] Pignatelli, *Consultationes Canonicae*, lib. IV, cons. 189, n. 10; De Justis, *De Disp. Matrim.*, II, c. 15, n. 28; Pontius, *De Sacramento Matrimonii*, VII, c. 48, n. 13; IX, c. 4, n. 13; Sylvius, *Commentarius in tertiam partem S. Thomae Aquinatis*, III, q. 59, art. 5, q. 2; Perrone, *De Matrim. Christ.*, III, p. 296, note 30; Billuart, *Theol. Dogmat.*, XIX, dissert. V, art. 5, q. 2: Tournely, *De Matrim.*, p. 249.

[112] Nicolaus de Tudeschis (Panormitanus), *Lectura in Decretales*, IV, *de divortiis*, c. 7, nn. 6, 7; c. 8, n. 15; cf. Pontius, *De Matrim.*, IX, c. 4, n. 16, for a list of authors holding this same opinion.

[113] *Commentaria in Libros V Decretalium*, IV, *de divortiis*, c. 7, n. 3. Jemolo thinks that Hostiensis was of the opposite opinion: "L'opinione che il matrimonio si sciolga solo con il nuovo matrimonio del convertito e seguita dall'Ostiense."—"Il Privilegio Paolino," *Studi Sassaresi*, II (1923), 315.

Creatoris of the infidel party.[114] Innocent's opinion has been followed generally since his time,[115] and it has definitely established in our day as the only possible one.[116]

Closely allied with the problem just treated was that of the right of the infidel to a second marriage. Authors of this period denied the infidel the right to a new marriage if the convert had failed to avail himself of the same privilege. However, if the latter had contracted another marriage, then there is a difference of opinion, for some writers permitted the unbeliever to do likewise, while others prohibited such an action. St. Thomas, for example, was strict in his teaching that the bond was equally dissolved for both parties, "quia matrimonium non claudicat quantum ad vinculum." But at the same time he denied permission to the infidel to remarry unless she also became a Christian.[117] St. Thomas undoubtedly held this view as a penalty imposed on the consort for having remained in infidelity; but the more common opinion is that which allows the unbeliever to contract a second marriage provided that the convert to Christianity has already done so.[118]

---

[114] Grandclaude, *Jus Canon.*, lib. IV, tit. XIX, p. 172.

[115] *Glossa Ordinaria,* ad v. "*compellitur*" in c. 8, X, *de divortiis,* IV, 19; St. Thomas Aquinas, *Summa,* III supplem., q. 59, art. 5, nn. 2, 3; Raymundus de Peneforte, *Summa,* IV, 10; Benedictus XIV, ep. "*Apostolici ministerii,*" 16 Sept., 1747, ad 4,—*Fontes,* n. 381; S. C. S. Off., (Cochinchin.), 1 Aug., 1759, ad 2,—*Fontes,* n. 810; Feije, *De Imped. et Disp. Matrim.*, n. 498; Hurter, *Theol. Dogmat.*, III, n. 760; "Divorce," *Cath. Encycl.*, V, 60; Fahrner, *Geschichte des Unauflöslichkeitsprinzips,* p. 168.

[116] Canon 1126; cf. *infra,* page 105.

[117] "Unde in poenam uxoris infidelis magis quam ex virtute matrimonii praecedentis, ei indicitur quod non possit cum alio contrahere; sed si postea convertatur, potest ei concedi dispensative, ut alteri nubat, si vir ejus aliam in uxorem duxit."—*Summa,* III supplem., q. 59, art. 5, n. 3; cf. De Justis, *De Disp. Matrim.*, II, c. 15, nn. 29-30; Sylvius, *Commentarium,* III, q. 59, art. 5, q. 1; Reiffenstuel, *Jus Canon. Univ.*, lib. III, tit. 34, n. 4; Schmalzgrueber, *Jus Eccles. Univ.*, lib. IV, tit. 19, n. 35; Cosci, *De Separatione Tori Conjugalis,* I, c. 16, nn. 309-315.

[118] "Ducor quod nullo iure interdicatur infideli hic transitus. Non enim humano ecclesiastico, cum Ecclesia careat jurisdictione in infideles; ius vero saeculare nullibi reperitur. Nec ius divinum naturale id infidelibus prohibet. Quia etsi peccaret violans ius divinum naturale legis prioris matrimonii, quis adstringebatur sequi priorem conjugem ad fidem conversum: at priori illo matrimonio iam penitus dissoluto nulla lex divina naturalis prioris matrimonii, quod iam nihil est, superest, qua hic infidelis arceatur ab alio matri-

ART. III. FROM THE COUNCIL OF TRENT TO THE CODE

During this period in the history of the Church a radical change is found in the legislation concerning the Pauline Privilege, for it had again become of practical necessity. A vast new field was opened up for the application of the institute because of the extensive discoveries made by the Spaniards and Portuguese, both in the East and in the West. This in turn excited missionary activity particularly in the New World, and the Privilege witnessed such an extension in its use that authors came to doubt if it was really being applied, or whether this was not the use of the Sovereign Pontiff's Apostolic power to dissolve a non-Christian marriage contract when one of the parties becomes a subject of the Church through the reception of Baptism.[119]

§1. *Constitution "Altitudo" of Paul III*

Up to this time there was thought to be only one method of procedure in a case where a man who had several wives was converted; unalterably he could retain only the first legitimate wife, even though he may have repudiated her before his conversion.[120] The first indication of a distinctive change in this legislation appeared in the Constitution *"Altitudo"* of Pope Paul III,[121] wherein the Pontiff broadened to some extent the teaching of canonists and theologians regarding polygamous marriages. Addressing this Constitution to the missionaries of the West Indies, Paul decided that in all cases of polygamous

---

monio."—Sanchez, *De Matrim.*, VII, disp. 77, n. 6; cf. Jemolo, "Il Privilegio Paolino," *Studi Sassaresi*, II (1923), 312; Gillmann, "Zum Problem vom Privilegium Paulinum," *AkKR*, CII (1922), 27-32; CIV (1924), 242-261.

[119] Benedictus XIV, *De Synodo Dioeces.*, XIII, c. 21, nn. 4-5; Sanchez, *De Matrim.*, II, disp. 17; Fahrner, *Geschichte des Unauflöslichkeitsprinzips*, p. 273; Biederlack, "Ueber das sog. Paulinische Privilegium," *ZKT*, VII (1883), 307, 318-320.

[120] Cf. Nicolaus de Tudeschis (Panormitanus), *Lectura in Decretales*, IV, *de divortiis*, c. 8, n. 15; Pirhing, *Jus Canon.*, lib. IV, tit. XIX, n. 43.

[121] *"Altitudo,"* 1 June, 1537,—*Docum.* VI, C. I. C.; cf. Mansella, *De Impedimentis Matrimonialibus*, p. 113; Feije, *De Imped. et Disp.*, n. 472; *infra*, page 84.

unions founded in infidelity, the convert may, if he cannot remember which was his first legitimate wife, choose any one of them and contract a new marriage. But if he is able to recall the woman with whom he first contracted a valid marriage, he is obliged to renounce all the others and to retain her. If it is necessary, according to the circumstances mentioned above, that the convert make a selection, then there is required a renewal of consent, even though this woman is considered to be his legitimate wife according to pagan customs.[122]

Under the discipline in force antecedently to this, it was required that the infidel declare himself unwilling to cohabit peacefully, so it is evident that a radical departure is contained in this Constitution. For no consideration whatever is shown to the infidel in the case posited by Paul, no demand is made that the unbeliever be questioned regarding his intentions, and the convert is free without any further effort to enter a new marriage.

§2. *Constitution "Romani Pontificis" of Pius V*

This legislation was again extended in some respects by the next occupant of the See of Rome, Pope St. Pius V, whose Constitution *"Romani Pontificis"* [123] also enveloped the question of polygamous marriages contracted among the pagan Indians. When these infidels accepted Christianity they had been permitted by the missionaries to retain that wife who consented to be baptized with her husband. But the validity of many of these unions was doubtful because, in numerous instances, the woman retained by the convert was not the first with which he had legitimately contracted marriage. When this practice was brought to the attention of Pius, he realized the presence of great difficulties almost impossible of solution; the impossibility of ascertaining the whereabouts of the first wife, and the danger of losing the convert incurred by dissolving such a union. Moreover, the missionaries had become

---

[122] Cf. Benedictus XIV, *De Synodo Dioeces.*, XIII, c. 21, n. 6.

[123] *"Romani Pontificis,"* 2 Aug., 1571,—*Docum.* VII, C. I. C.; cf. Mansella, *De Imped. Matrim.*, p. 114; *infra*, page 84.

scrupulous about this condition of affairs, so to ease their consciences, as well as to establish a practical principle, the Pontiff sanctioned this practice of the past and approved it as the *modus agendi* for the future. Again in this case the matrimonial consent must be renewed if the woman selected was not the first legitimate wife.[124] This legislation differed from that enacted by Paul III in the permission that, whether or not the first legitimate wife was known, the convert could retain the one who was baptized with him. The only requisite was that she also receive the Sacrament of Baptism, which condition was not demanded by the Constitution *"Altitudo."*

Neither of these Constitutions required that the infidel party be subjected to any form of interpellation; in truth, the disposition of the first spouse was not even considered, for the Pope dissolved[125] the first bond "motu proprio et ex certa scientia Nostra et apostolicae potestatis plenitudine."[126] Most authors concluded from this that the Pope was exercising his Apostolic power in this case, and that the application of the Pauline Privilege in no way occupied his mind.[127]

§3. *Constitution "Populis" of Gregory XIII*

A purer and more canonical notion of the Privilege was manifested a few years later by Pope Gregory XIII, in his Constitution *"Populis."*[128] This was addressed and restricted

---

[124] "Quod si in Apostolicis litteris, aut in praedicta formula, de eo consensu iterando nulla fit mentio; satis tamen id ex sacrarum legum sanctionibus aperte deducitur; nec ullus esse potest locus dispensationi, quae a consensus renovatione in huiusmodi casibus eximat."—Benedictus XIV, *De Synodo Dioeces.*, XIII, c. 21, n. 6.

[125] Cf. Mansella, *De Imped. Matrim.*, pp. 114, 115, note 1; De Smet, *De Spons. et Matrim.*, n. 355.

[126] *"Romani Pontificis,"—Docum.* VII, C. I. C.

[127] Cf. Benedictus XIV, *De Synodo Dioeces.*, XIII, c. 21, n. 4; Fahrner, *Geschichte des Unauflöslichkeitsprinzips*, p. 275; Ione, "Die Interpellationen bei Anwendung des Paulinischen Privilegs," *LQS*, LXXX (1927), 336-338; *infra*, page 85.

[128] *"Populis,"* 25 Jan., 1585,—*Docum.* VIII, C. I. C.; cf. Mansella, *De Imped. Matrim.*, p. 111; Benedictus XIV, *De Synodo Dioeces.*, XIII, c. 21, n. 3; Feije, *De Imped. et Disp. Matrim.*, n. 474; Ione, "Die Interpellationen bei Anwendung des Paulinischen Privilegs," *LQS*, LXXX (1927), 340-342; *infra*, pages 85-86.

to the mission countries of Angola, Ethiopia, Brazil and India, in which districts it was a common occurrence to have married infidels captured and carried off to distant countries, thus making it almost impossible to carry out the interpellations if one of these infidels was converted and wished to remarry.

Gregory was firm in his belief that marriages contracted in infidelity were true unions, but they were not so firm but that, *necessitate suadente,* they could be dissolved. Hence, he granted faculties to the Ordinaries and missionaries of these districts, and to those members of the Society of Jesus who were approved by their Superiors to hear confessions, whereby these men might dispense from the interpellations under these circumstances. This dispensation enabled the convert who was married before his Baptism to contract another marriage with a Catholic after his conversion, provided that at least summary or extra-judicial evidence was produced to show that the first wife could not be interpellated; or, if interpellated, she could not give her answer within the specified time. Furthermore, all marriages that were contracted by converts under these conditions were declared to be valid, even if it became known afterwards that the former partner had been prevented from giving an answer, or had been likewise converted to Christianity at the time the second marriage was entered into.[129]

Unless special permission was obtained from the Holy See, it was not allowed, under pain of invalidity, that the regulations contained in the Constitutions "*Romani Pontificis*" and "*Populis*" be extended to localities other than those to which

---

[129] "Nonnulli habent: *tempore contracti secundi matrimonii,* sed melius legitur: *tempore transacti secundi matrimonii.* Et sensus est matrimonium valere, etsi postea innotuerit conjugem priorem infidelem baptizatum fuisse *post* contractum a fideli secundum matrimonium. E contrario, Benedictus XIV, *De Syn.,* lib. XIII, cap. XXI, n. 5, ita verba Gregorii XIII intellexit ut matrimonium valeret, etsi postea innotuerit conjugem priorem infidelem baptizatum fuisse *ante* contractum a fideli secundum matrimonium; qui intellectus est manifeste erroneus, tum quia Gregorius XIII loquitur de conversione ad fidem *tempore transacti secundi matrimonii,* quod tempus, stricte loquendo, tum incipit, cum secundum matrimonium contractum fuit, tum quia secus sequeretur Gregorium XIII, momento secundi matrimonii, solvisse matrimonium etiam consummatum inter duos fideles."—Gasparri, *De Matrim.,* n. 1349.

they were addressed.[130] But when the occasion arose and necessity demanded that they be applied in places in which these extraordinary conditions were present, the Holy See readily granted permission for their use by means of special indults, demanding, however, that a summary or extra-judicial investigation be made.[131] Thus, for example, Pope Paul V granted a like faculty to the Bishop of Naples for a particular case; [132] Benedict XIV allowed the same permission to the Nuntio of Venice,[133] and today the Code of Canon Law extends the regulations of these Constitutions to all countries where the exact conditions exist.[134]

§4. *Canonists and Theologians of this Period*

Following these Constitutions, further extensions of the Pauline Privilege were sought without avail. Canonists and theologians from the Council of Trent to the promulgation of the Code were almost unanimous [135] in agreeing upon the fundamental principles of the Privilege as established in the early

---

130 Benedictus XIV, *De Synodo Dioeces.*, XIII, c. 21, nn. 3, 6; Mansella, *De Imped. Matrim.*, p. 108.

131 Mansella, *op. cit.*, p. 107.

132 "Ut possit dispensare cum hac Juvene, quae ante susceptum Baptismum in partibus Turcarum matrimonium contraxerat, ut, superstite etiam conjuge Turca, et consensu ipsius minime requisito, et responso non expectato, matrimonium cum quovis fideli contrahere possit, ita ut etiam postea, si ipse infidelis vel ad Christianam Religionem converteretur, vel cum ea cohabitare paratus esset sine injuria Creatoris, tamen hoc matrimonium posterius ratum, et indissolubile maneat, dummodo tamen ipsi Illustrissimo Ordinario summarie, et extraiudicialiter constet, conjugem absentem moneri legitime non posse."—S. C. C., *Instructio,* 21 June, 1611,—Benedictus XIV, *De Synodo Dioeces.*, XIII, c. 21, n. 6.

133 Benedictus XIV, ep. *"In suprema,"* 16 Jan., 1745,—*Fontes,* n. 353.

134 Canon 1125; cf. *infra,* page 87.

135 Cajetan, *Opera,* V, 106, expressed surprise that the Doctors should give such an interpretation to *I Cor.*, 7:12, when they refuse the same concession to the husband in the case proposed by Christ in *Matthew,* 19:9. According to Sarpi, *Historia del Conc. di Trento,* VII, p. 684, this opinion of Cajetan was followed to such an extent by Dominicus Soto that the latter doubted the ability of the Pauline Privilege to dissolve infidel marriages, and he called upon the Fathers of the Council to decide this. But this part of Soto's plea before the Fathers is absent in the record of Le Plat, *Monumenta ad Histor. Conc. Trid.* (ampliss. collectio), V, p. 687.

days of the Church, although argument was still in evidence concerning a few of the minor questions. Thus, to quote but one author, who expresses the minds of those who followed him: "Matrimonii inter infideles contracti vinculum solvitur ubi alter ex conjugibus ad Christi Fidem convertitur, alter vero requisitus, ut vel eamdem Fidem amplectatur, vel thori societatem sine contumelia Creatoris servare consentiat, utramque conditionem obfirmate recusat." [136] And in like manner they are all opposed to the view that the Privilege may be applied to Christian marriages in which one party has apostatized.

§5. *Decisions of the Holy See*

The Holy See was the recipient of two questions which were definitely settled now for all time, the first of which was whether a catechumen, who had been abandoned by his infidel partner out of hatred for the Faith, could have recourse to the *Casus Apostoli* and contract a new marriage. Rome answered this query in the negative,[137] which goes to show that the valid reception of Baptism is necessary in order that the Privilege be invoked. The second inquiry concerned itself with a marriage entered into between a Christian and an infidel with a dispensation from the impediment of Disparity of Cult, and it was asked whether the Christian spouse might avail himself of the Privilege if the infidel deserted or refused to cohabit *sine contumelia Creatoris.* If the Privilege were extended to apply to cases under these given circumstances it would open the way to many abuses, and could only be looked upon as a sanction placed upon a practice of which the Church severely disapproves.[138] Hence, the Holy Office declared that in this case a dissolution of the bond was not admissible and as long as the infidel party lived the Christian consort could not contract

---

[136] Benedictus XIV, *De Synodo Dioeces.*, XIII, c. 21, n. 1; cf. Pirhing, *Jus Canon.*, lib. IV, tit. XIX, n. 39; Sanchez, *De Matrim.*, VII, disp. 73, 74; Schmalzgrueber, *Jus Eccles. Univ.*, lib. IV, tit. 19, n. 20; De Coninck, *De Sacram. et Censur.*, disp. XXVI, dub. 5, n. 58; Reiffenstuel, *Jus Canon. Univ.*, lib. III, tit. 34, n. 4; Gasparri, *De Matrim.*, n. 1327.

[137] S. C. de Prop. Fide, (ad C. P. pro Sin.), 16 Jan., 1803, ad 1,—*Coll.* n. 665; cf. *infra*, page 57.

[138] Wernz, *Jus Decretalium*, IV, n. 702, note 59.

another marriage.[139] Contrary to these explicit answers of the Holy See, the opposite view appeared to be held by Kenrick, for under these circumstances he was in favor of permitting the dissolution of the matrimonial bond.[140]

With the promulgation of the Code of Canon Law the point has been reached where the purpose of this brief historical conspectus has been fulfilled, namely, to establish the principles of the Pauline Privilege as they became evident throughout the evolution of the institute. A variation of theories and opinions had eventually become crystallized into definite legislation during the period immediately preceding the Code, and this discipline has once for all been promulgated for our observance. Further consideration of the legislation contained in the Code shall be made in subsequent chapters.

---

139 S. C. S. Off., (Cochinchin.), 1 Aug., 1759, ad 4,—*Fontes*, n. 810: (Nankin.), 5 March, 1852,—*Fontes*, n. 918; (Siam), 4 July, 1855,—*Fontes*, n. 931; instr. (ad Ep. S. Alberti), 9 Dec., 1874,—*Fontes*, n. 1036; cf. Zitelli, *De Disp. Matrim.*, p. 121; Perrone, *De Matrim. Christ.*, II, p. 323; Vecchiotti, *De Matrim.*, p. 410; Gasparri, *De Matrim.*, n. 1340.

140 "Quando vero ex Ecclesiae dispensatione conciliatae sunt nuptiae inter fidelem et hominem non baptizatum, dubitare potest utrum solvi queant; *nobis autem videtur semper solvi potest*, si renuat infidelis cum fideli habitare, sine contumelia Creatoris; de eo enim dici potest: 'Quod si infidelis discedit, discedat.' "—*Theologia Moralis*, II, tract. 21, c. IV, n. 110.

PART III
PRESENT LEGISLATION IN THE CODE

CHAPTER III

FUNDAMENTAL ELEMENTS

CANON 1120

§1. Legitimum inter non baptizatos matrimonium, licet consummatum, solvitur in favorem fidei ex privilegio Paulino.

§2. Hoc privilegium non obtinet in matrimonio inter partem baptizatam et partem non baptizatam inito cum dispensatione ab impedimento disparitatis cultus.

ART. I. DEFINITION AND ORIGIN OF THE PAULINE PRIVILEGE

It is well to begin the discussion of present legislation on the Pauline Privilege, or *Casus Apostoli,* with a comprehensive definition of all that it entails. The Privilege, therefore, may be defined as a special concession granted by St. Paul in consequence of a power divinely conceded to him, by virtue of which a marriage validly contracted and even consummated in infidelity may be dissolved if one of the parties receives Baptism and the one remaining in infidelity departs. But only when the convert enters a new marriage is the former bond dissolved.[1]

The foundation of the name "Pauline" is evident, for the terms of the Privilege are to be found in St. Paul's First Epistle to the Corinthians.[2] And it is called the *Casus Apostoli* for the reason that the Apostle proposed and decided a case of mixed marriage entirely different from any determined by

[1] Vermeersch, *De Casu Apostoli,* n. 1; Wernz-Vidal, *Jus Canon.,* V, n. 631; Petrovits, *The New Church Law on Matrimony,* n. 553; Cappello, *De Sacram.,* III, n. 767; Vermeersch-Creusen, *Epitome,* II, n. 427.

[2] I Cor., 7:12-15; Canon 1120, §1.

Christ in His doctrine on matrimony.[3] In the definition it has been called a "divinely conceded power," for Catholic doctrine teaches us that human authority, even of an ecclesiastical nature, is incapable of itself to affect the bond of a true marriage; that every power which the Church exercises in this regard, even through the medium of the Holy Father, springs from the positive will and grant of God. In such matters, therefore, the province of the Church is to act merely in her ministerial capacity.[4]

Nevertheless, there is a two-fold opinion regarding the origin of the Privilege, wherein some authors [5] think that it is of *immediate divine Law* given by Christ and promulgated by St. Paul, and others [6] prefer to speak of it as being of *apostolic right,* introduced by the Apostle of the Gentiles for the Corinthians and later extended to the universal Church by St. Peter. The former opinion is more common and its strength is enhanced by favorable instructions of the Roman Congregations, for the style of the Roman Curia is wont to call the Privilege "divine, granted by Our Lord and promulgated by the Apostle, St. Paul." [7] Moreover, it is held by all those who deny to

---

[3] Cf. *supra,* page 4.

[4] Vermeersch, *De Casu Apostoli,* n. 2.

[5] Benedictus XIV, *De Synodo Dioec.,* VI, c. 4, n. 3; Sanchez, *De Matrim.,* VII, disp. 74, n. 4; Perrone, *De Matrim.,* II, 312; Pesch, *Praelect. Dogmat.,* n. 790; Biederlack, "Ueber das sog. Paulinische Privilegium," *ZKT,* VII (1883), 320-321; Braun, "Auflösung der von Ungläubigen abgeschlossenen Ehe," *AkKR,* XLVI (1881), 385; Ott, "Card. C. Tarquini über das Paulinische Privileg," *AkKR,* L (1883), 232, 235; Ojetti, *Synopsis Rerum Moralium,* III, n. 3281; Noldin, *De Jure Matrimoniali,* p. 34; Wernz-Vidal, *Jus Canon.,* V, n. 631, note 56; Vlaming, *Praelectiones Juris Matrimonii,* n. 718; Billot, *De Sacramentis,* II, 394; Vermeersch-Creusen, *Epitome,* II, n. 427; Petrovits, *The New Church Law,* n. 553; Cerato, *Matrimonium,* n. 120.

[6] *Disputatio Apostolicae Sedi Exhibitae a Patribus S. J.*—Zitelli, *De Disp. Matrim.,* Appendix XI; Cornely, *Comment. in I Ep. ad Cor.,* p. 181; Lemhkuhl, *Theol. Moral.,* II, nn. 929-932; Scherer, *Handbuch des Kirchenrechts,* II, 136, note 64; Gasparri, *De Matrim.,* n. 1329; Vermeersch, *De Casu Apostoli,* n. 2; Fahrner, *Geschichte des Unauflöslichkeitsprinzips,* p. 284; De Smet, *De Spons. et Matrim.,* n. 341; Cappello, *De Sacram.,* III, n. 767; Creusen, "Privilège Paulinien et Mixtes Mariages," *NRT,* L (1923), 88.

[7] S. C. de Prop. Fide, instr. (Tunkin), 5 Mar., 1816, ad 1,—*Coll.* n. 704; S. C. S. Off., instr. (pro Vic. Ap. ad Gallas), 20 June, 1866,—*Fontes,* n. 994; instr. (Natal), 11 July, 1866, ad 8,—*Fontes,* n. 996.

the Roman Pontiff the power to dissolve the marriages of infidels.

But on the other hand, once this power of dissolving infidel unions, even if consummated, is admitted in the Pope, there is no apparent need of a special intervention immediately and directly from God; for the dissolution of the bond is best explained by the extraordinary power of the Apostle and the ordinary power of the Sovereign Pontiff. In like manner the latter opinion appears at an advantage because it seems to be more in conformity with the context of the Apostolic dispensation and with the expositions of the text as afforded by the Fathers. The words, "For the rest, I speak, not the Lord," are evidently significant of what is to follow and they seem to indicate apostolic authority rather than divine. The weight of the argument drawn from the style of the Roman Curia dwindles when it is correctly understood that the Congregations did not examine this question *ex professo,* but rather called the Privilege "divine" in as much as it is contained in Sacred Scripture and as such it is from God.[8] For these reasons the latter opinion is more probable, although both sides present solid arguments and are represented by learned authors. In either case it may be said that the doctrine has divine authority, for St. Paul wrote this letter in the exercise of that apostolic authority which he had received from the Lord and under the inspiration of the Holy Ghost.[9]

The Pauline dispensation is rightly termed a "privilege" because it was evoked precisely to aid conversions to the Faith. When the Apostle decreed that "if the unbeliever depart, let him depart; for a brother or sister is not under servitude in

[8] Gasparri, *De Matrim.*, n. 1329; Cappello, *De Sacram.*, III, n. 767; Wernz-Vidal, *Jus Canon.*, V, n. 631, note, 56.

[9] "Idcirco otiosa videtur controversia utrum privilegium hoc sit origine immediata divinum atque a Paulo solummodo promulgatum, an ab hoc concessum ex potestate ministeriali sub Deo, in charismate apostolatus contenta: atque ita non pro solis corinthiis concessum, sed approbante etiam Petro, pro tota Ecclesia. Uno enim alterove transmissionis modo, privilegium est aeque divinum, nec aestimandum et exercendum nisi in correlationem cum plenitudine Pontificii ministerialis quidem sub Deo, sed supremi relate ad ceteros omnes in Ecclesia, Petro a Christo Domino traditi."—Arendt, "Nota Circa Canonem 1127," *Eph. Th. Lov.*, I (1925), 179, note 12.

such cases, but God hath called us in peace," [10] he had in mind the separation and consequent dissolution of the marriage bond effected by the desertion of the infidel party. Exegetes unanimously interpret the sense of the text to mean that in such cases of abandonment a brother or sister is not under servitude to the unbaptized party as regards the conjugal bond.[11] This is the prerogative that Christians enjoy under the circumstances stated; the advantage of the faith which was necessary in order to make everything more favorable for conversion to the faith. Were this Privilege unattainable to married infidels, their conversion would be greatly deterred in the event that they were bound to a life of continency after separation from their unbaptized spouses. Thus, the concession is a privilege in the sense that it affords a deserted convert conjugal freedom and tranquillity of mind in the knowledge that the bond of his marriage contracted in infidelity is absolutely broken.[12] This doctrine has been the common teaching of exegetes, theologians and canonists.

§1. *Efficacy of the Privilege in Non-Catholic Baptism*

Although the Pauline Privilege is said to be granted in favor of the faith, some doubt might arise as to the capacity of those who join a Christian denomination by the valid reception of Baptism. The solution of this problem is found in the principle that *the Privilege is attached to the Sacrament of Baptism.* Therefore, it is applicable to all who are converted from infidelity and are the recipients of valid Baptism, either in the Catholic Church or in a non-Catholic sect. Such is the opinion of the majority of authors and rightly so, since the foundation of the Privilege is not the acceptance of the True Faith but rather the valid reception of Baptism, through which marriage is given greater strength. Furthermore, many of the older

---

[10] I Cor., 7:15.

[11] Cf. *supra,* page 7.

[12] St. Thomas, *Commentaria in Omnes Epistolas D. Pauli A.,* I, 321; Hurter, *Theol. Dogmat.,* III, 760; Benedictus XIV, const. "*Apostolici ministerii,*" 16 Sept., 1747, ad 4,—*Fontes,* n. 381; Perrone, *De Matrim.,* II, 315.

authors interpret the terms "brother" and "sister" in the text of St. Paul to include generally all who are baptized, and even St. Augustine in the early days of the Church appears to have understood the passage in this sense.[13]

Rosset[14] denies that the Privilege is applicable to baptized non-Catholics, and Vlaming[15] is in agreement with him on the grounds that the interpretation of verses 12 to 14 of the Pauline text and the phrase *in favorem fidei* of Canon 1120, §1 should be construed to include *both* Baptism and the profession of the True Faith as the foundation of the Privilege. Nevertheless, Könings and other authors of wide repute[16] assert that the Privilege is to be granted in such a case, and that a practical decision to that effect has been made by a Roman Congregation.[17]

---

[13] St. Augustine, *Enarratio in Psalmnum XXXII* (ad finem),—*MPL*, XXXVI, 299; cf. Palmieri, *De Matrim.*, pp. 224-226; Feije, *De Imped. et Disp. Matrim.*, n. 502; Ferreres, *Theol. Moral.*, II, n. 1115; Ott, "Card. C. Tarquini über das Paulinische Privileg," *AkKR*, L (1883), 225-229, 232-234; Biederlack, "Ueber das sog. Paulinische Privilegium," *ZKT*, VII (1883), 305.

[14] *De Sacramento Matrimonii*, I, n. 616.

[15] *Praelectiones*, n. 720, note 3.

[16] Könings, *Theologia Moralis*, II, 394, note d; Ballerini-Palmieri, *Opus Theol. Moral.*, VI, 457; Braun, "Auflösung der von Ungläubigen abgeschlossenen Ehe," *AkKR*, XLVI (1881), 404-413; Fahrner, *Geschichte des Unauflöslichkeitsprinzips*, p. 290; De Smet, *De Spons. et Matrim.*, n. 345; Wernz-Vidal, *Jus Canon.*, V, n. 631, note 55; Chelodi, *Jus Matrimoniale*, n. 157; Cappello, *De Sacram.*, III, n. 767; Cerato, *Matrim.*, n. 120; Vermeersch, "Interpretatio Canonis 1127," *Periodica*, X (1922), (28); Vermeersch-Creusen, *Epitome*, II, n. 428; Farrugia, *De Matrimonio*, n. 320; Gasparri, *De Matrim.*, n. 1331. Cardinal Gasparri has seemingly undergone a change of mind since his work was last published in 1904, for in a *votum* prepared for a particular case and presented to the Holy Office on August 21, 1929, he quotes the words of Pope Innocent III and denies the Apostolic concession to the person who was baptized validly in a non-Catholic sect. As the Consultors and Auditors interested in this case were evenly matched in the disagreement, the Holy Father has decided nothing and the case is still pending. Cf. "Si enim alter infidelium conjugum *ad fidem catholicam convertatur*, etc."—Innocent III, ep. "*Quanto te magis*," 1 May, 1199,—c. 7, X, *de divortiis*, IV, 19.

[17] Könings states, *Theol. Moral.*, II, 394, that such a decision was given by the Holy See for a particular case in 1876, but he does not give full information as to which Congregation, on what day, or in what form this was done. Cf. Braun, "Auflösung der von Ungläubigen abgeschlossenen

But in order that the Privilege may be used in this case, all of its conditions must be fulfilled. For non-Catholics are truly in a less favorable position than Catholics because a dispensation from the interpellations is frequently necessary, and this is never granted by the Holy See to non-Catholics.[18]

Hence, heretical or schismatical spouses may avail themselves of the Privilege if it is certain that they were not baptized before marriage, and if it is proved that only later on one of them was converted and baptized.[19]

ART. II. THE OBJECT OF THE PRIVILEGE

A few preliminary remarks concerning the various kinds of marriage may help to clarify somewhat the notion of the exact object of the Privilege. Marriage is said to be ratified, legitimate, or consummated. It is called ratified when contracted validly and sacramentally between two baptized persons, or when, having been entered into between unbaptized persons, it later becomes a Sacrament by the Baptism of both parties. Marriage is termed legitimate when it has been validly contracted between two unbaptized persons and has not as yet become sacramental through the Baptism of both parties.[20] Consummated or not consummated is that valid union which has or has not been followed by the conjugal act suitable of itself for the purpose of generation. Now, if a ratified marriage is followed by consummation, it is said to be *matrimonium ratum et consummatum;* if a legitimate union is consummated, it is known as *matrimonium legitimum consummatum;* and if the conjugal act follows upon a legitimate marriage in which both parties are later baptized, that union is then classified as *matrimonium legitimum consummatum et ratum.* Thus, the

---

Ehe," *AkKR,* XLVI (1881), 413, note 4. De Angelis, *Praelectiones,* IV, thesis 19, n. 11, says that he consulted the Holy Office on an identical case, but after a series of investigations nothing was decided, and therefore either opinion may be held.

[18] Perrone, *De Matrim.,* II, 315; Feije, *De Imped. et Disp. Matrim.,* n. 503; Gasparri, *De Matrim.,* n. 1331; Wernz-Vidal, *Jus Canon.,* V, n. 631, note 55.

[19] Cappello, *De Sacram.,* III, n. 769.

[20] Canon 1015, §3.

reception of Baptism by both parties is the existing distinction between ratified and legitimate marriage. Gratian harbored a distinction radically foreign to this, for he called *matrimonium legitimum* that which was contracted according to the legal institutions or customs of a country, whether it was between baptized or unbaptized persons. According to his categories if the parties to the union were baptized, the marriage was *legitimum et ratum;* if they were unbaptized, it was *legitimum non ratum.* And if baptized persons married without observing the required legal institutions and ceremonies, their marriage was not to be considered even legitimate, but only ratified.[21] These differences have been entirely discarded now, and Canon 1120, §1 restricts the use of the *Casus Apostoli* to a marriage validly contracted between unbaptized persons, whether it has been consummated or not. Under the designation of "infidel" are to be included all persons who are not validly baptized, whether they be pagans, Jews, Mohammedans or adherents to some Christian sect.

§1. *The Privilege Dissolves Only a Valid Marriage*

It must be borne in mind that the Pauline Privilege is a concession whereby a marriage *validly* contracted between two unbaptized persons may be dissolved. But if the union has been entered into *invalidly* there is place, not for the Privilege, but rather for a simple declaration of nullity. To judge of the validity or invalidity of these marriages is frequently a very difficult task and demands a serious investigation in individual cases.[22] Thus, it must be determined whether or not there was

[21] *Dictum* ad c. 17, C. XXVIII, q. 1.

[22] S. C. S. Off., (Siouxormen.), 18 May, 1892, ad 1, 2,—*Fontes*, n. 1155. The Holy Office decreed that this preliminary examination could not be omitted even in the case of persons belonging to a *savage* tribe, and observed that "it is neither certain nor proved that there is no marriage valid in the natural law among such tribes, that all unions are indiscriminately concubinal, and that every idea, however confused, of the difference between marriage and concubinage has been lost to them. It is not right to pass a judgment like that upon them, upon an entire foreign race without having made a careful investigation of their customs, and such a judgment should be based on weighty arguments drawn from ascertained facts; otherwise we must

any diriment impediment of the natural, divine or civil laws,[23] and if the usual solemnities which are customary in different countries have been fully observed. In this manner the Holy Office has declared that "we must consider as valid those marriages celebrated with the usual ceremonies of the country when the mutual and present consent of the parties has been sufficiently expressed according to the common estimation of the locality." [24] The same Congregation has also stated that "infidels occasionally marry without observing the customary local ceremonies, so that in the beginning these unions must be regarded as concubinal. But things turn out well and they live together faithfully, . . . leading a conjugal life which they will not give up, because they love one another, have children, and separation would cause them both serious injury. This is why the Cardinals declare that it is necessary to examine not only the initial circumstances and the way in which the marriage was contracted, but also its duration and the other circumstances which may have subsequently intervened; namely, the birth of children, mutual love, its continuance and growth, and so forth. If such indications either singly or by their collective weight show certainly or almost certainly that the parties in question will remain united until death, though it may be evident that in the beginning there was only an irregular union, it must, nevertheless, be held as certain, or at least

---

keep to the *praesumptio juris*. For in the absence of certain proof, nature, which as the Apostle says (*Romans*, 2:14), has implanted the first conception of marriage in the hearts of all, cries out in behalf of these tribes, however abandoned they may be. All things considered, therefore, it is impossible to establish a general rule permitting the omission of particular inquiry, and to decree that the marriages of infidels in this country, and of such Catholics as happen to be in like ignorance, are to be considered as cases of mere concubinage. On the contrary, a special inquiry must be made into each particular case."—S. C. S. Off., instr. (ad Ep. S. Alberti), 9 Dec., 1874, ad 2, 11,—*Fontes*, n. 1036.

[23] S. C. S. Off., instr. (ad Ep. S. Alberti), 9 Dec., 1874, ad 8-11,—*Fontes*, n. 1036; instr. (ad Ep. Nesquallien.), 24 Jan., 1877,—*Fontes*, n. 1050. In these Instructions the Sacred Congregation pays especial attention to the possibility that these marriages may have been entered into under the burden of some suspensive condition contrary to the substance of a valid union.

[24] S. C. S. Off., (Niger), 17 Aug., 1898,—*Fontes*, n. 1205.

as probable, that such an illicit union has passed into a legitimate marriage in the course of time." [25] Hence, it must be borne in mind that where the Civil Law fully recognizes the so-called "Common Law" marriage, it is truly a legitimate union. If, after a careful investigation, the marriage still remains doubtful, the doubt must be solved in favor of the faith [26] so as to leave the convert to Christianity at liberty and free to enter a new marriage.

§2. *It Does Not Apply Among Baptized Persons*

The Privilege can in no way affect the marriage of *two baptized persons* when one of them, through hatred of the Faith, has apostatized and embraced infidelity. Pope Celestine appeared to have dissolved such a marriage,[27] but if his opinion was to be looked upon as a Pontifical decision it was quickly recalled by his successor, Pope Innocent III.[28] This is likewise the mind of all authors,[29] in accordance with the declaration of the Holy See.[30]

§3. *Application to Catholic Mixed Marriages*

Nor may the Privilege be applied so as to dissolve the bond of a marriage validly entered into between a Catholic and an

---

[25] S. C. S. Off., (Siam), 22 Nov., 1871, ad finem,—*Fontes*, n. 1019, and, instr. (ad Ep. S. Alberti), 9 Dec., 1874, ad 17,—*Fontes*, n. 1036.

[26] Canon 1127; S. C. S. Off., (Cochinchin.), 1 Aug., 1759, ad 2,—*Fontes*, n. 810; instr. (ad Archiep. Quebecen.), 16 Sept., 1824, ad 1,—*Fontes*, n. 866; instr. (ad Ep. S. Alberti), 9 Dec., 1874, ad 13,—*Fontes*, n. 1036; 18 May, 1892, ad 1, 2,—*Fontes*, n. 1156; 19 April, 1899,—*Fontes*, n. 1220, 26 April, 1899,—*Fontes*, n. 1222; cf. *infra*, page 112.

[27] Celestine III, ep. "*Laudabilem*," a. 1191,—c. 1, X, *de conversione infidelium*, III, 33.

[28] Innocent III, ep. "*Quanto te magis*," 1 May, 1199,—c. 7, X, *de divortiis*, IV, 19; cf. *supra*, page 32.

[29] Cf. Benedictus XIV, *De Synodo Dioec.*, XIII, c. 21, n. 1; Pirhing, *Jus Canon.*, lib. IV, tit. XIX, n. 39; Sanchez, *De Matrim.*, VII, disp. 73, 74; Schmalzgrueber, *Jus Eccles. Univ.*, lib. IV, tit. 19, n. 20; Reiffenstuel, *Jus Canon. Univ.*, lib. III, tit. 34, n. 4; De Coninck, *De Sacram. et Censur.*, disp. XXVI, dub. 5, n. 58; Gasparri, *De Matrim.*, n. 1327; De Smet, *De Spons. et Matrim.*, n. 342; Cappello, *De Sacram.*, III, n. 768.

[30] S. C. de Prop. Fide, (Iaponiae), 7 Dec., 1626,—*Coll.* n. 2245.

infidel when the proper dispensation from the impediment of Disparity of Cult has been obtained.[31] For once such a marriage has been consummated it is indissoluble for all practical purposes; [32] the marital bond remains and the only possible relief is in the separation advised by the Holy Office.[33]

§4. *Application to Mixed Marriages of Non-Catholics*

A question of prime importance today is whether or not the Privilege can be given to a validly baptized non-Catholic who has validly married an infidel since May 19, 1918. The former has never belonged to the Catholic Church, but now he is converted to that Faith. Is his case to be considered within the ambit of the Pauline Privilege? One writer has answered this problem in the affirmative,[34] but the negative opinion [35] is common and most probable for several reasons.

In the first place, the text of the Code itself specifically excludes such a possibility when it confines the use of the Privilege to the non-baptized.[36] Furthermore, from the manner in

---

[31] Canon 1120, §2; S. C. S. Off., (Cochinchin.), 1 Aug., 1759, ad 4,—*Fontes*, n. 810; (Nankin.), 5 Mar., 1852,—*Fontes*, n. 918; (Siam), 4 July, 1855,—*Fontes*, n. 931; instr. (ad Ep. S. Alberti), 9 Dec., 1874,—*Fontes*, n. 1036; cf. Fahrner, *Geschichte des Unauflöslichkeitsprinzips*, p. 290; Creusen, "Privilège Paulinien et Mixtes Mariages," *NRT*, L (1923), 89; Arendt, "Nota Circa Canonem 1127," *Eph. Th. Lov.*, I (1924), 183, note 30.

[32] Schenk, *Mixed Religion and Disparity of Cult*, p. 185, fails to distinguish between the exercise of ecclesiastical law and of divine Law. Many authors are of the opinion that at least *theoretically* the Sovereign Pontiff can dissolve any marriage which is not both sacramental and consummated, though *in practice* it is true that he is averse to the use of this power.

[33] S. C. S. Off., (Cochinchin.), 1 Aug., 1759, ad 4,—*Fontes*, n. 810. "Nec fideles, qui post obtentam dispensationem ab impedimento disparitatis cultus celebrant nuptias cum infideli; secus privilegium in favorem fidei concessum potius cederet in praemium nequitiae et fraudem sibi tentaminis causa assumendi coniugem."—Wernz-Vidal, *Jus Canon.*, V, n. 631, note 55; cf. Cappello, *De Sacram.*, III, n. 768.

[34] *Ami du Clergé* (1920), 669; (1921), 69.

[35] Wernz-Vidal, *Jus Canon.*, V, n. 631, note 55; Cappello, *De Sacram.*, III, n. 769; Vermeersch-Creusen, *Epitome*, II, n. 428; Chelodi, *Jus Matrim.*, n. 157; Creusen, "Privilège Paulinien et Mixtes Mariages," *NRT*, L (1923), 88-95.

[36] Canon 1120, §1.

which the Fathers have always interpreted the words of St. Paul it has ever been the practice of the Church to exclude such heretics. As has been said above, the Privilege is a concession granted to a convert from infidelity in order that he might not be slavishly bound by a marriage contracted *in infidelity*. Since valid Baptism, rather than the profession of the true Faith, is the basis of the Privilege, it is always to be understood as embracing *two infidels* in a valid marriage, one of whom is converted while the other remains in infidelity.[37] Hence, the marriage in this case is valid[38] and cannot be dissolved by the Pauline Privilege.

Art. III. Necessary Conditions

For the valid use of the Privilege there must be present four conditions. Two of these have been spoken of previously; namely, the requirement that the marriage must have been founded while the parties were still infidels, and the necessity of conversion and the reception of valid Baptism by one of the parties while the other spouse elects to remain in infidelity. Canon 1120, §2 expressly states that the Privilege does not obtain in a marriage between a baptized person and one not baptized, even when the proper dispensation has been procured. Considering all possible aspects, circumstances and forms of marriage, the basic principle of the Privilege strongly reasserts itself: *the Pauline Privilege is attached to the reception of valid Baptism.* It is for this reason that the Holy See has decreed that catechumens cannot avail themselves of the concession, even though they are necessarily forced by their infidel relatives to lead a life of sin.[39] Here it may be remarked that a catechumen, validly married, who wishes to take ad-

---

[37] This traditional interpretation of the Fathers is discussed at length by Arendt, "La Tradizione catt. del Priv. Paolino," *Gregorianum*, IV (1923), 241 sq., 329 sq.

[38] Canon 1070, §1.

[39] S. C. de Prop. Fide, (ad C. P. pro Sin.), 16 Jan., 1803, ad 1,—*Coll.*, n. 665; S. C. S. Off., 13 March, 1901,—*ASS*, XXXIII, 549-550; cf. Wernz-Vidal, *Jus Canon.*, V, n. 631, note 55; Cappello, *De Sacram.*, III, n. 768.

vantage of the Privilege may not be admitted to Baptism unless he consents to retain his legitimate spouse, if she is willing and agreeable to continue in a peaceful married state.[40]

The third condition which must be fully established is the desertion of the party remaining in infidelity, for from the text of St. Paul it is evident that the use of the term *discedit* refers to a separation effected by this infidel spouse. That this condition may be considered as fulfilled, it is further necessary that the unconverted party persevere in his infidelity and that he refuse to continue peaceful cohabitation with the convert. These concurrent acts point to the infidel's wish for separation, for in either case he may evidence a desire to cohabit with the believer, while in doing so he would subject the latter to unpleasant and sinful temptations.

§1. *Physical and Moral Departure*

The concession may be granted to the converted party if the departure of the infidel is physical or moral. *Physical* desertion is present if the unbeliever unjustly leaves a faithful spouse who has given no cause for departure, if he contracts marriage with another person, if he is detained by a second consort or is bound by a creditor because of unpaid debts, and, finally, if he leaves purely out of hatred for the Christian Faith.[41]

Moral departure, on the other hand, is said to be effected by one or more of the following actions or like circumstances: when the infidel party refuses to live with the believer without blaspheming the Holy Name of God; [42] when he refuses to give

---

[40] S. C. S. Off., (Cochinchin.), 6 Aug., 1856,—*Fontes*, n. 939; 30 April, 1908,—*Periodica*, IV (1908), 181-184. However, good faith and a sincere acceptance of Christianity may be presumed on the part of a convert. Cf. Vermeersch, *De Casu Apostoli*, n. 37; De Smet, *De Spons. et Matrim.*, n. 345, note 5; *HPR*, XXX (1929), 64.

[41] S. C. S. Off., (Cochinchin.), 12 June, 1850, ad 1,—*Fontes*, n. 910; (Siam), 4 July, 1855,—*Fontes*, n. 931; (Cochinchin.), 1 Aug., 1759, ad 2,—*Fontes*, n. 810; S. C. de Prop. Fide, (ad Vic. Ap. Sutchuen.), 30 Jan., 1807,—*Coll.*, n. 690; cf. Laemmer, "Die Interpellatio Conjugis Infidelis," *AkKR*, XI (1864), 246; Ione, "Die Anwendung des Paulinischen Privilegs," *LQS, LXXX* (1927), 135.

[42] S. C. S. Off., (Siam), 4 July, 1855,—*Fontes*, n. 931.

up a life of concubinage, which condition is likewise an offense against God; [43] in the event that he denies to the offspring of the union a Catholic education; [44] if he attempts to lead the convert into idolatry; [45] if he himself tries to tempt the believer to grave sin, especially against the chastity to be observed in the marital state; [46] and lastly, should the infidel create an unhappy married life in which severe quarrels continually arise, dissensions which in no way are caused by the convert or if so caused they have already been propitiated, moral departure is thought to have taken place if such a family condition is serious and proves a handicap to the faithful party.[47]

Hence, from an investigation of the modes of departure stated above, it may be concluded that physical desertion on the part of the infidel for any reason at all suffices in order that the Privilege may be granted to the believer. The Holy See does not require that the departure take place solely on account of malice or hatred for the Faith, but it recognizes as well any reason because of which the infidel is detained, as long as the converted partner is not the cause of such detention.[48]

---

[43] S. C. S. Off., (Siam), 4 July, 1855,—*Fontes*, n. 931; (Natal), 11 July, 1866, ad 2,—*Fontes*, n. 996.

[44] S. C. S. Off., (Tunkin. Occident.), 14 Dec., 1848, ad 2,—*Fontes*, n. 908; (Natal), 11 July, 1866, ad 4,—*Fontes*, n. 996.

[45] S. C. S. Off., (Cochinchin.), 1 Aug., 1759,—*Fontes*, n. 810; S. C. de Prop. Fide, 5 March, 1816, ad 6,—*Coll.*, n. 704.

[46] S. C. de Prop. Fide, 5 March, 1816, ad 6,—*Coll.*, n. 704. In this decision it is stated that if the temptation towards sin is not on the part of the infidel husband himself toward his converted wife, but rather that it arises from others who live in his house, e.g., from the father-in-law or mother-in-law, the converted party may withdraw from that house if there are no other means at hand; but she cannot dissolve that marriage and enter another. Cf. Ione, "Die Anwendung des Paulinischen Privilegs," *LQS*, LXXX (1927), 134.

[47] S. C. S. Off., (Cochinchin.), 1 Aug., 1759, ad 2,—*Fontes*, n. 810; 26 April, 1899,—*Fontes*, n. 1222.

[48] "Quidam ad fidem nuper conversi interpellant coniugem infidelem, an velit converti vel saltem habitare pacifice. Respondet illa se quidem velle, sed detineri a secundo marito vel a creditore, qui illam abire non sinunt. Quaeritur, utrum in hoc casu coniux conversus possit ad alias transire nuptias." Resp:—"Affirmative, nempe conversum, de quo agitur, si non est legitime ab Apostolica Sede dispensatus, teneri ex divino praecepto ad faciendam in praesenti casu una vice interpellationem alteri coniugi, posse autem pluries ex mera caritate. Expleta autem a converso hac divinitus iniuncta conditione,

§2. *Perseverance in Infidelity*

Separation effected by the unbeliever must be evident, for if he should also be converted and receive valid Baptism before the Christian spouse has entered a second marriage, the Privilege is not applicable to their union.[49] In such a case the original marriage has now become *ratum* because of the Baptism of both parties, and therefore it is subject to the laws governing Christian marriage.[50] Nevertheless, the converted party would not forfeit his right to enter a second marriage if at the time he exercises this privilege the other spouse is still an infidel, even though he expresses a disposition to embrace the Faith.[51]

§3. *Refusal of Peaceful Cohabitation*

Three possible hypotheses may present themselves, any one of which would constitute a case indicating the unbeliever's unwillingness to continue peaceful cohabitation with the converted party.

(1) If the infidel is entirely set against the idea of continu-

---

si pagana uxor ad ipsum non redierit intra iustum aliquod et rationabile temporis spatium, posse praefatum conversum licite et valide alias inire nuptias cum muliere tamen christiana, dummodo *vir non sit causa impedimenti*, quo mulier detineatur."—S. C. S. Off., (Cochinchin. Occident.), 12 June, 1850, ad 1,—*Fontes*, n. 910; cf. Cappello, *De Sacram.*, III, n. 770; Wernz-Vidal, *Jus Canon.*, V, n. 631, note 58; Vermeersch, *De Casu Apostoli*, n. 45; Chelodi, *Jus Matrim.*, n. 157; De Smet, *De Spons. et Matrim.*, n. 347; Vlaming, *Praelect.*, n. 721.

[49] "Quod si conversum ad fidem et illa conversa sequatur antequam propter causas praedictas legitimam ille ducat uxorem, eam recipere compelletur."—Innocent III, ep. "*Gaudemus in Domino*,"—c. 8, X, *de divortiis*, IV, 19; cf. S. C. S. Off., instr. (ad Vic. Ap. pro Gallas), 20 June, 1866,—*Fontes*, n. 994; (Natal), 11 July, 1866, ad 8,—*Fontes*, n. 996; (Siouxormen.), 18 May, 1892, ad 2,—*Fontes*, n. 1155.

[50] Canons 1118, 1119.

[51] S. C. S. Off., (Siam), 22 Nov., 1871,—*Fontes*, n. 1019; (Victoriae Nyanzae), 8 July, 1891, ad 1, 2,—*Fontes*, n. 1140; 26 April, 1899,—*Fontes*, n. 1222; 30 April, 1908, ad 2, 3,—*Periodica*, IV (1908), 262. The Holy See requires that the Bishop is to decide whether or not there is possible the application of the Privilege in those cases wherein prolonged delay on the part of the infidel party in receiving Baptism may cause suspicion that he is not sincere or that the faith of the converted party is in danger. Cf. S. C. S. Off., (Tunkin. Orient.), 4 July, 1855,—*Fontes*, n. 930; (Mongoliae), 29 Nov., 1882, ad 3,—*Fontes*, n. 1075.

ing cohabitation with the Christian, even though the former expresses a desire to embrace the Faith.[52] It matters not what motive has prompted him to arrive at such a conclusion, so long as the believer has provided no just and reasonable cause for separation after his baptism.[53] However, if the converted party has been guilty of some act sufficient in itself to provide the infidel with a just cause for separation, for example, by the commission of adultery after Baptism, the former may not take advantage of the Privilege.[54] But, on the other hand, if the adultery was committed before conversion, the infidel spouse has not been furnished with a legitimate excuse for separation, because the stain of the sin is looked upon as having been washed away by Baptism. In reply to the question: "Are faults committed after Baptism an obstacle to the use of the Privilege by the baptized party if they are inconsequential in the eyes of the infidel or even entirely unknown to him?" the Holy Office declared that its previous decrees of August 1, 1759, and of January 16, 1797, should be consulted; and it stated the principle that in a case of doubt the decision must always be rendered to the advantage of the Faith.[55]

---

52 "Vir fidelis mulierem infidelem in ipsius viri infidelitate ductam habet, quae quidem vult converti, sed nullo modo cum eo habitare consentit." Quaeritur: "An vir uti privilegio paulino, et facta interpellatione de cohabitandi voluntate, ad alias nuptias transire possit." Resp.: "Affirmative—dummodo uxor in infidelitate permaneat."—S. C. S. Off., (Victoriae Nyanzae), 8 July, 1891, ad 1,—*Fontes*, n. 1140; cf. 26 April, 1899,—*Fontes*, n. 1222.

53 Quaeritur: "An id (Privilegium Paulinum) solum habeat locum quando infidelis discedit odio fidei, an etiam quando discedit propter discordias, vel aliam causam a fide diversam." Resp.: "Cum militet ex parte coniugis conversi favor fidei, eo potest uti quacumque ex causa, dummodo iusta sit, nimirum si non dederit iustum ac rationabile motivum alteri coniugi discendendi."—S. C. S. Off., (Cochinchin.), 1 Aug., 1759, ad 2,—*Fontes*, n. 810; cf. 26 April, 1899,—*Fontes*, n. 1222; Canon 1123.

54 Canon 1123; S. C. de Prop. Fide, (ad C. P. pro Sin.), 16 Jan., 1797, ad 2,—*Coll.*, n. 634; (ad Vic. Ap. Sutchuen.), 30 Jan., 1807,—*Coll.*, n. 690; Jombart, "Casus de Dissolutione Matrimonii Paganorum," *Periodica*, XIV (1925), (72)-(73).

55 S. C. S. Off., 19 April, 1899, ad 1, 2,—*Fontes*, n. 1220; cf. (Cochinchin.), 1 Aug., 1759, ad 1,—*Fontes*, n. 810; S. C. de Prop. Fide, 16 Jan., 1797, ad 2,—*Coll.*, n. 634; (ad Vic. Ap. Sutchuen.), 30 Jan., 1807,—*Coll.*, n. 690. From a study of these decrees it is evident that the converted

(2) In the second hypothesis the infidel is considered to refuse peaceful cohabitation if he freely consents to continue community of bed and board, but at the same time he rejects the promise that he will live peaceably and *sine contumelia Creatoris.* This blasphemy of the Creator has been spoken of in preceding paragraphs,[56] and is verified whenever the infidel has the intention of endangering the faith of the convert, either by acts which might persuade him to renounce his faith entirely[57] or in the participation of which he would commit sin.[58] A refusal to relinquish the practice of concubinage or the denial of a Christian education to any children would thus constitute a grave insult to the Creator.[59]

(3) The third hypothesis giving rise to the conclusion that the unbeliever refuses peaceful cohabitation presents itself when the infidel willingly accedes to all the conditions required by law, but for some physical reason, even if involuntary, he is prevented from resuming the conjugal state with the convert. But again in these circumstances it is necessary that the convert be innocent, since Baptism was received, of causing the obstacle which so prevents the resumption of the marital relationship. Verification of this possibility is had in the event that the unbeliever is forcibly detained against his will, e.g., by a creditor or a second spouse; [60] and even if he has been taken away beyond

---

party does not jeopardize his right to a new marriage under these circumstances. Cf. Vlaming, *Praelect.*, n. 721; Cappello, *De Sacram.*, III, n. 770; Braun, "Auflösung der von Ungläubigen abgeschlossenen Ehe," *AkKR*, XLVI (1881), 388; Arendt, "De Clausula Restrictiva Canoni 1123 Adiecta," *Eph. Th. Lov.*, III (1926), 328-337; Ione, "Die Anwendung des Paulinischen Privilegs," *LQS*, LXXX (1927), 136.

[56] Cf. *supra*, pages 16, 18, 27, 29, 34, 35, 42, 58.

[57] S. C. S. Off., (Mongoliae), 29 Nov., 1882, ad 3,—*Fontes*, n. 1075.

[58] S. C. de Prop. Fide, (ad C. P. pro Sin.), 5 March, 1816, ad 6,—*Coll.*, n. 704.

[59] S. C. S. Off., (Natal), 11 July, 1866, ad 2-4,—*Fontes*, n. 996; (Tunkin. Occident.), 14 Dec., 1848, ad 2,—*Fontes*, n. 908.

[60] S. C. S. Off., (Cochinchin. Occident.), 12 June, 1850, ad 1,—*Fontes*, n. 910. From the tenor of this decree the convert is required to make at least one interpellation out of justice, and charity might bind him to several. Only after a lapse of a just and reasonable time in which the infidel fails to return is the convert free to enter a second union.

all hope of recovery or sold, provided that such sale was consummated *before* the conversion of the Christian partner.[61] The Sacred Congregation of the Propaganda has also admitted perpetual insanity in an infidel spouse as sufficient cause to allow of a dispensation from the interpellations and permission for the convert to enter a second marriage.[62]

It must be noted that the convert to Christianity is in no way at liberty to take advantage of the Pauline Privilege and to contract a second marriage if the infidel party is willing to live peaceably and to abide by all the conditions of the law, although at the same time he refuses to become a convert. Any opinion affirming such a principle cannot readily be admitted when stated so absolutely and in these general terms, for it is nowhere supported in the Pauline passage, in the legislation of the Church, or in the teaching of theologians.[63] It cannot be broadly stated that cohabitation with an infidel always carries with it the danger of perversion for the baptized party, for it would follow that St. Paul erred in advising the latter not to depart from an unconverted spouse.[64] In a particular case, judging the circumstances of place and persons, there may be evidence of this danger to faith,[65] and then there is truly a place

[61] S. C. S. Off., (Victoriae Nyanzae), 8 July, 1891, ad 1, 2,—*Fontes*, n. 1140.

[62] S. C. de Prop. Fide, (ad C. P. pro Sin.), 5 March, 1787, ad 1,—*Coll.*, n. 589. Although the Holy See has not as yet been questioned regarding the application of the Privilege to a convert who is unable to live with an infidel spouse because of the infamy and loss of good name attendant on the latter's various crimes, Vermeersch, *De Casu Apostoli*, n. 48, is of the opinion that such a case fully merits the concession. His kindly interpretation rests solely on the argument that the circumstances of the case seem to be on a par with the physical impediment whereby the infidel spouse is detained against his will. In practice the solution of a similar problem should be left to the decision of the Holy See. *Cf.* Cappello, *De Sacram.*, III, n. 773.

[63] St. Thomas, *Summa*, pars III, q. LIX, art. 5; Schmalzgrueber, *Jus Eccles. Univ.*, lib. IV, tit. XIX, n. 35; Rosset, *De Matrim.*, n. 604; Sanchez, *De Matrim.*, VII, disp. 74, n. 8; Pesch, *Theol. Dogmat.*, VII, n. 788; Wernz-Vidal, *Jus Canon.*, V, n. 631, note 58 ad 2; Cappello, *De Sacram.*, III, n. 773.

[64] I Cor. 7: 12-13.

[65] S. C. S. Off., littera, 7 Aug., 1891,—*Fontes*, n. 1142; Cf. Cappello, *De Sacram.*, III, n. 773; De Smet, *De Spons. et Matrim.*, n. 348.

for the concession. But in practice the doubt should be forwarded to the Holy See.[66]

The fourth and last condition necessary for the application of the Privilege is that by means of an interpellation made to the infidel party, it is fully established that he separates. The following chapter shall treat of this condition in its various phases.

---

[66] De Becker, *De Spons. et Matrim.*, p. 447; Michel, *Questions Practiques sur le Mariage dans les Missions*, p. 55; De Smet, *De Spons. et Matrim.*, n. 348; note 1; Cappello, *De Sacram.*, III, n. 773.

CHAPTER IV

THE INTERPELLATIONS

CANON 1121

§1. Antequam coniux conversus et baptizatus novum matrimonium valide contrahat, debet, salvo praescripto can. 1125, partem non baptizatam interpellare:

1°. An velit et ipsa converti ac baptismum suscipere;

2°. An saltem velit secum cohabitare pacifice sine contumelia Creatoris.

§2. Hae interpellationes fieri semper debent, nisi Sedes Apostolica aliud declaraverit.

Some sort of interpellations must have been implicitly contained in all the legislation evoked throughout the evolution of the Pauline Privilege,[1] for from the time of St. Augustine it was necessary to determine whether or not the infidel partner was willing to cohabit peacefully. Interpellations were indirectly referred to in two letters of Pope Innocent III,[2] but they acquired definite form only in the period closely following the Council of Trent. In a response offered by the Sacred Congre-

[1] Santi, *Praelectiones Juris Canonici*, III, p. 174, n. 10, is of the opinion that the first interpellations were introduced by the Fourth Council of Toledo, (a. 633). He says: "Verum ex Conciliis Toletanis habemus primam faciendam esse interrogationem parti infideli, ita ut pars conversa possit post primam interpellationem reiectam ab infideli ad alia vota transire."

[2] Ep. "*Quanto te magis,*" 1 May, 1199; ep. "*Gaudemus in Domino,*" a. 1201,—c. 7, 8, X, *de divortiis*, IV, 19; cf. Wernz, *Jus Decretalium*, IV, n. 702, note 72; De Angelis, *Praelectiones*, IV, 19, *de divortiis*, n. 8; Manscella, *De Imped. Matrim.*, p. 105; Gasparri, *De Matrim.*, n. 1336.

gation of the Council, January 23, 1603, there is found the first clear and unmistakable legislation on this requirement.[3] According to this decree the infidel[4] must be asked if he is willing to accept Christianity and if he will agree to continue a peaceful married life with the convert without offering insult to Almighty God.

Art. I. Origin and Necessity of the Interpellations

Authors are rather confusing in their contentions regarding the divine or ecclesiastical origin of the interpellations, although in general they reach their respective conclusions in accordance as they posit divine or apostolic origin of the Privilege itself.[5] Those writers who stand for apostolic origin of the institution are necessarily bound to hold that the interpellations are founded purely and simply in human or ecclesiastical law, while others who support the theory of divine institution claim that the convert is bound to interpellate the infidel party by a divine precept. A few among the latter class secede from the pure doctrine of their confrères and teach that the necessity of making the interpellations arises only from the ecclesiastical law in a case where the departure of the infidel is made certain through the medium of knowledge other than that afforded by the answers to the interpellations.[6]

---

[3] "Sacra Congregatio censuit ita respondendum, minime posse praedictos ad veram Fidem conversos accipere alias fideles uxores, nisi prius constiterit, utrum primae voluerint cum eis permanere, vel non. Quod si noluerint cohabitare, vel si voluerint, non tamen absque contumelia Creatoris, vel ut conversos ad mortale peccatum pertrahant, tunc posse eos alias fideles accipere uxores. Si cohabitare absque Creatoris contumelia velint, at absque eo quod conversos ad mortale peccatum pertrahant, quamvis veram agnoscere Fidem noluerint, non posse conversos alias fideles accipere uxores. Non sufficere ea, quae proponuntur, nempe loci distantiam, difficultatem, ac praesumptionem, quum constare debeat de voluntate ipsarum uxorum infidelium."—Benedictus XIV, *De Synodo Dioec.*, XIII, c. 21, n. 1; Cf. Feije, *De Imped. et Disp. Matrim.*, n. 475; S. C. de Prop. Fide, (ad C. P. pro Sin.), 16 June, 1797,—*Coll.*, n. 634.

[4] Where a polygamous union was being considered, only the first legitimate wife was to be interpellated.

[5] Cf. *supra*, pages 48-49.

[6] Sanchez, *De Matrim.*, VII, disp. 74, nn. 11-17; Feije, *De Imped. et Disp. Matrim.*, nn. 487, 493; Putzer, *Comment. in Facultates Apostolicas*, n. 128; Vermeersch-Creusen, *Epitome*, II, nn. 430, 434; Wernz-Vidal, *Jus Canon.*, V, n. 632, note 68; De Smet, *De Spons. et Matrim.*, n. 351.

The second opinion, which insists on immediate divine origin, is apparently supported by a Roman decision,[7] but in considering this it must be again borne in mind that the Sacred Congregation did not intend to offer a dogmatic definition, but rather a merely disciplinary response. Hence, it is stated that the necessity of making the interpellations is founded purely on ecclesiastical law,[8] and as the author of this requirement the Church is capable of dispensing and does dispense from both or only one question as she sees fit.[9] D'Annibale[10] makes a distinction between the first and second questions which comprise the interpellations, saying that the divine law demands that the infidel be asked if he wishes to be converted, whereas the query whether or not he will consent to live peacefully is only a requirement of the ecclesiastical law. But D'Annibale provides no serious reasons for his arbitrary assertion, and therefore, it must be looked upon as lacking any sound foundation.

Since the interpellations are the normal means by which the dispositions of the infidel party are ascertained, it follows that they must always be made.[11] The only two exceptions to this steadfast rule are the possibilities that a case may come under the provisions of Canon 1125, or that the Holy See may dispense.[12] All authorities are agreed that for the *licit* use of the Privilege there is required an interpellation made at least in the private form; and the Holy See is very strict on this formality even when it is evident that the interrogations are useless or

---

7 "Affirmative: nempe conversum de quo agitur, si non est legitime ab Apostolica Sede dispensatus, teneri *ex divino praecepto* ad faciendam in praesenti casu una vice interpellationem alteri coniugi; . . . . expleta autem a converso hac *divinitus* iniuncta conditione, etc."—S. C. S. Off., (Cochinchin. Occident.), 12 June, 1850, ad 1,—*Fontes*, n. 910; Cf. instr. (ad Archiep. Quebecen.), 16 Sept., 1824, ad 3,—*Fontes*, n. 866.

8 Gasparri, *De Matrim.*, n. 1337; Cappello, *De Sacram.*, III, n. 777; Chelodi, *Jus Matrim.*, n. 158; Scherer, *Handbuch des Kirchenrechts*, p. 563, note 68; Lemhkuhl, *Theol. Moral.*, II, nn. 929-932.

9 Canons 1121, §2; 1123; De Smet, *De Spons. et Matrim.*, n. 353; Wernz-Vidal, *Jus Canon.*, V, n. 632, note 70; Cerato, *Matrim.*, n. 121.

10 *Summula Theol. Moral.*, III, n. 476; cf. Cappello, *De Sacram.*, III, n. 777; Wernz-Vidal, *Jus Canon.*, V, n. 632, note 68.

11 Canon 1121.

12 Canons 1121, § 2; 1123; cf. *infra*, pages 76-83.

impossible to execute, or when the departure of the infidel is known as a certainty by some other means.[13]

Authors writing before the Code disagreed as to the necessity of the interpellations *ad validitatem*, for some sought to prove that the necessity of making the interpellations ceased when a presumption arose which afforded moral certainty of the infidel's departure. Such a presumption was regarded by these authors[14] as born of facts which attested the desertion of the infidel, such as the procurement of a civil divorce and the entrance into a second civil marriage. But it may be said in turn that such a presumption is merely arbitrary, that it is not invulnerable to particular contrary facts,[15] and that the Holy See does not admit its efficacy in determining the certain will of the infidel.[16] Rome always insisted that a dispensation from the interpellations be asked for, even in a case where it was difficult or impossible to make them properly, or when their execution

---

[13] "Non satis tutam in praxi appellare opinionem illam, quae ponit iudicialem interpellationem licite omitti posse quoties aut fieri reipsa nequit, aut, si fierit, nullius utilitatis fore reputatur; etiam in casu quod coniux infidelis in longinquas abierit regiones, aut ita latitet ut interpellari nequeat, adhuc opus esse dispensatione Summi Pontificis, cuius est declarare in quibusnam circumstantiis desinat obligare praeceptum divinum quo praedicta interpellatio videtur iniuncta."—S. C. S. Off., instr. (ad Archiep. Quebecen.), 16 Sept., 1824, ad 3,—*Fontes*, n. 866. It was also decided that the interpellation must be made or a dispensation obtained in a case where the convert had been publicly repudiated by the infidel party. Cf. S. C. de Prop. Fide, (Tunkin. Occident.), 5 March, 1816, ad 3,—*Coll.*, n. 704; 13 March, 1901,—*ASS*, XXXIII, 549-550; Gasparri, *De Matrim.*, n. 1337; Cappello, *De Sacram.*, III, n. 776.

[14] Sanchez, *De Matrim.*, VII, disp. 74, n. 13; Pesch, *Theol. Dogmat.*, n. 793; Ballerini-Palmieri, *Theol. Moral.*, VI, n. 434; Laemmer, "Die Interpellatio Coniugis Infidelis," *AkKR*, XI (1864), 247-250; Biederlack, "Ueber das sog. Paulinische Privilegium," *ZKT*, VII (1883), 304-322.

[15] Wernz-Vidal, *Jus Canon.*, V, n. 632, note 68; Cappello, *De Sacram.*, III, n. 776.

[16] S. C. C., 23 Jan., 1603,—Benedictus XIV, *De Synodo Dioec.*, XIII, c. 21, n. 1; S. C. S. Off., (Chen-si et Chan-si), 23 Nov., 1769,—*Fontes*, n. 825; instr. (ad Archiep. Quebecen.), 16 Sept., 1824, ad 1,—*Fontes*, n. 866; (Cochinchin. Occident.), 12 June, 1850, ad 1.—*Fontes*, n. 910; S. C. de Prop. Fide, litt. (ad Vic. Ap. Siam), 20 March, 1836,—*Coll.*, n. 2265; cf. Laemmer, "Die Interpellatio Coniugis Infidelis," *AkKR*, XI (1864), 247.

would involve danger or inconvenience for the convert.[17] A few authors did not sufficiently acknowledge that this judgment of fact regarding impossibility or inutility is solely the prerogative of the Roman Pontiff, and as such it is reserved to him. But all agreed that if the departure of the infidel party did not exist, or at least was doubtful, the convert could not validly enter a second marriage if the interpellations were omitted without proper dispensation.

Since the Code the law is evident and requires that in *all* cases the interpellations must be made, and that *ad validitatem*. The wording of Canon 1121, §1, demands this when it says: "Antequam coniux conversus . . . *valide* contrahat, debet . . . partem non baptizatam interpellare"; and §2: "Hae interpellationes fieri *semper* debent." In an identical tone Canon 1122, §2, follows up this same idea by stating: "Interpellationes etiam privatim factae ab ipsa parte conversa *valent*." [18] There can be no doubt but that this is the mind and the positive law of the Church.

But what is to be decided in a particular case such as the following? One partner of a valid union contracted in infidelity is converted and baptized; the one remaining in infidelity is known by certain proof to have deserted, but the convert neglects to make the necessary interpellation required by law nor does he obtain a dispensation from the Holy See. The convert then enters a second marriage. Now, does the omission of the interpellations render that second marriage invalid or not? Some authors think that the failure to make the interpellations in this case necessarily invalidates the second marriage, for they claim that by the wording and intent of the canons quoted above the convert is disqualified from validly contracting a second union. And they insist that since this inhability

---

[17] S. C. S. Off., 8 June, 1836,—*Fontes*, n. 874; (Portland), 18 June, 1884,—*Fontes*, n. 1088; S. C. de Prop. Fide, (ad Vic. Ap. Sutchuen.), 17 Jan., 1836, ad 2,—*Coll.*, n. 845.

[18] Wernz-Vidal, *Jus Canon.*, V, n. 632, note 68; Cappello, *De Sacram.*, III, n. 776; Vermeersch-Creusen, *Epitome*, II, n. 430; De Smet, *De Spons. et Matrim.*, n. 352; Cerato, *Matrim.*, n. 122; Petrovits, *The New Church Law*, n. 560; Chelodi, *Jus Matrim.*, n. 158; Augustine, *A Commentary on Canon Law*, V, 353; Vlaming, *Praelect.*, n. 722.

arises from the positive law of the Church, it perseveres unless the interpellation is made or legitimately dispensed.[19] This theory was true undoubtedly under the old discipline[20] and it has the same weight today for all practical purposes, although a decisive argument in its favor cannot be gleaned from the responses of the Roman Congregations.

Several prominent writers[21] contend that in the case posited above the second marriage may be presumed valid at least theoretically until a decisive answer is received from Rome. Cappello[22] urges Canons 1014 and 1127 in support of this theory, but it is difficult to see what strength they carry in the argument. For Canon 1121 requires that the interpellations be made in every case (*fieri semper debent*) before a convert may validly contract a new marriage. No provision is made by Canon 1121 for the omission of the interpellations when the objective departure of the infidel is certainly known through some other medium, but it is simply stated that they must *always* be made. Canons 1014 and 1127, therefore, have no foothold, since they respectively refer to the *favor iuris* which accrues to a convert when the validity of his first or second

---

[19] Fahrner, *Geschichte des Unauflöslichkeitsprinzips*, p. 288; Vermeersch-Creusen, *Epitome*, II, n. 430; De Becker,—*Eph. Th. Lov.*, II (1925), 274; Petrovits, *The New Church Law*, n. 560; De Smet, *De Spons. et Matrim.*, n. 352; Laemmer, "Die Interpellatio Coniugis Infidelis," *AkKR*, XI (1864), 246.

[20] S. C. C., 23 Jan., 1603,—Benedictus XIV, *De Synodo Dioec.*, XIII, c. 21, n. 1; S. C. S. Off., instr. (ad Superior. Mission. Peguan.), 11 June, 1760,—*Fontes*, n. 811; (Chen-si et Chan-si), 23 Nov., 1769,—*Fontes*, n. 825; instr. (ad Archiep. Quebecen.), 16 Sept., 1824, ad 1,—*Fontes*, n. 866; (Cochinchin. Occident.), 12 June, 1850, ad 1,—*Fontes*, n. 910; 11 Aug., 1859,—*Fontes*, n. 954; (Coreae), 11 Sept., 1878, ad 1, 2,—*Fontes*, n. 1057; (Portland), 18 June, 1884,—*Fontes*, n. 1088; 17 Jan., 1901,—*Anal. Eccl.*, VIII (1901), 105; S. C. de Prop. Fide, (ad Vic. Ap. Sutchuen.), 17 Jan., 1836,—*Coll.*, 845; (ad Vic. Ap. Siam), 20 Mar., 1836,—*Coll.*, n. 2265.

[21] Wernz-Vidal, *Jus Canon.*, V, n. 632, note 68; Vermeersch, *Theol. Moral.*, III, n. 818, note 4; *De Casu Apostoli*, nn. 52, 56; Cappello, *De Sacram.*, III, n. 776; Chelodi, *Jus Matrim.*, n. 158; Ione, "Die Unterlassung der Interpellationen bei Anwendung des Paulinischen Privilegs," *LQS*, LXXX (1927), 348; *L'Ami du Clerge*, XXXI (1928), 520-523, quoted in *Apollinaris*, I (1928), 435.

[22] *De Sacram.*, III, n. 776.

marriage is doubtful or when any doubt affects the integrity of his marriage. But the illegitimate omission of the interpellations does not produce a doubt concerning the validity of the second marriage; the positive law of the Church in Canon 1121 renders that union certainly invalid.

The argument brought forward by advocates of this theory in support of its intrinsic probability is stated briefly that, the condition of the Pauline Privilege is the infidel's *departure,* rather than the *proof* of that departure. But, on the other hand, proof of the infidel's desertion is *also* a condition of the Privilege which the Church demands *de facto* by means of the interpellations. And she insists that this condition be fulfilled in the manner stated, with the alternative that to a second marriage there will be attached the penalty of nullity. Hence, *in practice* the interpellations must always be made[23] unless the proper dispensation has been obtained from the competent authority.[24]

ART. II. THE TIME APPOINTED FOR THE INTERPELLATIONS

The Code in unmistakable terms gives the general rule by which the convert is to be guided in appointing the time suited to the valid and licit use of the interpellations. The text states that the ordinary period is after the baptism of the convert (*coniux conversus et baptizatus*), and before he has entered a second valid marriage (*antequam . . . novum matrimonium valide contrahat*).[25] This, then, is the general law which has

---

[23] Canon 1121, §2; Chelodi, *Jus Matrim.*, n. 158; Vlaming, *Praelect.*, n. 722, note 1; Petrovits, *The New Church Law*, n. 562; Wernz-Vidal, *Jus Canon.*, V, n. 632, note 68; De Smet, *De Spons. et Matrim.*, n. 352; Farrugia, *De Matrim.*, n. 322.

[24] The only competent authority is the Holy See, as stated in Canons 1121, §2, and 1123, or its delegate to whom the faculty of dispensing has been granted. This privilege may also be gained from the common law, Canon 1125, of which more later.

[25] Canon 1121, §1; cf. Cappello, *De Sacram.*, III, n. 778; Wernz-Vidal, *Jus Canon.*, V, n. 632; De Smet, *De Spons. et Matrim.*, n. 349; Gasparri, *De Matrim.*, n. 1336; Chelodi, *Jus Matrim.*, n. 158; Cerato, *Matrim.*, n. 121.

frequently been insisted upon by the Holy See.[26] Nevertheless, the Supreme Pontiff has granted the faculty to propose the interpellations during the catechumenate in extraordinary cases, where the abode of the infidel was unknown or where a separation of great distance would reduce the possibility and certainty of the interpellation to a minimum.[27] But since a catechumen is not a subject of the Church and is thus really incapable of receiving a dispensation, it must be understood that under these circumstances the Church ratifies after Baptism the interpellation which she permitted to be made before.[28]

Should the interpellation be made improperly before the reception of Baptism, its validity would not be impaired so long as the interrogation evidenced the fact that the obdurate will of the infidel would persevere even after the convert's baptism.[29]

It is hardly necessary to say that the interpellation must be made before the infidel spouse is also converted and baptized, for if that should be effected there is no place for the use of the Privilege and the original marriage still stands.

The law requires that the interpellation be made only once and, if that is done in the proper manner, it need not be re-

[26] S. C. S. Off., (Cochinchin. Orient.), 6 Aug., 1856,—*Fontes*, n. 939; (Pondichery), 20 June, 1858,—*Fontes*, n. 947; (Tchely Orient.), 13 Apr., 1859,—*Fontes*, n. 951; instr. (ad Vic. Ap. Sutchuen. Orient.), 3 June, 1874,—*Fontes*, n. 1030; S. C. de Prop. Fide, (ad C. P. pro Sin.), 5 March, 1816,—*Coll.*, n. 704.

[27] S. C. S. Off., instr. (ad Vic. Ap. Sutchuen. Orient.), 3 June, 1874,—*Fontes*, n. 1030; 13 March, 1901,—*ASS*, XXXIII (1901), 549; cf. Gasparri, *De Matrim.*, n. 1336, note 1; De Smet, *De Spons. et Matrim.*, n. 349; "Permittendi ut, accedente gravi causa, *interpellatio* coniugis infidelis *ante baptismum* partis quae ad fidem convertitur fieri possit."—Faculty granted by the Congregation of the Propaganda, *Formula* III, n. 27,—*Vide* Vermeersch, *Commentaria de Formulis Facultatum S. C. P. F.*, p. 111.

[28] Vermeersch, *De Casu Apostoli*, n. 55; De Smet, *De Spons. et Matrim.*, n. 349, note 4; Cappello, *De Sacram.*, III, n. 778; Augustine, *A Commentary*, V, 352.

[29] S. C. S. Off., instr. (ad Vic. Ap. Sutchuen. Orient.), 3 June, 1874,—*Fontes*, n. 1030; cf. Petrovits, *The New Church Law*, n. 563; Vermeersch, *De Casu Apostoli*, n. 55; Vermeersch-Creusen, *Epitome*, II, n. 431; Wernz-Vidal, *Jus Canon.*, V, n. 632, note 70; Vlaming, *Praelect.*, n. 725; Ione, "Wie müssen die Interpellationen bei Anwendung des Paulinischen Privilegs gemacht werden," *LQS*, LXXX (1927), 345.

peated unless charity demands, even though a long period of time has elapsed before the convert enters a second marriage.[30]

Art. III. The Object of the Interpellation

The discipline regarding the nature and substance of the interpellation has been the same for centuries[31] and remains constant even after the Code.[32] Two questions are to be put to the infidel consort, namely, if he wishes to be converted and baptized, and, if he wishes at least to live peacefully without blaspheming God. It is neither licit nor valid to ask only one or the other of the questions, but *both* must always be offered,[33] unless the Holy See declares otherwise.

§1. *Responses of the Infidel*

In providing an answer to the interpellation, the infidel spouse may follow one of several courses. He may: (1) answer

---

[30] S. C. de Prop. Fide, (Sutchuen.), 26 June, 1820,—*Coll.*, n. 743; S. C. S. Off., (Cochinchin. Occident.), 12 June, 1850, ad 1,—*Fontes*, n. 910; cf. Cappello, *De Sacram.*, III, n. 778; Petrovits, *The New Church Law*, n. 564; Chelodi, *Jus Matrim.*, n. 158; Cerato, *Matrim.*, n. 121; De Smet, *De Spons. et Matrim.*, n. 349; Vermeersch-Creusen, *Epitome*, II, n. 431; Wernz-Vidal, *Jus Canon.*, V, n. 632; Vermeersch, *De Casu Apostoli*, n. 57.

[31] Innocent III, ep. *"Quanto te magis"*; ep. *"Gaudemus in Domino,"*—c. 7, 8, X, *de divortiis*, IV, 19; S. C. C., 23 Jan., 1603,—Benedictus XIV, *De Synodo Dioec.*, XIII, c. 21, n. 1; Benedictus XIV, const. *"Apostolici ministerii,"* 16 Sept., 1747, ad 3,—*Fontes*, n. 381; S. C. de Prop. Fide, (Sutchuen.), 17 Jan., 1836, ad 1,—*Coll.*, n. 845; S. C. S. Off., (Cochinchin.), 1 Aug., 1759,—*Fontes*, n. 810; (Cochinchin. Occident.), 12 June, 1850, ad 1,—*Fontes*, n. 910; (Natal), 11 July, 1866, ad 2,—*Fontes*, n. 996; (Victoriae Nyanzae), 8 July, 1891, ad 1,—*Fontes*, n. 1140; 26 Apr., 1899,—*Fontes*, n. 1222; Wernz, *Jus Decret.*, IV, n. 703; Gasparri, *De Matrim.*, n. 1336.

[32] Canon 1121, §1.

[33] *"Hae interpellationes* fieri semper debent."—Canon 1121, §2; S. C. de Prop. Fide, (ad C. P. pro Sin.), 3 Jan., 1777,—*vide* Bucceroni, *Enchiridion Morale*, p. 471; (ad C. P. pro Sin.), 5 Mar., 1816, ad 2,—*Coll.*, n. 704; S. C. S. Off., 10 Dec., 1885, ad 2,—*Fontes*, n. 1097; cf. Wernz-Vidal, *Jus Canon.*, V, n. 632, note 69; Cappello, *De Sacram.*, III, n. 775; Vermeersch, *De Casu Apostoli*, n. 54; Vermeersch-Creusen, *Epitome*, II, n. 431; Chelodi, *Jus Matrim.*, n. 158; De Becker, *De Spons. et Matrim.*, n. 420.

both questions either in the affirmative or in the negative; (2) answer one in the affirmative, but the other in the negative; (3) refuse to give any response whatever.

In the event that the unbeliever answers both questions affirmatively, to the effect that he is both willing to accept Christianity and to continue peaceful marital relations, the marriage contracted in infidelity remains active; unless the promises cannot be fulfilled by the infidel within the time specified by the Ordinary.[34] On the contrary, if the unbaptized party has answered both questions negatively, then there arises for the Christian the right to enter a second marriage.[35]

In the second hypothesis, the unbeliever may answer the first question negatively and the second one affirmatively; that is, he may refuse to be baptized but is quite willing to continue cohabitation in a peaceful manner. If such a response is made the Christian party may discontinue the marital life if she so wishes; but she may not contract another marriage as long as her spouse lives, unless the Ordinary decides that the common life of this couple would constitute a grave spiritual danger fully warranting both answers of the infidel to be construed as negative.[36] And if the Ordinary is fully aware that this is the case at the time when the interpellation is being made, he may dispense from the second question if he has the faculty to do so.[37] Some authors go so far as to claim that cohabitation with an infidel is unlawful at all times, and hence, when he refuses to embrace Christianity the Privilege may be used by the con-

---

[34] S. C. S. Off., (Cochinchin. Occident.), 12 June, 1850, ad 1,—*Fontes*, n. 910; (Siam), 22 Nov., 1871,—*Fontes*, n. 1019; (Victoriae Nyanzae), 8 July, 1891, ad 2,—*Fontes*, n. 1140; cf. Ojetti, *Synop. Rerum Moral.*, III, n. 3284; Vermeersch, *De Casu Apostoli*, n. 60.

[35] Canon 1123; Benedictus XIV, const. "*Apostolici ministerii*," 16 Sept., 1747,—*Fontes*, n. 381; S. C. S. Off., (ad Vic. Ap. Yunnan), 23 June, 1847, ad 1,—*Fontes*, n. 903; (Siam), 17 July, 1850,—*Fontes*, n. 911; (Siam), 4 July, 1855,—*Fontes*, n. 931; cf. De Smet, *De Spons. et Matrim.*, n. 354; Gasparri, *De Matrim.*, n. 1336.

[36] The Third Synod of Lima, in which this question was so decided, was approved by the S. C. S. Off., (Mongoliae), 29 Nov., 1882, ad 3,—*Fontes*, n. 1075; cf. Gasparri, *De Matrim.*, nn. 1336, 1352; Feije, *De Imped. et Disp. Matrim.*, n. 490.

[37] S. C. S. Off., (Mongoliae), 29 Nov., 1882, ad 2,—*Fontes*, n. 1075.

verted party.[38] This assertion is mostly based on a general prohibition of the Fourth Council of Toledo, forbidding cohabitation between Jews and Christians because of the greater danger of perversion for the Christian and little hope of conversion for the infidel.[39] This presumption still prevails even in modern times,[40] and the practice is to permit cohabitation within infidel countries while refusing it among Christian nations.[41] Nevertheless, such prohibitions are suppressed by the common law which demands both interpellations, and in practice the particular case should be referred to Rome.[42]

If the infidel agrees to be baptized but refuses to continue in a happy domestic life, without any just cause for this refusal being given by the Christian after her baptism, then the unbeliever is thought to be insincere in his responses and the Christian is free to enter another contract.[43]

Lastly, in the third hypothesis, if the infidel pays no attention to the interpellation and refuses to answer, such action is to be considered as a negative reply, unless it is known that he was legitimately impeded.[44]

---

[38] Sanchez, *De Matrim.*, VII, disp. 74, n. 9; Feije, *De Imped. et Disp. Matrim.*, nn. 490-491; Palmieri, *De Matrim.*, p. 218; Vermeersch, *De Casu Apostoli*, n. 45; Vlaming, *Praelect.*, n. 729.

[39] C. 10. C. XXVIII, q. 1.

[40] This presumption of the danger of perversion is evidenced today in the Faculties given to American Bishops, wherein they may not grant a dispensation from the impediment of Disparity of Cult to a Catholic contracting marriage with a Jew or Mohammedan. Cf. Schenk, *Mixed Religion and Disparity of Cult*, n. 254.

[41] Feije, *De Imped. et Disp. Matrim.*, n. 491; Mansella, *De Imped. Matrim.*, pp. 120-122; Gasparri, *De Matrim.*, n. 1336; Vermeersch, *De Casu Apostoli*, n. 70.

[42] De Smet, *De Spons. et Matrim.*, n. 340, note 1; Gasparri, *De Matrim.*, n. 1336; Petrovits, *The New Church Law*, n. 561; De Becker, *De Spons. et Matrim.*, p. 420, note 1; Cappello, *De Sacram.*, III, nn. 771-772; Perrone, *De Matrim.*, II, p. 321.

[43] Petrovits, *The New Church Law*, n. 561; Cappello, *De Sacram.*, III, n. 770; Gasparri, *De Matrim.*, n. 1336; De Smet, *De Spons. et Matrim.*, n. 347; Vermeersch, *De Casu Apostoli*, n. 60; S. C. S. Off., (Victoriae Nyanzae), 8 Július, 1891, ad 1,—*Fontes*, n. 1140; 26 April, 1899,—*Fontes*, n. 1222.

[44] Wernz-Vidal, *Jus Canon.*, V, n. 632; Gasparri, *De Matrim.*, n. 1336; Feije, *De Imped. et Disp. Matrim.*, n. 495; Vermeersch, *De Casu Apostoli*, n. 60; S. C. de Prop. Fide, (ad C. P. pro Sin.), 5 March, 1816, ad 1, 3,—*Coll.*, n. 704; S. C. S. Off., 11 Aug., 1859,—*Fontes*, n. 954.

It is naturally to be supposed that the responses of the unbeliever are given seriously and sincerely. But if it is known for a certainty that his answers were offered with a feigned or bad will, those affirmative replies are to be considered as negative. Such circumstances might arise if the infidel failed to reply within the time appointed, if he tacitly gave a negative answer,[45] if he continually requests postponements which will avail nothing, or if he remains in hiding lest he be reached. Looking at any of these possibilities and their attendant circumstances, it may be taken for granted that he wishes neither to be converted nor to live peacefully.[46]

Art. IV. Dispensation from the Interpellation

Although the general rule demands that the interpellation be made in every case, even when there is sufficient evidence to prove that the infidel has no intention of being baptized or that he has already obtained a civil divorce and has remarried according to the laws of the State, the Roman Pontiff may dispense from the interpellation[47] for a just cause. Such a dispensation may be either plenary or partial; it may be given by the Holy See directly or indirectly through its delegate, and in the modern discipline it may be granted either by means of special faculties and indults[48] or it may arise purely from the common law.[49]

When speaking of the relaxation of the necessity of interpellating, the Code abstains from the use of the term *dispensare*, using in its stead the word *declarare*. Hence, the text reads:

---

[45] Canon 1123.

[46] S. C. S. Off., (Mongoliae), 29 Nov., 1882, ad 2, 3,—*Fontes*, n. 1075; 28 Nov., 1894,—*ASS*, XXIX (1894), 564; Regulae #25, #31, R. J. in VI°; Braun, "Auflösung der von Ungläubigen abgschlossenen Ehe," *AkKR*, XLVI (1881), 391; Vermeersch, *De Casu Apostoli*, n. 60; Chelodi, *Jus Matrim.*, n. 158; Cappello, *De Sacram.*, III, n. 780; Wernz-Vidal, *Jus Canon.*, V, n. 632.

[47] Canons 1121, §2; 1123.

[48] Formul. Facult. S. C. de Prop. Fide, *form.* III (*Maior*), nn. 25, 26, 27; *form.* III (*Minor*), nn. 24, 25, 26; S. C. S. Off., 8 June, 1836,—*Fontes*, n. 874; (Siam), 22 Nov., 1871,—*Fontes*, n. 1019; (Mongoliae), 29 Nov., 1882,—*Fontes*, n. 1075; (Siouxormen.), 18 May, 1892,—*Fontes*, n. 1155.

[49] Canon 1125.

"Nisi Sedes Apostolica aliud *declaraverit*" (Canon 1121, §2), and, "Si interpellationes *ex declaratione* Sedis Apostolicae omissae fuerint" (Canon 1123). The true meaning of *declarare* is most broad and must be defined in individual cases, for it may signify more than a dispensation. Thus, when the interpellations are useless because it is definitely known that the infidel has departed, the Church declares them so by divine law and at the same time dispenses from the ecclesiastical law demanding them. Or if it is impossible to make the interpellation because of the certain objective departure of the unbeliever, again the Church declares that the divine law does not bind and dispenses from the ecclesiastical law. But if the objective departure of the infidel is not certain, the Church then gives a pure and true dispensation from the interpellation. It is evident that where the marriage is truly doubtful or when the bad will of the infidel is certain, the interpellation would be superfluous from the nature of things, and hence, a dispensation would be nothing more than a comprehensive declaration of the Privilege.[50] However, in accord with the common way of speaking, the use of the term "dispensation" shall be continued.

§1. *Dispensation by the Roman Pontiff*

The Holy See has frequently dispensed from both questions, so that without giving any warning whatever to his infidel consort a Christian partner may licitly and validly enter into a new union with a third person.[51] Moreover, when this power of relieving from both interpellations is conceded to the Holy

---

[50] Cf. Cappello, *De Sacram.*, III, n. 781; Vermeersch-Creusen, *Epitome*, II, n. 434; Vermeersch, *De Casu Apostoli*, n. 74; Chelodi, *Jus Matrim.*, n. 160; Wernz Vidal, *Jus Canon.*, V, n. 635.

[51] Gregory XIII, const. *"Populis,"* 25 Jan., 1585.—*Docum.* VIII, C. I. C., Benedictus XIV, ep. *"In suprema,"* 16 Jan., 1745, ad 2,—*Fontes*, n. 353; const. *"Apostolici ministerii,"* 16 Sept., 1747, ad 2,—*Fontes*, n. 381; S. C. S. Off., (Cochinchin.), 1 Aug. 1759, ad 5,—*Fontes*, n. 810; 16 Aug., 1895,—*ASS*, XXIX (1895), 564; S. C. de Prop. Fide, (ad C. P. pro Sin.), 3 Jan., 1777,—*Coll.*, n. 517; cf. Putzer, *Comment. in Facult. Apost.*, n. 130; Gasparri, *De Matrim.*, n. 1342; Feije, *De Imped. et Disp. Matrim.*, n. 488; Petrovits, *The New Church Law*, n. 566; Cappello, *De Sacram.*, III, n. 781; De Smet, *De Spons. et Matrim.*, n. 353; Cerato, *Matrim.*, n. 121.

Father, a fortiori he is also able to dispense from one or the other question. Therefore, if a negative answer is supplied to the query whether the infidel wishes to be converted, the dispensation may excuse the question whether the infidel wishes to continue peacefully in that marriage; and again the convert may licitly and validly contract a second union.[52]

A. *In Case of Urgent Necessity*

If an urgent case should arise which would not allow of sufficient time for recourse to Rome, any Ordinary, acting as the delegate of the Holy Father, may dispense from the interpellations if he is certain that the infidel has departed.[53] Such an urgency would appear to be the same as that which allows Bishops to dispense from matrimonial impediments.[54]

B. *Just Causes for Dispensation*

A dispensation from the interpellations cannot be conceded by the Holy Father unless there is present a just and reasonable cause, which fact has been ascertained at least by a summary and extra-judicial investigation. In general terms the Holy See has adduced as just causes for dispensation the impossibility or inutility of making the interpellation and the grave danger which might arise for the convert if he attempts to interpellate.[55]

---

[52] S. C. S. Off., (Cochinchin.), 1 Aug., 1759, ad 3,—*Fontes*, n. 810; (Siam), 4 July, 1855,—*Fontes*, n. 931; instr. (pro Vic. Ap. ad Gallas), 20 June, 1866,—*Fontes*, n. 994; cf. Wernz-Vidal, *Jus Canon.*, V, n. 633; Cappello, *De Sacram.*, III, n. 781; Chelodi, *Jus Matrim.*, n. 160; Petrovits, *The New Church Law*, n. 566; De Becker, *De Spons. et Matrim.*, p. 425; Facultates Apostolicas, *Formula* I, n. 11,—apud Putzer, *Comment.*, n. 130.

[53] S. C. S. Off., 11 Aug., 1859,—*Fontes*, n. 954; (Portland), 18 June, 1884,—*Fontes*, n. 1088; cf. Gasparri, *De Matrim.*, n. 1353; Putzer, *Comment.*, n. 130; Vermeersch, *De Casu Apostoli*, n. 52; *Commentaria de Formulis Facultatum*, n. 120; Vromant, *Commentaria Facultates Apostolicae*, n. 81; Petrovits, *The New Church Law*, n. 571; Blat, *Comment.*, III, pars I, n. 531; Ayrinhac, *Marriage Legislation in the New Code*, n. 300.

[54] Cf. Canons 81; 1043; S. C. S. Off., instr. (ad Superior. Mission. Peguan.), 11 June, 1760,—*Fontes*, n. 811.

[55] "Iustae autem huiusmodi causae tunc aderunt cum ex processu saltem summario et extraiudiciali moraliter constet coniugem infidelem interpellari non posse, aut interpellationem vel inutilem vel graviter periculosam futuram

In particular, however, such causes are to be divided into two classes, ordinary and extraordinary.[56]

Among the *ordinary* just causes which permit of dispensation there may be listed the following: (1) if the infidel's place of residence is unknown to the convert;[57] (2) if the infidel's home is located at some far distant place to which safe access cannot be gained because of a state of war or because that region is infested with robbers;[58] (3) if the distance to the infidel's domicile is so excessive as to cause great difficulty for the convert in presenting the interpellations, which difficulty may consist in the necessary length of the journey, its cost, inconvenience and consequent damage suffered; (4) if the infidel does not respond within the time appointed;[59] (5) if a polygamous convert cannot remember which of his wives was the first and legitimate one, or if he is uncertain whether or not he has truly given full matrimonial consent to any of those wives[60] (6) if the first legitimate wife is unknown and it is difficult to locate her.[61]

Just causes which are considered as being of an *extraordinary* nature may present themselves in a case where the infidel party may be reached easily enough, but if the interpellation is made there may arise a manifest danger of grave loss to the convert, to his children, or to other Christians.[62] This danger may evi-

esse."—S. C. S. Off., (ad Vic. Ap. Iaponiae Merid.), 4 Feb., 1891, ad finem,—*Fontes*, n. 1130; cf. 16 Aug., 1895,—*ASS*, XXIX (1895), 565; Gasparri, *De Matrim.*, n. 1349.

[56] Cf. S. C. S. Off., (Mongoliae), 29 Nov., 1882,—*Fontes*, n. 1075.

[57] Cf. Wernz-Vidal, *Jus Canon.*, V, n. 633, note 80; Vermeersch, *De Casu Apostoli*, n. 78.

[58] Cf. Gregory XIII, const. "*Populis*," 25 Jan., 1585,—*Docum.* VIII, C. I. C.; S. C. S. Off., (Mongoliae), 29 Nov., 1882,—*Fontes*, n. 1075.

[59] Cf. S. C. S. Off., (Mongoliae), 29 Nov., 1882,—*Fontes*, n. 1075; Vermeersch, *De Casu Apostoli*, nn. 77-78; Vromant, *Comment. Facult. Apost.*, n. 80.

[60] Cf. Paul III, const. "*Altitudo*," 1 June, 1537,—*Docum.* VI, C. I. C.; S. C. S. Off., 8 June, 1836,—*Fontes*, n. 874; (Siouxormen.), 18 May, 1892,—*Fontes*, n. 1155.

[61] Cf. Pius V, const. "*Romani Pontificis*," 2 Aug., 1571,—*Docum.* VII, C. I. C.; S. C. S. Off., (Siam), 22 Nov., 1871,—*Fontes*, n. 1019; Krasa, "Privilegium Paulinum," *LQS*, LXXV (1922), 97.

[62] S. C. S. Off., (Chen-si et Chan-si), 23 Nov., 1769, ad 4,—*Fontes*, n. 825; Facultates S. C. de Prop. Fide, *Formula* III (*Maior*), n. 26; (*Minor*), n. 25.

dence itself even if it is supposed that the infidel may respond to the interpellations in the affirmative, but the damage resulting must be foreseen and founded on solid reasons rather than on mere presumptions.[63] It is not necessary that the danger entail the loss of life, but it suffices that liberty or material fortune be imperiled.[64]

C. *Renewal of Dispensation*

Under the former discipline if a dispensation from the interpellations was granted, but the convert failed to take advantage of it by entering a second marriage within one year, it was then necessary to secure a new dispensation.[65] The same requirement exists today for the liceity of a second marriage,[66] although its validity would not seem to be imperiled since the Code is silent on the necessity of such a renewal. Moreover, it would appear that a dispensation once granted would remain in force as long as the unbeliever continues in infidelity, since there is the analogy that once the interpellations are made they need not be repeated nor must a dispensation be obtained, even if the convert refrains from entering a new union for a considerable time.[67]

If a dispensation from the interpellations was granted to a convert to enter marriage with a *specified* person, that dispensation could not be used to permit the convert's union with *any other* party. For dispensations are to be interpreted strictly.

---

[63] S. C. S. Off., (Chen-si et Chan-si), 23 Nov., 1769, ad 1-3,—*Fontes*, n. 825.

[64] For a discussion of just causes, ordinary and extraordinary, their gravity and existence, consult the following authors:—Gasparri, *De Matrim.*, n. 1347; Cappello, *De Sacram.*, III, n. 781; Wernz-Vidal, *Jus Canon.*, V, n. 633, note 80; Petrovits, *The New Church Law*, n. 567; Vermeersch, *De Casu Apostoli*, nn. 77-80; *Comment. Formul. Facult.*, nn. 120-122; Vlaming, *Praelect.*, n. 724; Vromant, *Comment. Facult. Apost.*, nn. 80-88; Winslow, *Vicars and Prefects Apostolic*, pp. 110-115; Farrugia, *De Matrim.*, n. 322.

[65] S. C. de Prop. Fide, (C. P. pro Sin.), 26 June, 1820,—*Coll.*, n. 743.

[66] Vlaming, *Praelect.*, n. 725; Wernz-Vidal, *Jus Canon.*, V, n. 632; Cappello, *De Sacram.*, III, n. 781; Vermeersch, *De Casu Apostoli*, nn. 75-76; Farrugia, *De Matrim.*, n. 325, nota; De Smet, *De Spons. et Matrim.*, n. 353.

[67] Petrovits, *The New Church Law*, n. 566; Cappello, *De Sacram.*, III, n. 781.

However, if the dispensation was granted simply and merely stated the permission to remarry, the convert could enter another union with any Catholic person he desired.[68]

§2. *By Special Faculties and Indults*

Beyond the individual indults permitting of dispensation from the interpellations which the Holy See may grant directly to Ordinaries, there are also special faculties addressed to the Ordinaries of particular regions which contain this privilege. Formerly these special faculties were given by the Sacred Congregation of Propaganda for missionary countries, where it frequently happened that extraordinary cases arose without sufficient time for appeal to Rome.[69] With the advent of the Code, however, these faculties were withdrawn, for the common law was thought to be adopted to modern situations and the power of the Ordinaries had been extended wherever it was necessary. Hence, to avoid confusion and to secure a greater uniformity in Church law, Pope Benedict XV recalled on April 25, 1918, all faculties for the external forum which had been granted to Ordinaries subject to the common law. The same Pontiff, however, confirmed on February 6, 1919, a new set of faculties which the Congregation of Propaganda addressed to definite Ordinaries as in force from January 1, 1920.[70]

The Ordinaries of the United States were formerly beneficiaries under the original faculties,[71] but today unless they are the recipients of particular indults[72] they must depend on the common law or appeal to Rome for individual cases. For the

[68] Vermeersch, "Quaesita de Usu Privilegii Fidei," *Periodica*, XVII (1928), 241*-243*.

[69] For a comprehensive history of the origin and development of these faculties, consult Vermeersch, *Comment. Formul. Facult.*, nn. 1-29.

[70] Cf. Ayrinhac, *General Legislation in the New Code*, nn. 169-170; Vermeersch, *Comment. Formul. Facult.*, n. 29; Winslow, *Vicars and Prefects Apostolic*, p. 76.

[71] Facultates Apostolicae, *Formula* I, *C, D, E*,—Cf. Putzer, *Comment.*, n. 1.

[72] Individual Bishops in the United States have been granted the faculty of dispensing from the interpellations without the necessity of appealing to Rome.

special faculties in force since 1920 are in no way directed to Ordinaries in this country.[73]

Where the faculties in use before the Code were divided into "ordinary" and "extraordinary," the present schema classifies three Formulas, of which the Second and Third are subdivided into *"Maior"* and *"Minor."* This classification of major and minor is founded on a distinction of persons, for the former are addressed to Vicars and Prefects who enjoy the Episcopal character, while the latter are intended for the use of lesser personages.[74]

Among these special faculties those which respect a dispensation from the interpellations are to be found in the Third Formula, both major and minor, listed as Numbers 25, 26, 27, and 24, 25, 26, respectively.[75] Since they are of no practical

---

[73] This more recent set of faculties was distributed for the following countries:

(1) Formulam primam obtinet:—Suecia, Norvegia, Dania, Smyrna, Constantinopolis, Hierusalem, Aleppa, Ispahan, Babylonia (Bagdad), Arabiae Vicariatus Apostol., Aegyptus, Lybia (Tripoli), Maroquium.

(2) Formulam alteram consequuntur:—Tasmania, Wellingtonium (N. Zelandia), Dioeceses Coloniarum Galliae in Africa, Dioeceses Americae Centralis, Martinica (Roseau), Coloniae Anglicae in Africa.

(3) Formulam tertiam impetrant:—Sinae, Indosinae, Japonia, Insulae Oceaniae, Sandwich, Carolinae, Mariannae Carolinae, Guam, Tahiti, Africa (excepta Lybia, Aegypto, Dioecesibus Gallicis et Coloniis Anglicis), Indiae, Malaca, Americae Vicariatus Praefecturae.

Cf. Vermeersch, *Comment. Formul. Facult.*, n. 31; Vromant, *Comment. Facult. Apost.*, n. 4; Winslow, *Vicars and Prefects Apostolic*, p. 76.

[74] Iglesias, *Brevis Commentarius in Facultates*, p. 16.

[75] #25:—"Dispensandi super interpellatione coniugum in infidelitate relictorum pro omnibus casibus ordinariis, dummodo scilicet adhibitis antea omnibus diligentiis, etiam per publicas ephemerides ad reperiendum locum ubi coniux infidelis habitat, iisque in irritum cessis, constet saltem summarie et extraiudicialiter coniugem absentem moneri legitime non posse, aut monitum infra tempus in monitione praefixum suam voluntatem non significasse."

#26:—"Itemque dispensandi super interpellatione coniugis in infidelitate relicti, siquidem certo constiterit, saltem summarie et extraiudicialiter, interpellationem fieri non posse sine evidenti gravis damni aut coniugi iam ad fidem converso, aut christianis inferendi periculo."

#27:—"Permittendi ut, accedente gravi causa, interpellatio coniugis infidelis ante baptismum partis quae ad fidem convertitur fieri possit; nec non, gravi pariter de causa, ab eadem interpellatione, ante baptismum partis quae convertitur, dispensandi, dummodo hoc in casu ex processu saltem summario et extraiudiciali constet interpellationem fieri non posse, vel fore inutilem."

value in the United States a thorough discussion of details is not to be attempted here,[76] for the only purpose in mentioning them is to show that the Holy See is wont to grant dispensations from the interpellations by means of such special faculties. It is difficult, however, to understand the purpose of the Holy See in granting these faculties in such a manner, for the common law of Canon 1125 comprises every favor which they entail. As Vermeersch, Vromant and Ione so aptly remark, their appropriateness may lie in the fact that they are merely meant to act as norms supplying a prudent interpretation of the Apostolic Constitutions contained in Canon 1125, for in themselves they certainly appear to grant no further concessions.[77] Moreover, it should be remembered that the Holy See has ever been most solicitous for the welfare of missionary countries and the clergy who labor therein, and these particular faculties may merely embody a continuation of that solicitude.

§3. *By the Common Law*

The third and last source of a dispensation from the interpellations is contained in common law as exemplified in

CANON 1125

Ea quae matrimonium respiciunt in constitutionibus Pauli III *Altitudo,* 1 June, 1537; S. Pii V *Romani Pontificis,* 2 Aug., 1571; Gregorii XIII *Populis,* 25 Jan., 1585, quaeque pro peculiaribus locis scripta sunt, ad alias quoque regiones in eisdem adiunctis extenduntur.

Formerly there was some doubt as to whether these Papal Constitutions could be applied to all places or only to those countries to which they were addressed. But the Code has dis-

[76] For a detailed commentary on these faculties, consult Vromant, *Commentaria Facultates Apostolicae;* Vermeersch, *Commentaria de Formulis Facultatum;* Iglesias, *Brevis Commentarius in Facultates;* Winslow, *Vicars and Prefects Apostolic;* Blat, *Comment.*, III, pars I, n. 532.

[77] Vermeersch, *Comment. Formul. Facult.*, n. 120; Vromant, *Comment. Facult. Apost.*, n. 81; Ione, "Die Interpellationen bei Anwendung des Paulinischen Privilegs," *LQS*, LXXX (1927), 338-340.

pelled any cloudy controversy and states that they may be applied in any part of the world as long as the circumstances which they enumerate are present. Hence, the favors contained in these Constitutions now arise from the law itself, and they may be employed without the necessity of any further recourse to Rome.

A controversy of magnificent proportions has endured among canonists and theologians for centuries as to whether, aside from the limits of the Pauline Privilege, the Roman Pontiff by the plenitude of his power can dissolve the bond of a marriage contracted and consummated in infidelity, when that marriage later becomes a mixed union by the baptism of one party and even if it is consummated after the reception of the Sacrament. It is not within the purpose of this work to investigate closely the arguments for and against the question of Papal power in this respect,[78] but rather to confine itself within the limits of the Pauline institution. Whereas the dispositions of these three Constitutions have been spoken of previously,[79] present mention shall be restricted to a brief resumé of the indults and a consideration of those parts wherein there is granted a dispensation from the interpellations.

All three decrees refer to the objective validity of the second marriage, for in their effects they grant a real dissolution of the original marriage rather than a mere presumption that that union is dissolved. The constitution "*Altitudo,*" of Paul III, granted to a convert who had many wives before his conversion the right to choose one of those spouses and to enter a new marriage with her, if he did not remember which was his first legitimate wife. Pope Pius V, in his "*Romani Pontificis,*" permitted a convert who had been polygamous to retain that wife who was baptized with him or who wished to be baptized, even if he remembered which one was legitimately his first wife. While both of these constitutions regarded the state of polyga-

---

[78] For a lengthy discussion of this phase of Papal power, consult Cappello, *De Sacram.*, III, nn. 789-792; Vlaming, *Praelect.*, nn. 730-732; Gasparri, *De Matrim.*, nn. 1355-1361; Feije, *De Imped., et Disp. Matrim.*, n. 602; Wernz-Vidal, *Jus Canon.*, V, nn. 635-636.

[79] Cf. *supra*, pages 37-41.

mists, they are entirely diverse from the Pauline Privilege as such. For neither of them grants a place for the interpellations, the necessity of which has disappeared by virtue of the law itself.[80] In fact, the wishes of the infidel partner are in no way considered, and the dissolution of the marital bond can only be explained by the exercise of the Roman Pontiff's power. Furthermore, it must be kept in mind that a marriage is dissolved in virtue of the Pauline Privilege only at the moment when the convert enters a second union.

In like manner it is said that the constitution *"Populis,"* of Gregory XIII, is entirely lacking in its presentation of the conditions necessary for the use of the Pauline Privilege and, therefore, it is merely an execution of pontifical power as are the two preceding constitutions. By the terms of this decree, which concerned all infidels, Pope Gregory allowed a convert to enter a new union with another Catholic without making any pretense at interpellation, and he proclaimed that the second marriage remained valid even though it was later discovered that after the time of its contraction the infidel partner of the first union had also been converted and baptized. Surely the Pontiff did not mean to advert to the use of the Pauline Privilege in issuing this Constitution, for its contents do not verify the conditions of the Privilege. The only explanation is that he too intended to exercise Papal power, for the infidel spouse may have been fully prepared to cohabit peacefully. And of greater moment is the argument that the Privilege can be invoked only when the infidel has departed and *remains unbaptized*. But in his decree Gregory holds a second marriage as valid even if it is later found that the infidel was also baptized. Hence, from the terms of the Constitution it is evident that the Pope exercised a power far beyond the confines of the Pauline Privilege.[81]

---

[80] Wernz-Vidal, *Jus Canon.*, V, n. 633; Vlaming, *Praelect.*, n. 730; Cappello, *De Sacram.*, III, nn. 787-791; Chelodi, *Jus Matrim.*, n. 160; Augustine, *A Commentary*, V, 363; Vermeersch-Creusen, *Epitome*, II, n. 436; De Becker, *De Spons. et Matrim.*, p. 432.

[81] Vlaming, *Praelect.*, n. 730; Petrovits, *The New Church Law*, n. 577; Wernz-Vidal, *Jus Canon.*, V, n. 635; Cappello, *De Sacram.*, III, n. 791;

Nevertheless, a dispensation from the interpellations arises from this Constitution which, by the promulgation of the Code, is now a part of common law. And it is a most ample concession, having as its effect the dissolution of a marriage founded in infidelity. In accordance with this declaration the Holy See, through the medium of the common law, authorizes all Ordinaries, pastors and those members of the Society of Jesus who are approved to hear confessions, to dispense from the interpellations when it is evident that the infidel party cannot be reached, or that he has not given his reply within the specified time. The only restriction to this concession is the necessity of proving at least by a summary and non-judicial investigation that this impossibility or failure to respond truly exists. The text does not allow the omission of the interpellations under any other circumstances, e.g., when their inutility is foreseen for any reason, but its sole allowance is "dummodo constet, etiam summarie et extra-iudicialiter, coniugem absentem moneri legitime non posse, aut monitum, intra tempus eadem monitione praefixum, suam voluntatem non significasse." Such a case might arise when the infidel partner has his residence at a place so far distant that the execution of the interpellations would become impossible or at least very difficult because of the intervening distance or because the inhabitants of that region are hostile.

This extensive power may be used by Ordinaries and pastors toward their subjects wherever the latter may be, and in favor of all persons who are actually residing within their territories. Since this is now common law, it becomes a part of ordinary power attached to these respective offices and as such it may be delegated habitually.

Jesuit confessors may exercise this power toward all persons, not only in the act of confessing but also outside of confession for the external forum. For no restriction in this regard is mentioned either in the Constitution itself or in Canon 1125.

Gasparri, *De Matrim.*, n. 1359; Blat, *Comment.*, III, pars I, n. 536; De Becker, *De Spons. et Matrim.*, p. 431; De Smet, *De Spons. et Matrim.*, n. 355.

But if they grant the dispensation for the external forum the convert must be able to prove that concession, for a document to that effect is necessary to establish the convert's freedom to remarry. It may be that this power granted to the Society of Jesus may also be extended to other religious by way of a special privilege, but it is certain that none other than the Jesuits obtain it from the common law.[82]

It must be borne in mind that these three constitutions are extended by the Code to all countries wherein the *same* conditions exist,[83] and since they were granted originally to meet the circumstances of *countries* rather than of cases, those same conditions must now prevail in the *region* rather than merely among persons. Augustine[84] is of the opinion that for practical use in the United States it can hardly be claimed that any of these conditions exist today. However, if our Indian Reservations and Negro colonies in the South may be considered as "regions" (a classification which seems fully warranted), there appears to be no solid reason for denying the use of Canon 1125 among these peoples. For actual conditions indicate the presence of circumstances identical to those mentioned in the Pontifical constitutions. Polygamy is still the rule rather than the exception among many of the Indian tribes, and pastors working among the Negroes testify that it is a common occurrence to find converts who cannot remember how many consorts they have had or when and under what conditions they entered these various unions. Hence, Ordinaries who are met with these conditions common to the territory (not merely to individuals), should not hesitate in applying Canon 1125.

---

[82] Cappello, *De Sacram.*, III, n. 787; Vermeersch-Creusen, *Epitome*, II, n. 435; Petrovits, *The New Church Law*, n. 577; Gasparri, *De Matrim.*, n. 1349; Chelodi, *Jus Matrim.*, n. 160, note 6; Wernz-Vidal, *Jus Canon.*, V, n. 633; Vermeersch, *De Casu Apostoli*, n. 77; De Smet, *De Spons. et Matrim.*, n. 353; Vromant, *Comment. Facult. Apost.*, n. 80; Farrugia, *De Matrim.*, n. 324; Blat, *Comment.*, III, pars I, n. 536.

[83] Similarity of circumstances would not suffice, for the Code states that the declarations and dispensations of the constitutions are extended "ad alias quoque regiones *in eisdem adiunctis*."—Canon 1125; cf. Vermeersch, "De Canone 1125 Eiusque Vi Extensiva," *Periodica*, XX (1931), 1*-5*.

[84] *A Commentary*, V, 364.

Art. V. Effect of Dispensation from Interpellations

The general rule regarding the extraordinary effect or force of a dispensation from the interpellations is that the converted party gains the right to enter a second marriage; [85] and, moreover, this second union stands as valid even if it is later discovered that the infidel consort was prevented from declaring his mind, or that he had also embraced the Faith after the second marriage was contracted. That this singular effect ensues from the dispensation is best proved by the following quotations, which describe the mind of the Church and the style and practice of the Roman Curia. Thus:

> Quae quidem matrimonia, etiamsi postea innotuerit coniuges priores infideles suam voluntatem iuste impeditos declarare non potuisse, et ad fidem etiam tempore transacti secundi matrimonii conversos fuisse, nihilominus rescindi nunquam debere, sed valida et firma, prolemque inde suscipiendam legitimam fore decernimus.[86]

And again:

> Praeterea matrimonia inter neophytos huiusmodi, et alios fideles, et Catholicos alias rite contracta, etiamsi postmodum innotuerit priores coniuges infideles, . . . suam voluntatem significare, minime potuisse, vel ad fidem etiam tempore secundi matrimonii conversos fuisse, ullo unquam tempore rescindi minime debere, sed illa semper firma, valida, et inviolabilia existere et fore, dicto auctoritate decernas et declares.[87]

Furthermore, in his capacity as a private author, Benedict XIV says:

> Primum enim matrimonium eo ipso momento, et quidem irrevocabiliter, solutum remanet, quo coniux conversus ad alias nuptias cum fideli transivit; sive

---

[85] "Si interpellationes ex declarationes Sedis Apostolicae omissae fuerint, . . . pars baptizata ius habet novas nuptias . . . contrahendi."—Canon 1123; cf. Vlaming, *Praelect.*, n. 726.

[86] Gregory XIII, const. "*Populis,*" 25 Jan., 1585,—*Docum.* VIII, C. I. C.

[87] Benedict XIV, ep. "*In suprema,*" 16 Jan., 1745,—*Fontes*, n. 353.

> quia in hoc libertatem vindicatus fuerit Iure Divino, propterea quod infidelis coniux, iudicialiter interpellatus, evangelicae veritati, aut innocuae cohabitationi se denegaverit; sive quia peculiares rerum circumstantiae viam aperuerint Indulto Apostolico, quo sublata fuit interpellanda necessitas: quod quidem Indultum, quum nulli conditioni sit alligatum, secundi matrimonii validitatem et firmitatem perpetuo asserit, et reditum intercludit ad prima connubia, etiamsi quis probare contenderet, primo coniugi interpellato non fuisse liberum respondere, vel eum iam tunc Christianae Religioni amplectendae paratum fuisse, immo ante illam diem, qua secundum matrimonium a coniuge converso celebratum fuit, ipsum quoque Christo nomen dedisse, et baptismum suscepisse.[88]

And lastly:

> Matrimonium vero eius cum quo dispensatum fuerit, etiamsi postea innotuerit coniugen infidelem suam voluntatem iuste impeditam declarare non potuisse, et ad fidem etiam tempore initi matrimonii conversum fuisse, nihilominus numquam rescindi, sed validum esse debebit.[89]

It is true that the Pauline Privilege in itself does not attain such an extraordinary and far reaching juridic effect, but it is in the process of settling this point that authors disagree. Some argue that a dispensation from the interpellations is nothing more than an extensive declaration of the Privilege which the Pope rightfully gives in virtue of his supreme power, while others insist that he grants a true dispensation. This problem is likewise interwoven with the question concerning the ability of the Sovereign Pontiff to dissolve *a matrimonium legitimum* which has been consummated after the conversion of one party, and therefore, it will not be investigated here. Whichever side of the controversy is supported, the final solution is the same

[88] *De Synodo Dioecesana,* XIII, c. 21, n. 5.

[89] S. C. S. Off., (ad Vic. Ap. Iaponiae Merid.), 4 Feb., 1891,—*Fontes,* n. 1130. Cf. Wernz-Vidal, *Jus Canon.,* V, n. 634; Chelodi, *Jus Matrim.,* n. 160; Cappello, *De Sacram.,* III, n. 782; Petrovits, *The New Church Law,* n. 570; Vermeersch, *De Casu Apostoli,* n. 84; Vromant, *Comment. Facult. Apost.,* n. 79; Vermeersch-Creusen, *Epitome,* II, n. 136; Farrugia, *De Matrim.,* n. 322.

and admits the absolute severance of the first marriage and the validity of the second.[90]

ART. VI. THE PRESCRIBED FORM

CANON 1122

§1. Interpellationes fiant regulariter, forma saltem summaria et extraiudiciali, de auctoritate Ordinarii coniugis conversi, a quo Ordinario concedendae sunt quoque coniugi infideli, si quidem eas petierit, induciae ad deliberandum, eo tamen monito, fore ut, induciis inutiliter praeterlapsis, responsio praesumatur negativa.

§2. Interpellationes etiam privatim factae ab ipsa parte conversa, valent, imo sunt etiam licitae, si forma superius praescripta servari nequeat; hoc tamen in casu de ipsis, pro foro externo, constare debet duobus saltem testibus vel alio legitimo probationis modo.

Just as the Church demands that the interpellations must always be made or dispensed from, she also presents the canonical form or manner in which they must be executed in order to safeguard the liceity and validity of a second marriage. According to the Code, the form prescribed may be either *private* or *judicial*. If the latter method is employed it may bear the aspect of a strictly judicial proceeding or it may be merely summary and extra-judicial.

§1. *Strictly Judicial Form*

The formal judiciary method may be followed, and in that case all the formalities of any regular canonical hearing will be observed. This will entail an examination before a lawfully competent judge, with the convert, infidel, sworn witnesses, citations and notaries involved. It must be remembered that

[90] Cf. Wernz-Vidal, *Jus Canon.*, V, n. 635; Cappello, *De Sacram.*, III, nn. 789-792; Petrovits, *The New Church Law*, n. 570; Vlaming, *Praelect.*, nn. 731-732.

this is merely an examination to determine the dispositions of the infidel, and that it is not a strictly contentious process which would have to be sent to the Holy Office for decision.[91]

§2. *Extra-Judicial Form*

However, in regard to the interpellations the Church is not insistent on a rigorous canonical procedure, but she allows a summary and extra-judicial process for the purpose at hand. This juridic form is demanded at least, and it is to be instituted by the convert's Ordinary or his delegate.[92]

In accordance with the form of such a procedure, a letter signed by the Ordinary and Chancellor should be sent to the infidel party demanding his presence before an authorized person, in order that he may answer orally the two questions which constitute the interpellations. And the structure of this notification should contain all the formalities required of an official document. Therefore, there must be inserted the names of the party summoned and summoning, and of the judge who is appointed to ask the questions. The nature of the cause and the questions to be asked should be clearly stated; the place and date of service should be acknowledged and the location and date of answer must be appointed. The infidel is to be warned that the convert has the intention of contracting another marriage if a negative response is given. Finally, a peremptory period of time should be specified so that the infidel will realize that hesitation in answering is tantamount to his forfeiture of all later claims.[93]

---

[91] Vlaming, *Praelect.*, n. 723, note 3, suggests that where convenience allows, the formal judicial method should be carried out.

[92] Cf. Canon 94; De Becker, *De Spons. et Matrim.*, p. 422; Wernz-Vidal, *Jus Canon.*, V, n. 632; Cappello, *De Sacram.*, III, n. 779; De Smet, *De Spons. et Matrim.*, n. 350; Chelodi, *Jus Matrim.*, n. 158; Vermeersch-Creusen, *Epitome*, II, n. 432; Cerato, *Matrim.*, n. 122; Gasparri, *De Matrim.*, n. 1337; Feije, *De Imped. et Disp. Matrim.*, n. 487; S. C. S. Off., instr. (ad Superior. Mission. Peguan.), 11 June, 1760,—*Fontes*, n. 811; instr. (ad Archiep. Quebecen.), 16 Sept., 1824, ad 1,—*Fontes*, n. 866.

[93] Cf. Putzer, *Comment. in Facult. Apost.*, nn. 129, 132; Augustine, *A Commentary*, V, 355; Petrovits, *The New Church Law*, n. 563; Mansella, *De Imped. Matrim.*, p. 430; Michel, *Questions Pratiques sur le Mariage dans les Missions*, p. 62.

When the infidel appears for questioning he should be asked directly[94] by the Ordinary, or his appointee, and in the presence of two witnesses whether he wishes to be converted; and if that is answered negatively, the second question should be proposed, whether he consents to peaceful cohabitation. If a negative answer is supplied to both interrogations, then the judge should declare the convert free to enter a second marriage. All the acts of the case are to be recorded, signed by the judge, notary and witnesses and then placed in the Episcopal archives for future reference.[95]

Although the above procedure is to be preferred because of its similarity to a true judicial trial and for the reason that a personal appearance of the infidel provides an opportunity to understand better his dispositions in the matter, the interpellations and responses may be made entirely in writing. In this fashion a letter containing the following points should be sent to the unbeliever: notice that his wife has been baptized in the Catholic Church; her exhortation that he also be converted, or at least consent to live peacefully without blaspheming the Creator, that is, without leading her into mortal sin; the advice that if he answers both questions negatively the convert intends to enter another marriage; the demand that the infidel provide in writing an answer to the questions within one month from date, and if he fails to do this his silence will be construed as a negative reply; the date and place of the letter's origin and the

---

[94] "Quid censendum de responso negativo a parte infideli obtento, scilicet non velle converti aut pacifice cohabitare cum sua parte conversa, si istud responsum non quidem cordate sed quasi oblique obtentum fuerit?" Resp.: "In posterum interpellationes esse omnino faciendas iuxta formas ab Ecclesia praescriptas."—S. C. S. Off., (Mongoliae), 29 Nov., 1882, ad 4,—*Fontes*, n. 1075; cf. S. C. de Prop. Fide, (Sutchuen.), 17 Jan., 1836,—*Coll.*, n. 845; Cappello, *De Sacram.*, III, n. 779; Wernz-Vidal, *Jus Canon.*, V, n. 632; Ione, "Wie müssen die Interpellationen bei Anwendung des Paulinischen Privilegs gemacht werden," *LQS*, LXXX (1927), 343.

[95] Cf. Vermeersch-Creusen, *Epitome*, II, n. 432; Petrovits, *The New Church Law*, n. 563; Wernz-Vidal, *Jus Canon.*, V, n. 632; Putzer, *Comment. in Facult. Apost.*, n. 129; Chelodi, *Jus Matrim.*, n. 158; Cerato, *Matrim.*, n. 122; Gasparri, *De Matrim.*, n. 1337; Zitelli, *De Disp. Matrim.*, p. 122; Ayrinhac, *Marriage Legislation*, n. 301; Michel, *Questions Pratiques*, p. 62; S. C. S. Off., instr. (ad Superior. Mission. Peguan.), 11 June, 1760, —*Fontes*, n. 811; Conc. Plen. Baltim. III, p. 287, §45.

signatures of the Ordinary, or his delegate, and Chancellor, with the Curial seal; the address to which the infidel must send his letter of reply. This communication should be posted to the unbeliever by registered mail with the request that the addressee's receipt of delivery be returned to the official who sends the letter. Done in this manner it is certain that the infidel has personally received the notification. If no answer is forthcoming after the lapse of one month, the Ordinary or his delegate may declare the convert free to enter another union, and all the acts of the case should be recorded and kept in the diocesan archives for future reference.

The Code permits the Ordinary to grant the infidel a period of time for reflection and deliberation, *if* the latter requests it. Since this request is a right of the unbeliever which arises from the law,[96] charity and justice demand that it always be granted whenever it is sought or peculiar circumstances indicate a respite. Only the Ordinary or his delegate is authorized to permit or refuse this time for deliberation, and he may refuse the permission if an extension of time would seriously endanger the faith or morals of the convert.[97]

Furthermore, the Code constitutes the Ordinary or delegate as the only person capable of defining the time to be allowed for reflection. As individual cases and circumstances may differ he is to use his own judgment, though in general it may not be amiss to suggest a period of one month[98] as a suitable and sufficient extension. And it would seem best that this be considered as *tempus utile*,[99] for unforeseen circumstances might prevent a well-meaning infidel from expressing his wishes in time. However, in the act of granting this time allowance the Ordinary must also warn the infidel that if he fails to return an answer within the allotted period his silence will be construed as a negative answer.[100]

---

[96] Canon 1122, §1; cf. S. C. S. Off., (Cochinchin. Occident.), 12 June, 1850, ad 1,—*Fontes*, n. 910.

[97] Blat, *Comment.*, III, pars I, n. 533; Petrovits, *The New Church Law*, n. 564.

[98] Vermeersch, *De Casu Apostoli*, n. 59.

[99] Cf. Canon 35; Cappello, *De Sacram.*, III, n. 780.

[100] Canon 1122, §1; "Mora sua cuilibet nociva est."—Regula #25, R. J. in VI°.

§3. *Private Form*

Although Canon 1122, §1, prescribes at least a summary legal form, §2 permits of some relaxation in this matter. For it may not always be feasible to attend to the abbreviated judicial process, or the infidel may erect a barrier by refusing to heed a legal summons. In such a case the interpellations may be made validly and licitly in the private form, that is, by the convert himself or his proxy.[101] But if the legal process could be carried out without grave inconvenience, then private interpellations would be valid but illicit.[102]

If the interpellations are made privately by the convert or his delegate, the Code continues to say that the truth of the answers must be attested by at least two witnesses[103] or by some other

---

[101] Although Canon 1122, §2, includes the term *ipsa*, it is evidently placed there to denote the exercise of private interpellations by the convert in opposition to interrogations instituted by the Ordinary. Were it the intention of the legislator to restrict this privilege to the convert personally, it is probable that a more significant and qualifying term would have been employed, e.g., *unice, solus*. Furthermore, there seems to be no solid reason why a delegate may not effect that which the convert is empowered to do. In fact, the Holy See issued a warning that some responsible third person be employed in making private interpellations, lest the convert be prejudiced in his own case. (Cf. *Monita ad Missionarios Provinciae Nankinensis*, n. 521, quoted in De Smet, *op. cit.*, n. 350, note 7.) Most authors either definitely state or take it for granted that the convert may engage a third party: thus, De Smet, *De Spons. et Matrim.*, n. 350, note 7; Petrovits, *The New Church Law*, n. 565; Ayrinhac, *Marriage Legislation*, n. 302; Vermeersch-Creusen, *Epitome*, II, n. 432; Cappello, *De Sacram.*, III, n. 779; Gasparri, *De Matrim.*, n. 1337; Wernz-Vidal, *Jus Canon.*, V, n. 632; Augustine, *A Commentary*, V, 355; Farrugia, *De Matrim.*, n. 322; Vlaming, *Praelect.*, n. 723; Chelodi, *Jus Matrim.*, n. 158. On the other hand, Blat appears to be alone in his contention that the convert must use this privilege personally, for he says: "Interpellationes etiam privatim . . . factae personaliter ab ipsa (cuius interest) parte conversa, non ab alia persona, etsi ei valde coniuncta, valent."—*Comment.*, III, pars I, n. 533.

[102] De Smet, *De Spons. et Matrim.*, n. 350; Cappello, *De Sacram.*, III, n. 779; Wernz-Vidal, *Jus Canon.*, V, n. 632; Gasparri, *De Matrim.*, n. 1337; S. C. de Prop. Fide, (Tunkin. Occident.), 21 July, 1841,—*Coll.*, n. 929.

[103] Canon 1122, §2; "Debet adhibere testes, quod illa non vult ei cohabitare, ne impediatur postea contrahans."—*Glossa Ordinaria*, ad v. "qui relinquitur" in c. 7, X, *de divortiis*, IV, 19; S. C. de Prop. Fide, (Tunkin. Occident.), 21 July, 1841,—*Coll.*, n. 929; Gasparri, *De Matrim.*, n. 1337; Farrugia, *De Matrim.*, n. 322.

legitimate form of proof. Under the category of "other legitimate forms of proof" there may be listed the testimony of a pastor by virtue of his office;[104] an affidavit produced by the infidel bearing witness to the truth of his responses; the testimony under oath of any Catholic.[105] This evidence is necessary in order that the refusal of the infidel may be proved in the external forum, for if such testimony were lacking, the convert's second marriage might be impeded or its validity attacked.[106] The Ordinary should be assured of the integrity and honesty of the witnesses employed; and if the infidel is permitted to make his reply by letter, accompanied by affidavits, the Ordinary must exercise every caution before accepting such documents as a form of proof.[107] For in these modern times a dwarfed conscience can be easily regulated by not a few persons, and it is not uncommon to discover that affidavits have been falsely sworn to and even forged.

After the responses have been received privately they are to be sworn to by the convert or his proxy and witnesses, and then returned to the Ordinary or his delegate. From the substance of the answers that official is then free either to permit remarriage or not.

Although the letter of the Code specifies the necessity of witnesses, documents and the like for absolute proof in the external forum, it places none of these restrictions in allowing private interpellations to be made secretly for the internal forum. Hence, for the forum internum it will suffice that the interpellations be made privately by the convert in person or his proxy, either orally or by letter, and without witnesses.[108] But again

---

[104] "Unius testis depositio plenam fidem non facit, nisi sit testis qualificatus qui deponat de rebus ex officio gestis."—Canon 1791, §1.

[105] Cf. Vlaming, *Praelect.*, n. 723, note 4; Roberti, *De Processibus*, II, nn. 342-343; Vermeersch-Creusen, *Epitome*, II, n. 432; De Becker, *De Spons. et Matrim.*, p. 423; Putzer, *Comment. in Facult. Apost.*, n. 129.

[106] Cf. Cappello, *De Sacram.*, III, n. 779; Wernz-Vidal, *Jus Canon.*, V, n. 632; Chelodi, *Jus Matrim.*, n. 158; Cerato, *Matrim.*, n. 122.

[107] Cf. Roberti, *De Processibus*, II, nn. 372-373; Ione, "Wie müssen die Interpellationen bei Anwendung des Paulinischen Privilegs gemacht werden," *LQS*, LXXX (1927), 343-345.

[108] Cf. Petrovits, *The New Church Law*, n. 565; Ayrinhac, *Marriage Legislation*, n. 302.

in this contingency the greatest caution should be exercised in accepting such testimony, especially when the convert communicates a negative answer.

In practice, then, it would be well to employ the services of some trustworthy third person when the interpellations are to be made privately.

CHAPTER V

TRANSITION TO A SECOND MARRIAGE AND DISSOLUTION OF THE BOND

CANON 1123

Si interpellationes ex declaratione Sedis Apostolicae omissae fuerint, aut si infidelis eisdem negative responderit expresse vel tacite, pars baptizata ius habet novas nuptias cum persona catholica contrahendi, nisi ipsa post baptismum dederit parti baptizatae iustam discedendi causam.

CANON 1124

Coniux fidelis, licet post susceptum baptismum denuo matrimonialiter cum parte infideli vixerit, ius tamen novas celebrandi nuptias cum persona catholica non amittit, ideoque potest hoc iure uti, si coniux infidelis, mutata voluntate, postea discedat sine iusta causa, vel iam non cohabitet pacifice sine contumelia Creatoris.

CANON 1126

Vinculum prioris coniugii, in infidelitate contracti, tunc tantum solvitur, cum pars fidelis reapse novas nuptias valide iniverit.

In preceding paragraphs there have been discussed all the conditions which must be accounted for on the part of the infidel; but now there remains to be considered the immediate effect which their presence may have for the converted party. It is not to be thought that because the Pauline Privilege is a concession granted in favor of the faith the convert may blithely go his way. Certain considerations must be afforded to the infidel according to the form defined by the Church, but above all these requirements there still remain definite rules which govern the future life of the convert.

Canon 1123 grants to the convert not merely a permission but a right to enter a second marriage, but only after two of its three determined conditions have been fulfilled. For the law requires that before this right may be used, either an authorization must be obtained from the Holy See permitting the omission of the interpellations or it must be certain that the infidel has replied to them in the negative, whether expressly or tacitly. And thirdly, this right is denied the convert if after the reception of Baptism he presented the infidel with a just cause for departure. There is no necessity of repeating what has been said before concerning the power of the Church to dispense,[1] the definitely or tacitly negative responses of the unbeliever,[2] or the provision of a just cause for desertion.[3] Hence, there remains only the consideration of the convert's subsequent status.

ART. I. THE RIGHT TO ENTER A SECOND MARRIAGE

Canon 1123 grants to the convert the right to enter a new marriage when it is definitely known that the infidel has unjustly deserted, but this right does not comprise in itself a dissolution of the marital bond contracted in infidelity. Moreover, it demands that this new union be arranged only with another Catholic.

§1. *"Cum Persona Catholica"*

This condition must be fulfilled in order to safeguard the liceity and validity of a second marriage, although when the Code states the general rule demanding this, the practice of the Church opens the way to rare exceptions when she grants a

---

[1] Cf. *supra*, page 76.

[2] Cf. *supra*, pages 75-76.

[3] Cf. *supra*, page 61; Cappello, *De Sacram.*, III, n. 770.

dispensation from the impediment of Disparity of Cult or of Mixed Religion.[4] If the Pauline Privilege is a concession in favor of the Faith it hardly seems fitting that permission be given to enter a new union unless it be entirely to the advantage of that Faith. Therefore, the new spouse should be a Catholic, as is evident from the general tone of the Roman decisions,[5] the wording of the Code[6] and the contention of most authors.[7] It is understood that marriage with a non-Catholic would be valid and licit if a dispensation from the impediment of Disparity of Cult or Mixed Religion had been obtained from the Holy See, but otherwise such an attempted marriage would be illicit if with a baptized non-Catholic and invalid if with an infidel.[8]

Although the Holy See has granted these dispensations under such circumstances, it hesitates to make this a practice. The special faculties granted to missionaries whereby they may dispense from the interpellations do not include a dispensation from these impediments; nor may the missionaries use their regular faculties for these impediments in order that a convert availing himself of the Pauline Privilege may contract a second union with a non-Catholic spouse. And the same is true of the Quinquennial Faculties granted to Ordinaries. In both cases quite a special dispensation must be obtained from the Holy See, which rarely grants them for Mixed Religion and almost never for Disparity of Cult.[9]

---

[4] S. C. S. Off., (Coreae), 12 Sept., 1855, ad 1,—*Fontes*, n. 934; instr. (ad Vic. Ap. pro Gallas), 28 Mar., 1860, ad 6, 9,—*Fontes*, n. 957.

[5] S. C. S. Off., (Cochinchin. Occident.), 12 June, 1850, ad 1,—*Fontes*, n. 910; (Siam), 17 July, 1850,—*Fontes*, n. 911; instr. (ad Vic. Ap. Sutchuen. Orient.), 3 June, 1874,—*Fontes*, n. 1030.

[6] Canons 1123, 1124.

[7] Cf. Cappello, *De Sacram.*, III, n. 786; Wernz-Vidal, *Jus Canon.*, V, n. 631; De Smet, *De Spons. et Matrim.*, n. 354; Petrovits, *The New Church Law*, n. 568; Vermeersch, *De Casu Apostoli*, n. 62; Vlaming, *Praelect.*, n. 727; Augustine, *A Commentary*, V, 359; Cerato, *Matrim.*, n. 123; Chelodi, *Jus Matrim.*, n. 159, note 6; De Becker, *De Spons. et Matrim.*, p. 424, note 1; Blat, *Comment.*, III, pars I, n. 534; Farrugia, *De Matrim.*, n. 323.

[8] Vlaming, *Praelect.*, n. 727; Wernz-Vidal, *Jus Canon.*, V, n. 631.

[9] S. C. de Prop. Fide, instr. (Siam), 28 May, 1846,—*Coll.*, n. 1007; S. C. S. Off., (Siam), 17 July, 1850,—*Fontes*, n. 911; (Coreae), 12 Sept.,

Nevertheless, it is possible that in danger of death or when faced with the qualified circumstances of Canons 1043, 1044, 1045, Ordinaries and those priests specified may dispense from these impediments without having recourse to Rome. Intrinsic probability is afforded this contention, since the Canons cited specifically include these impediments; and extrinsic probability is not wanting, for the authors are either silent on this question or expressly confirm it.[10] It might be reasonably objected that the above Canons cannot be used under these circumstances, since the Church is not wont to dispense from Disparity of Cult or Mixed Religion in connection with the Pauline Privilege. But answer may be made that the Church *does* grant the dispensation at least rarely in cases *other* than danger of death; and, furthermore, although she is not accustomed to grant a dispensation for a deacon or sub-deacon to marry, that very dispensation is included in Canon 1043 for such a cleric in danger of death.[11]

If a baptized Protestant were to use the Pauline Privilege,[12] it would not be necessary for him to secure a dispensation from the impediments of Mixed Religion or Disparity of Cult in the event that he sought to establish a second marriage with another baptized non-Catholic or with an infidel. For the prohibitive impediment has never existed for him and he is no longer affected by the diriment impediment of Disparity of Cult.[13]

Hence, the convert has the right of contracting new matrimonial bonds with a Catholic. But exactly who are to be

---

1855, ad 1,—*Fontes*, n. 934; (Nankin.), 29 Aug., 1866,—*Coll.*, n. 1279; (Siam), 22 Nov., 1871,—*Fontes*, n. 1019; Vermeersch, *De Casu Apostoli*, nn. 62, 83; *Comment. Formul. Facult.*, n. 119; "Facultas ad decennium concessa alicui Vicario Apostolico," *Periodica*, XIV (1925), 114; XIX (1930), 77x-82x; Vermeersch-Creusen, *Epitome*, II, nn. 433-435; De Becker, *De Spons. et Matrim.*, p. 424, note 1; Vlaming, *Praelect.*, n. 727; Wernz-Vidal, *Jus Canon.*, V, n. 631; Cappello, *De Sacram.*, III, n. 786; Vromant, *Comment. Facult. Apost.*, n. 57, note 1, n. 79.

10 Vermeersch-Creusen, *Epitome*, II, n. 433.

11 Cappello, *De Sacram.*, III, n. 232; Vermeersch-Creusen, *Epitome*, II, n. 306.

12 Cf. *supra*, pages 50-51.

13 Canons 1060; 1070, §1; cf. Schenk, *Mixed Religion and Disparity of Cult*, pp. 98-99.

considered in the category of that term "Catholic"? It is a matter of common knowledge that among the members of the Church there are the majority who practically and externally profess their faith, while others are tepid and lax or even renounce their religion. Catholics are divisible, therefore, and the term may be understood in the strict or broad sense. In a matter such as the Pauline Privilege, where the very foundation and reason of the concession is always the advantage which accrues to the Faith, we believe that the designation "Catholic" should be construed only in the strict sense, to the exclusion of all others. Otherwise the legislator might not have been so insistent on the inclusion of the term in Canons 1123 and 1124. Schenk, in an able and serious dissertation, gives the very classification of a Catholic as constituted in the strict sense of the word; a classification which, though arranged in conjunction with the impediment of Mixed Religion, is every whit applicable to the present problem. For if the convert seeks to enter a new union with a person not a Catholic, that contract would be manifestly a mixed marriage, and hence the term "Catholic" should be interpreted in the light and sense of Canon 1060.[14] Nevertheless, if the convert insists on entering a second marriage with one who is excluded from the term "Catholic," he may do so with the permission of the Ordinary according to the declarations of Canons 1065 and 1066; for the prohibition mentioned there is not to be regarded as an impediment.[15] To quote Schenk in full:

> The following, therefore, are included in the *strict* sense of the term "Catholic": (a) those who have been baptized in, or converted to, the Catholic Church and who at the time of marriage are actual, professed Catholics; (b) those Catholics who are occult heretics; (c) those Catholics who are suspected of heresy; (d) those who have been excommunicated for moral delinquencies other than heresy or apostasy, and public sinners who refuse to be reconciled with the Church; (e) those Catholics who are mem-

[14] Cf. De Smet, *De Spons. et Matrim.*, n. 500; Blat, *Comment.*, III, pars, I, n. 455; Farrugia, *De Matrim.*, n. 131, nota.

> bers of condemned societies. The term "Catholic" excludes: (a) those who notoriously have left the Church as heretics or apostates; (b) those who by a declaratory or condemnatory sentence are recognized as heretics or apostates; (c) those Catholics who have joined an heretical or schismatic sect or a false religion.[16]

Furthermore, within the ambit of the designation "Catholic" there must be included not only members of the Latin Church, but also those who profess membership in any of the Eastern Uniate Churches.[17]

§2. *The Form of Marriage*

After permission has been given to take advantage of the Pauline Privilege, the convert from infidelity must celebrate his second marriage in accordance with the form prescribed by the Church.[18] Therefore, the union must be contracted before the proper Ordinary or pastor, or their delegate, and two witnesses.[19] The very rare cases mentioned in Canon 1098 [20] may arise, however, and under those circumstances the second marriage may be contracted if permission to avail oneself of the Privilege has *already* been received. Nevertheless, before marriage may be validly contracted in this way there must be

---

[16] *Mixed Religion and Disparity of Cult*, pp. 83-85.

[17] "Matrimonia cum quovis fideli alterius etiam ritus contrahere."—Gregory XIII, const. *"Populis,"* 25 Jan., 1585,—*Docum.* VIII, C. I. C.; S. C. de Prop. Fide, 18 Feb., 1783,—*Coll.*, n. 562; instr. (ad Ep. Graeco-Rumenos), a. 1858,—*Coll.*, n. 1154; S. C. S. Off., instr. (ad omnes Ep. Ritus Orient.), 12 Dec., 1888,—*Fontes*, n. 1112; Schenk, *Mixed Religion and Disparity of Cult*, p. 83, note 3.

[18] Canon 1099, §1, 1°; cf. Vermeersch, *De Casu Apostoli*, n. 62.

[19] Canon 1094.

[20] "Si haberi vel adiri nequeat sine gravi incommodo parochus vel Ordinarius vel sacerdos delegatus qui matrimonio assistant ad normam Canonum 1095, 1096:

1°. In mortis periculo validum et licitum est matrimonium contractum coram solis testibus; et etiam extra mortis periculum, dummodo prudenter praevideatur eam rerum conditionem esse per mensem duraturam;

2°. In utroque casu, si praesto sit alius sacerdos qui adesse possit, vocari et, una cum testibus, matrimonio assistere debet, salva coniugii validitate coram solis testibus."—Canon 1098.

present the conditions required by the Code and as interpreted by approved authors.[21]

Since Canon 1043 speaks of a dispensation from the form of marriage in danger of death, an Ordinary may grant this dispensation at the same time he allows permission to apply the Pauline Privilege. Canon 1044 extends this same faculty of dispensing from the form of marriage to the pastor, to the priest assisting at a marriage and to the confessor for the sacramental forum. But must permission to use the Pauline Privilege be *already* granted by the Ordinary before any of these priests may dispense from the matrimonial form, or may they also allow the use of the Pauline Privilege in danger of death? There seems to be no reason for denying them this power in such emergencies as long as they are certain that all the conditions of the Privilege, e.g., departure of the infidel, interpellations, etc., have been fulfilled. For after all, the Ordinary *strictly* does not permit a new marriage in a case of the Pauline Privilege; rather, he merely ascertains judicially that all the necessary conditions are present. And if all these requirements are verified, the convert's second marriage would be illicit but valid if entered into without the Ordinary's permission. Therefore, if any of the priests mentioned in Canons 1044 and 1098, 2° is positive that all the requirements of the Privilege are at hand, he may declare the use of the Privilege possible and a *valid* marriage would ensue. This holds only in danger of death and, as Canon 1044 demands, it must be impossible to reach the Ordinary.

Art. II. Perseverance of This Right

It may well happen that the common marital life founded in infidelity is continued, even after the reception of Baptism by one spouse. The convert had no thought of disrupting the union and did not interpellate the unbeliever. Nevertheless, the converted party has not been deprived of his right to a new marriage, regardless of the fact that he has continued to live

---

[21] Cf. Cappello, *De Sacram.*, III, nn. 690-697; Wernz-Vidal, *Jus Canon.*, V, nn. 543-549; Vermeersch-Creusen, *Epitome*, II, nn. 403-406; De Smet, *De Spons. et Matrim.*, nn. 130-134.

with the infidel over a period of years. For now the latter may initiate a belligerent domestic life, blaspheme the Name of God, and in general live a life which is a constant source of unhappiness for the convert. The interpellations may then be made; and if a negative answer is supplied, all the conditions of the Privilege are verified and the convert is free to leave and marry again.

Or, in a second hypothesis posited by Canon 1124, the converted partner may have received affirmative responses to the interpellations and then continued in the marital state with the unbeliever. But he has not forfeited his right to new nuptials if at any subsequent date the infidel divagates from his original promises, thereafter refusing to live peacefully and *sine contumelia Creatoris,* or if he departs without a just cause.[22] In both of these cases the favor of the faith should not be denied to the convert, for otherwise there would be imposed upon him the added affliction of contending with the deceits and profligacy of the infidel as well as the slavish obligation to remain celibate.

But if the infidel partner either receives or seriously intends to receive Baptism during the time the marital state has been continued, (this, after the baptism of the first convert), then the spouse first received into the Church is entirely deprived of his right to a second marriage. And if a separation from board and cohabitation has been in effect, the first convert is obliged to take up again the common life.[23] The reason for this demand is apparent in that some of the conditions of the Privilege are lacking, since the infidel member of the union is serious in his desire to abide by all the requirements of law or has already effected a sacramental union by his baptism.

---

[22] Canon 1124; cf. Cappello, *De Sacram.*, III, n. 784; Vlaming, *Praelect.*, n. 726; Gasparri, *De Matrim.*, n. 1340; De Smet, *De Spons. et Matrim.*, n. 348; Cerato, *Matrim.*, n. 124; Chelodi, *Jus Matrim.*, n. 159; Wernz-Vidal, *Jus Canon.*, V, n. 631; S. C. S. Off., (Cochinchin.), 1 Aug., 1759, ad 1,—*Fontes*, n. 810; (Oceaniae Occident.), 27 Sept., 1848,—*Fontes*, n. 907; (Natal), 11 July, 1866, ad 1,—*Fontes*, n. 996; *Synodus Sciarfensis Syrorum*, a. 1888, p. 169.

[23] Cf. c. 8, X, *de divortiis*, IV, 19; S. C. S. Off., (Natal), 11 July, 1866, ad 8,—*Fontes*, n. 996; Chelodi, *Jus Matrim.*, n. 159; Wernz-Vidal, *Jus Canon.*, V, n. 631; Cappello, *De Sacram.*, III, n. 784; Vermeersch, *De Casu Apostoli*, n. 64.

But what is the solution to the following problem? After the conversion of one party both spouses continue in the marital state; later on the infidel evinces her desire to receive Baptism, but at the same time refuses to continue cohabitation with her husband for no just cause, (or if offense were offered, sufficient satisfaction has been made). Now, must the deserting wife remain celibate, or may she invoke the Pauline Privilege? The Congregation of the Holy Office has declared that if the infidel is in danger of eternal damnation she may enter another marriage, but she must first interpellate her converted husband. By the same token, the convert husband of the above case may also avail himself of the Privilege, but he must do so before the baptism of his spouse.[24]

In the final analysis, Canon 1124 also qualifies the convert's right to a new marriage by stating that it must be *cum persona Catholica*. This, however, is not required *ad validitatem* if the proper dispensation has been provided.[25]

ART. III. DISSOLUTION OF THE BOND

Over a period of centuries canonists and theologians have held divergent views as to the exact moment when the bond of a marriage contracted in infidelity was dissolved by virtue of the Pauline Privilege. Some were of the opinion that the dissolution was effected by the very fact of the convert's baptism; others, that it arose out of the infidel's refusal to be converted and live peacefully; and lastly, there were those who correctly adhered to the principle that the marital bond was severed only by the entrance of the convert into a second marriage.[26]

Canon 1126 reaffirms the stand taken by the Church and the interpretation of all authors in recent years and states that the marriage founded in infidelity is dissolved in virtue of the

[24] S. C. S. Off., 26 April, 1899,—*Fontes*, n. 1222; cf. Cappello, *De Sacram.*, III, n. 784.

[25] Cf. *supra*, page 99.

[26] Cf. *supra*, pages 16, 22, 30, 35. Fahrner, *Geschichte des Unauflöslichkeitsprinzips*, p. 289; Biederlack, "Ueber das sog. Paulinische Privilegium," *ZKT*, VII (1883), 322.

Pauline Privilege only when the converted partner validly enters a new union.[27] It should be noted that the second marriage of the convert must be valid in all its aspects, for otherwise the bond of the first union is not dissolved.

Although the text of the Canon includes the word "*tantum*" when referring to dissolution (*tunc tantum solvitur*), it is our contention that this is a qualifying term referring only to the *time* when the dissolution is effected. It carries with it the idea that the bond is not severed by the baptism of the convert nor by the desertion of the infidel, but *only when (tunc tantum)* the second marriage is contracted. On the contrary, Augustine [28] interprets *tantum* as referring, not to time, but to the exclusion of any state of life other than marriage.

§1. *Reception of Solemn Vows or Sacred Orders*

Almost all authors are agreed that by Apostolic dispensation the convert may enter religion or receive Sacred Orders in lieu of contracting a second marriage. But those same authors are not one in deciding whether or not solemn profession in religion actually dissolves the bond of such a marriage. It is certain that the reception of Sacred Orders does not have this effect, and the competency of solemn profession hinges on whichever view is taken of the Roman Pontiff's power to dissolve matrimonium legitimum.[29] For practical purposes it is

---

[27] Benedictus XIV, ep. "*Postremo mense,*" 28 Feb., 1747, ad 58,—*Fontes*, n. 377; const. "*Apostolici ministerii,*" 16 Sept., 1747, ad 4,—*Fontes*, n. 381; S. C. C., *Florentina*, 27 July, 1726,—*Fontes*, n. 3321; *Florentina*, 29 March, 1727,—*Fontes*, n. 3324; S. C. S. Off., (Cochinchin.), 1 Aug., 1759, ad 2, 5,—*Fontes*, n. 810; S. C. de Prop. Fide, instr. (ad Vic. Ap. Sutchuen.), 30 Jan., 1807,—*Coll.*, n. 690; Hurter, *Theol. Dogmat.*, III, n. 760; Sanchez, *De Matrim.*, VII, disp. 75; Schmalzgrueber, *Jus Eccles. Univ.*, lib. IV, tit. XIX, n. 24; Feije, *De Imped. et Disp. Matrim.*, n. 498; Ojetti, *Synop. Rerum Moral.*, III, n. 3286; Wernz-Vidal, *Jus Canon.*, V, n. 631; Cappello, *De Sacram.*, III, n. 785; Chelodi, *Jus Matrim.*, n. 159; Gasparri, *De Matrim.*, n. 1333.

[28] *A Commentary*, V, 366; cf. Blat, *Comment.*, III, pars I, n. 537.

[29] Cf. Fahrner, *Geschichte des Unauflöslichkeitsprinzips*, p. 289; Cappello, *De Sacram.*, III, nn. 758-760, 792; Gasparri, *De Matrim.*, n. 1362; Feije, *De Imped. et Disp. Matrim.*, n. 500; Wernz-Vidal, *Jus Canon.*, V, n. 631, note 67; Sanchez, *De Matrim.*, VII, disp. 76; Noldin, *De Jure Matrim.*, n. 34.

sufficient to state that before the convert may be allowed to enter religion by solemn profession or Sacred Orders, a dispensation to that effect must be obtained from Rome.[80]

ART. IV. RIGHTS OF THE INFIDEL

It may well happen that the converted party declines to avail himself of the Pauline Privilege by entering a new union, since he prefers from now on to lead a life of celibacy. In such a contingency the infidel party is awarded no right to contract a second marriage herself, for there still exists the impediment of *ligamen* arising from the divine law. But if the infidel partner is also converted and baptized while the first convert is still confirmed in his celibate state, the latter is obliged by charity, if not by the demands of justice, to resume domestic life.[81] It is not an uncommon occurrence to find that the infidel gives serious attention only to the demands of the State, and once successful in obtaining a civil divorce he immediately attempts another marriage. Since he is not yet free,—for the convert has entered no new wedlock,—that marriage would be invalid.[82]

But once the converted party enters a second marriage, the bond of the union founded in infidelity is dissolved entirely for both persons. In this manner the infidel is indirectly freed, and consequently he may proceed himself to contract a new union.[83]

---

[80] Canons 542, 1°; 987, 2°; cf. Vermeersch-Creusen, *Epitome*, II, n. 433.

[81] Vermeersch, *De Casu Apostoli*, n. 64; Gasparri, *De Matrim.*, n. 1335; Feije, *De Imped. et Disp. Matrim.*, n. 499; Cappello, *De Sacram.*, III, n. 784.

[82] S. C. C., *Florentina*, 29 March, 1727,—*Fontes*, n. 3324.

[83] Benedictus XIV, const. "*Apostolici ministerii*," 16 Sept., 1747, ad 4,—*Fontes*, n. 381: "Principium autem iuris communis est: soluta a vinculo coniugali muliere, solutum remanere et virum. Quippe vinculum est inter duo, seu duorum in unum, idcirco libertas unius libertatem infert alterius."—S. C. S. Off., instr. (ad Archiep. Quebecen.), 16 Sept., 1824,—*Fontes*, n. 866; cf. Wernz-Vidal, *Jus Canon.*, V, n. 631; Cappello, *De Sacram.*, III, n. 785; Chelodi, *Jus Matrim.*, n. 159; Gasparri, *De Matrim.*, n. 1335; Vermeersch, *De Casu Apostoli*, n. 65; Vlaming, *Praelect.*, n. 728; De Becker, *De Spons. et Matrim.*, p. 425; Gillmann, "Zum Problem vom Privilegium Paulinum," *AkKR*, CII (1922), 27; Jombart, "Casus de Dissolutione Matrimonii Paganorum," *Periodica*, XIV (1925), (69); Ione, "Die Anwendung des Paulinischen Privilegs," *LQS*, LXXX (1927), 136.

CHAPTER VI

THE FAVOR OF THE FAITH

CANON 1127

In re dubia privilegium fidei gaudet favore iuris.

The principle contained in Canon 1127, that in doubtful matters the privilege of the faith enjoys the favor of the law, involves no innovation in the jurisprudence of the Church. It was clearly enunciated by Pope Benedict XIV [1] and has frequently borne repetition by the Roman Curia,[2] theologians and canonists as a safe and practical rule of action when the interests at heart are the conversion to and the practice of the True Faith. This general principle invoked by Benedict XIV is now taken up in Canon 1127, where it applies specifically to all cases wherein the continuation or maintenance of a marriage would prove an obstacle to the acquisition and profession of the Faith. Since the legislator has inserted it in the Code within the ambit of the Article *"De Dissolutione Matrimonii,"* (Liber III, Title VII), and as it follows closely upon Canon 1125 (which now extends the usage of the Sovereign Pontiff's power over *matrimonium legitimum*), Canon 1127 is applicable not only to the Pauline Privilege as such but to all cases where the marriage bond is dissolved in favor of the Faith.[3]

---

[1] "In re dubia in favorem fidei pronuntiandum esse constans regula est."—ep. *"Probe te,"* 15 Dec., 1751, ad 27,—*Fontes,* n. 418.

[2] S. C. S. Off., 8 June, 1836,—*Fontes,* n. 874; 5 July, 1853,—*Fontes,* n. 924; instr. (ad Ep. S. Alberti), 9 Dec., 1874, ad 13,—*Fontes,* n. 1036; (Mongoliae), 29 Nov., 1882,—*Fontes,* n. 1075; (Siouxormen.), 18 May, 1892, ad 1, 2,—*Fontes,* n. 1155; 19 Apr., 1899,—*Fontes,* n. 1220; 26 Apr., 1899,—*Fontes,* n. 1222.

[3] Creusen, "Baptême Douteaux et Mariage Indissoluble," *NRT,* LII (1925), 229; Arendt, "Quomodo in favorem fidei solvatur a S. Pontifice matrimonium in infidelitate Contractum," *Eph. Th. Lov.,* I (1924), 184, n. 35; Wernz-Vidal, *Jus Canon.,* V, n. 637; Vlaming, *Praelect.,* n. 733; Blat, *Comment.,* III, pars I, n. 538.

For a principle of such latitude, involving as it does a matter of supreme importance, the intent and interpretation of Canon 1127 have been sorely neglected by the majority of modern writers. Without claiming the virtue of investigating a field embracing every possibility, an attempt shall be made here to enhance the clarity of the principle and to signify its application to matrimonial difficulties which are constantly arising. With these definite objects in mind, the discussion of this norm of law shall be divided among the following points: (a) general interpretation of the principle; (b) what constitutes the *privilegium fidei;* (c) what is understood by *favor iuris;* (d) what is to be included among *res dubia.*

ART. I. GENERAL INTERPRETATION OF THE PRINCIPLE

When speaking of the general interpretation of the principle involved there is to be understood the positive manner in which it is to be applied to all possible cases. In other words, any principle of law may be considered and reduced to a working basis either in the strict or in the broad sense, according as it is deemed so by the jurisprudence of the Church and the common teaching of canonists. From the very nature of the thing it may be said that the rule of action,—in doubtful matters the privilege of the faith enjoys the favor of the law,—should always be understood in the *broad* sense.[4] For in what way would any benefit arise to the Faith if to this privilege or favor of the law there were attached a strict interpretation?

From the time of St. Paul the favor has been understood as a concession to an infidel person, assuring him of an aid to conversion and freedom from a life of servitude necessitated by a pagan atmosphere and possible infelicitous domestic arrangements. In all her decisions and instructions the Church has ever maintained this concessive attitude and the tone of her decrees proves beyond a doubt that in every possible way she wishes to make conversion and the practice of the True Faith easy for the infidel. Thus, for example, her lenient attitude is manifested wherein she considers an infidel spouse as having

[4] Vermeersch, "Interpretatio Canonis 1127," *Periodica,* X (1922), (25).

departed and permits a new marriage to the converted partner when the former has been physically detained for some reason,[5] even though he is perfectly willing to cohabit peacefully.[6] Hence, as a practical conclusion, the principle of Canon 1127 may be invoked by the Ordinary and a decision granted which will redound to the liberty of a converted partner; its confines are to be measured only by the limits of the power which the Sovereign Pontiff enjoys.

ART. II. WHAT CONSTITUTES THE *Privilegium Fidei*

In the broad sense of the phrase, the privilege of the faith may be understood as the right to choose in any doubtful case the probable solution which would be most favorable to the acquisition, profession and extension of the True Faith.[7] Thus, for example, a case was settled affirmatively by Benedict XIV, where the question concerned the power of a grandparent to have a grandson baptized over the opposition of his mother. The natural right of a parent over a child created a positive doubt as to the lawfulness of the grandparent's act, but Benedict ruled: "In re dubia in favorem fidei pronuntiandum esse constans regula est."[8] This principle stated by the Sovereign Pontiff was a general rule applicable to all cases, from the solution of which the True Faith would benefit as well as the individuals concerned.

But this norm of action is repeated nowhere in the Code except in Canon 1127, and there the position of the principle manifestly points to its application in matrimonial affairs. The *privilegium fidei* of Canon 1127 directly affects, then, only

---

[5] The permission in this case is qualified, however, in that after the reception of Baptism the convert provided the infidel with no just cause for deserting.

[6] S. C. S. Off., (Cochinchin. Occident.), 12 June, 1850, ad 1,—*Fontes*, n. 910; (Victoriae Nyanzae), 8 July, 1891, ad 2,—*Fontes*, n. 1140.

[7] Creusen, "Baptême Douteaux et Mariage Indissoluble," *NRT*, LII (1925), 229; "De Dubio Matrimonio ob Dubium Baptismum," *Periodica*, XVII (1928), 159*; Vermeersch-Creusen, *Epitome*, II, n. 427; Arendt, "De Clausula Restrictiva Canoni 1123 Adiecta," *Eph. Th. Lov.*, III (1926), 329, n. 3.

[8] Ep. "*Probe te*," 15 Dec., 1751, ad 27,—*Fontes*, n. 418.

marital difficulties. But its interpretation or meaning is again divisible into the broad and strict sense. Thus, according to the broad interpretation the *privilegium fidei* may refer to any judgment granted in favor of the faith whereby a marriage of doubtful validity is judged and looked upon as valid or invalid, according as that validity or invalidity opens the way to the reception of Baptism.[9] It was with this in mind that the Holy Office specifically repeated and applied the general principle of Benedict XIV, when it decreed: "Mens est ut in dubiis iudicium sit in fidei favorem," and again "Mens est ut in dubio iudicium sit in favorem fidei."[10]

On the other hand, the *privilegium fidei* is designated strictly as that faculty granted to a convert from infidelity whereby he may contract a second marriage after the reception of Baptism if his infidel consort departs, that is, if the latter refuses to be baptized or at least to live peacefully with the convert and without blaspheming God. It is in this sense that the phrase "privilege of the faith" is generally understood, and as such it refers directly to the Pauline Privilege. But when all the conditions of the Pauline concession are not *certainly* realized, then the Sovereign Pontiff may exercise the power which he has by divine law and dissolve a marriage which has not been consummated by two certainly baptized partners. And to facilitate conversion to the Faith and the practice thereof, he may authorize under these circumstances a new marriage for the convert.[11]

---

[9] S. C. S. Off., (Siouxormen.), 18 May, 1892, ad 2,—*Fontes*, n. 1155; Vromant, *Comment. Facult. Apost.*, n. 83; Vermeersch, *De Casu Apostoli*, n. 31; "Interpretatio Canonis 1127," *Periodica*, X (1922), (26); Wernz-Vidal, *Jus Canon.*, V, n. 631.

[10] S. C. S. Off., 19 Apr., 1899,—*Fontes*, n. 1220; 26 Apr., 1899,—*Fontes*, n. 1222; cf. instr. (ad Ep. S. Alberti), 9 Dec., 1874, ad 13,—*Fontes*, n. 1036, where the statement of Benedict XIV is repeated in reference to marital difficulties.

[11] Thus, e.g., the provisions of Canon 1125, and the dissolution of the *natural bond* of marriage as exemplified in the so-called "Helena Case." Cf. *AER*, LXX (1924), 59; LXXII (1925), 186, 405, 622; *Periodica*, XIV (1925), 19-21; *Nederlandsche Katholieke Stemmen* (1925), 53 sq.; *LQS*, LXXIX (1926), 568-579; *NRT*, LII (1925), 326-329; 499-500; *HPR*, XXX (1930), 864.

Hence, the privilege of the faith properly so called is not a judgment concerning the validity or invalidity of a marriage, but it is in truth the dissolution of the marital bond. Therefore, in Canon 1127 the privilege of the faith is to be understood as that grant of liberty which accrues to a convert to the Faith, whereby a doubtful marriage bond is dissolved or a marriage newly contracted is esteemed as valid, the while all other necessary conditions are observed.[12]

Art. III. What is Understood by *Favor Iuris*

Considered *objectively*, the favor of the law is to be understood as a certain propensity or bent evidenced in ecclesiastical legislation whereby the privilege of the faith as determined strictly may be invoked in doubtful cases. Thus, for example, Canon 1014 states that marriage enjoys the favor of the law, (that is, it is to be considered valid), and if a doubt of law or of fact concerning validity arises, the validity of the union is to be upheld until the contrary is proved *except in the case mentioned in Canon 1127.*[13] Hence, it is seen that this presumption in favor of validity (Canon 1014) cedes to a presumption in favor of the faith (Canon 1127), that is, to the liberty of a convert from infidelity.[14]

The presumption of Canon 1014 is not to be considered as *juris et de jure,* but merely as a *praesumptio juris* which gives

---

[12] Vermeersch, "Interpretatio Canonis 1127," *Periodica*, X (1922), (27); Donovan, "Doubtful Baptisms and Pauline Privilege," *AER*, LXXI (1924), 49; Farrugia, *De Matrim.*, n. 326; Vermeersch-Creusen, *Epitome*, II, n. 437; Cappello, *De Sacram.*, III, n. 788; Wernz-Vidal, *Jus Canon.*, V, n. 631; De Smet, *De Spons. et Matrim.*, n. 355.

[13] "Matrimonium gaudet favore iuris; quare in dubio standum est pro valore matrimonii, donec contrarium probetur, salvo praescripto can. 1127." —Canon 1014; "Quoad matrimonia infidelium istius regionis videri in hanc etiam opinionem devinisse, *in dubio* standum esse pro invaliditate matrimonii."—S. C. S. Off., instr. (ad Vic. Ap. Oceaniae Central.), 18 Dec., 1872,—*Fontes*, n. 1024; instr. (ad Ep. Nesquallien.), 24 Jan., 1877, ad 3,—*Fontes*, n. 1050; "Si vero pars una convertatur post conversionem alterius, et examinato casu particulari supersit dubium, stet pro nullitate matrimonii, in favorem fidei."—18 May, 1892, ad 1,—*Fontes*, n. 1156; 19 Apr., 1899,—*Fontes*, n. 1220; 26 Apr., 1899,—*Fontes*, n. 1222.

[14] Vermeersch, *De Casu Apostoli*, n. 28; Vromant, *Comment. Facult. Apost.*, n. 82.

way before a certain demonstration of truth.[15] Therefore, the presumption favorable to the liberty of a convert is likewise only *juris*. And if later on it is definitely and certainly known to be contrary to the objective order of truth, where the conditions of the Pauline Privilege are not verified, it would seem that then the power of the Sovereign Pontiff must be called upon in as far as it is necessary to dissolve the marital bond.[16]

Nevertheless, this presumption of invalidity in favor of the faith cannot be carried so far as to entail the risk of trampling on a divine law or an inviolable right. In every case in which the jurisprudence of Rome permits a convert to enter a new marriage when there is some doubt as to the verification of the conditions necessary for the Pauline Privilege, the Sovereign Pontiff does not rely on any presumption which exposes him to the danger of violating an inprescriptible right or a divine law. Therefore, the presumption supporting the invalidity of marriage in favor of the faith should be established and prudently applied in proportion to the danger attendant upon the violation of either of these two objects.

Looked upon *subjectively*, the favor of the law must be considered as a right arising purely from ecclesiastical law. It is determined definitely as a right derived from ecclesiastical law in the present Code, for Canon 1127 states the general rule allowing the favor of the law. Furthermore, it has been seen above that Canon 1014 safeguards the *privilegium fidei* from the warrant of validity by extending the *favor iuris*. Again, Canon 1069, §1 [17] concedes the favor of the law to a convert when it excepts the privilege of the faith as a species of the impediment of *ligamen*.

---

[15] Vermeersch-Creusen, *Epitome*, II, n. 279, Wernz-Vidal, *Jus Canon.*, V, n. 44; Chelodi, *Jus Matrim.*, n. 7; Cappello, *De Sacram.*, III, nn. 51-55.

[16] De Smet, *De Spons. et Matrim.*, n. 355; Wernz-Vidal, *Jus Canon.*, V, nn. 44, 631, note 61; Arendt, "Nota Circa Canonem 1127," *Eph. Th. Lov.*, I (1924), 180-181; Creusen, "Baptême Douteaux et Mariage Indissoluble," *NRT*, LII (1925), 235-236.

[17] "Invalide matrimonium attentat qui vinculo tenetur prioris matrimonii, quanquam non consummati, salvo privilegio fidei."—Canon 1069, §1. In the case of the Pauline Privilege a new marriage is permitted to the convert *before* the first matrimonial bond has been truly dissolved. In other words, the first union is broken *only* by a second valid marriage.

On the other hand, Vermeersch argues that the favor of the law may also be thought of as a derivative of the divine law, since Canon 1127 simply and without any distinction puts the proposition that in doubtful things the privilege of the faith enjoys the favor of the law. Furthermore, he says, authors are not agreed on the origin of the Pauline Privilege; for some contend that it is of immediate divine origin, while others bear witness that it is a concession granted by St. Paul in virtue of a power divinely conceded to him as an Apostle. Hence, it may be argued that since the privilege of the faith may be interpreted as arising either from divine law or from a divinely conceded power, the *favor iuris* may be understood as the favor of the divine law. Lastly, he adduces the argument that in allowing a Jewish infant to be baptized when presented by its grand-mother against the wishes of its mother, Benedict XIV formally declared that the privilege of the faith enjoyed the favor of the divine law.[18]

It is true that ultimately all law is derived from divine authority, but in the present case it can hardly be claimed as the source of Canon 1127 since this norm was stated purely by the human legislator.

ART. IV. WHAT IS TO BE INCLUDED AMONG "*Res Dubia*"

§1. *Defining a Doubtful Thing*

Before entering into a detailed discussion of those things which might be classified as doubtful, it would be well to determine definitely what is meant by a doubtful thing as well as the circumstances under which the principle of Canon 1127 may be applied.

Doubt, in general, is accepted as the state of mind concerning any given proposition in which the mind lacks certitude. Therefore, a person who is not certain about a thing is said to be doubtful when he suspends judgment entirely, when he inclines toward one opinion, or when he assents to one part of

[18] Vermeersch, "Interpretatio Canonis 1127," *Periodica*, X (1922), (26) ; cf. Benedictus XIV, ep. "*Probe te*," 15 Dec., 1751, ad 26,—*Fontes*, n. 418.

the proposition with the fear of the opposite being true.[19] In this sense doubt is opposed only to certitude.

In the strict sense a doubt exists when answers to both parts of a theme offer a probable reason for doubting. As such it is opposed to ignorance, which is present when no, or very slight, reasons for giving assent are at hand.

For the purpose at hand,—a doubt resolving in favor of the faith,—it is best that doubt be understood more broadly. Therefore, doubt is defined as the exclusion of moral certitude or the absence of any certain demonstration, even though it arises from presumptions.[20]

A. *Dubium Iuris Vel Facti*

By reason of the object concerned, the principle contained in Canon 1127 may be applied to a *dubium juris*, that is, when the doubt hinges on the existence of a law or a thing contained in the law; or to a *dubium facti*, namely, when the doubt is occupied with particular facts or conditions upon which the application of the law depends.[21] An example of the former is proposed by De Smet,[22] wherein marriage was contracted in infidelity within a degree of consanguinity in which marriage is probably invalid by the law of nature itself, e.g., marriage between brother and sister. In that case if one of the parties

---

[19] Cf. Noldin, *Summa Theologiae Moralis*, I, n. 222.

[20] "Dubium de quo agitur in canone 1127, certo certius non intelligitur sensu ita stricto ut opponatur ignorantiae, sed potius consentanee ad finem obtinendum in favorem fidei, complectitur absentiam cuiuscumque certae demonstrationis, sive probabiles tantum in utramque dubii partem, sive etiam nullae rationes huic inde suppetant, ne praesumptivae quidem, quarum completus defectus ignorantiam proprie dictam constituit; dubium igitur intelligo in praesenti, *certitudinis moralis* exclusionem."—Arendt, "Nota Circa Canonem 1127," *Eph. Th. Lov.*, I (1924), 181, n. 25; Cf. Vromant, *Comment. Facult. Apost.*, n. 82; Creusen, "Baptême Douteaux et Mariage Indissoluble," *NRT*, LII (1925), 230; S. C. S. Off., (Siouxormen.), 18 May, 1892, ad 1,—*Fontes*, n. 1155. On the other hand, Cappello, *De Sacram.*, III, n. 788, holds that doubt should be construed in the strict sense to the exclusion of ignorance.

[21] Vromant, *Comment. Facult. Apost.*, n. 83; Vermeersch, "Interpretatio Canonis 1127," *Periodica*, X (1922), (28); Arendt, "Nota Circa Canonem 1127," *Eph. Th. Lov.*, I (1924), 182.

[22] *De Spons. et Matrim.*, n. 343, note 4.

is converted and wishes to marry again, the marriage might be declared null and void quite apart from any application of the Pauline Privilege.[23] On the other hand, a sample of a *dubium facti* is had when it is doubted whether or not one of the conditions necessary for the application of the Privilege is verified, e.g., a valid marriage contracted in infidelity. In either doubt, whether of law or of fact, the marriage may be dissolved in favor of the faith.

From the very nature of things it is clearly evident that before the principle of Canon 1127 may be applied, the doubt must be dissipated if possible. This can be done only by means of a serious and diligent investigation, which cannot be omitted in a matter so highly important. If, after every reasonable avenue of examination is patrolled, the doubt persists, then the Ordinary may invoke the principle.[24]

§2. *"Res Dubia"*

We come now to the consideration of what is to be included in the category of doubtful matters. In general it may be stated that Canon 1127 may be advanced and applied whenever doubt arises in any way, whether it be of persons or circumstances, of law or of fact. More specifically, however, several authors propose a list of objects around which doubt may not be precluded. The points enumerated in these catalogues, to which we adhere, are practically in accord with each other, and the purpose of this work is sufficient guaranty for their reiteration at this time.

---

[23] "Nunquam matrimonium permittatur, si quod subsit dubium num partes sint consanguineae in aliquo gradu lineae rectae aut in primo gradu lineae collateralis."—Canon 1076, §3; cf. De Smet, *De Spons. et Matrim.*, nn. 343, note 4, 608; Augustine, *A Commentary*, V, 207-208; Gasparri, *De Matrim.*, nn. 769, 772.

[24] "Instituendum est in singulis casibus particularibus examen circumstantiarum et modi, quo coniugium primitus initum fuerit. Si vero pars una convertatur post conversionem alterius, et examinato casu particulari supersit dubium, stet pro nullitate matrimonii, in favorem fidei."—S. C. S. Off., 18 May, 1892, ad 1, 2,—*Fontes*, n. 1156; cf. instr. (ad Ep. S. Alberti), 9 Dec., 1874, ad 11, 17,—*Fontes*, n. 1036; Wernz-Vidal, *Jus Canon.*, V, n. 631; Vermeersch, *De Casu Apostoli*, n. 28; Vlaming, *Praelect.*, n. 733; Arendt, "Nota Circa Canonem 1127," *Eph. Th. Lov.*, I (1924), 182; Farrugia, *De Matrim.*, n. 326.

Hence, it is said that a doubt may stand upon: (a) the validity of a marriage contracted in infidelity; (b) the existence of a second marriage now founded: (c) the person of the first wife of a polygamous man; (d) the sincere response of the infidel party when the interpellations have been made; (e) the presence of sufficient cause for dispensing from the interpellations or from an expected answer; (f) the degree of cause for separation given by the convert to the infidel after Baptism; (g) the validity of the Baptism received *by one party.*[25]

With the exception of a doubt arising from the validity of Baptism, these others have been treated of before.[26] Hence, reconsideration is unnecessary, and discussion is here confined to the practical application of the Pauline Privilege in a marriage case where doubtful Baptism has been received by one or both parties.

ART. V. DOUBTFUL BAPTISM

It is not our intention to enter the field of controversy regarding Baptism as doubtful when administered in an heretical

[25] Cf. Vermeersch-Creusen, *Epitome,* II, n. 437; Wernz-Vidal, *Jus Canon.,* V, n. 631; Vromant, *Comment. Facult. Apost.,* nn. 84-85; Vermeersch, "Interpretatio Canonis 1127," *Periodica,* X (1922), (27); Arendt, "Nota Circa Canonem 1127," *Eph. Th. Lov.,* I (1924), 182-184, nn. 26-34; Cappello, *De Sacram.,* III, n. 788; Farrugia, *De Matrim.,* n. 326; Cerato, *Matrim.,* n. 127. In the schedules of Cappello and Farrugia there is added a more or less general doubt, namely, a doubt whether or no there are present *all* the conditions necessary for the use of the Privilege. When this is dissected it will be found to be contained among the doubts specifically enumerated above. A few authors are content to explain the doubt in briefer language. Thus: "Quodsi dubius apparet valor, dubim est solvendum *in favorem fidei,* seu libertatis partis conversae."—De Smet, *De Spons. et Matrim.,* 343. Again: "Certum est etiam in re dubia partem conversam iuvare, quia gaudet *favore iuris.*"—Chelodi, *Jus Matrim.,* n. 156. Lastly: "Dubium quod . . . . aut de valore prioris vinculi aut de verificatis conditionibus privilegii Paulini applicandi aut denique de verificatis adiunctis canonis 1125, remaneat, id solvendum est in favorem partis ad fidem conversae."—Vlaming, *Praelect.,* n. 733.

[26] For a discussion of the doubts enumerated and their solution, consult the following: (a) validity of marriage contracted in infidelity,—*supra,* page 53; (b) the existence of a second marriage,—*supra,* page 112; (c) the person of the first wife of a polygamous man,—*supra,* page 84; (d) sincerity of the answers to the interpellations,—*supra,* page 76; (e) sufficient warrant for dispensing from the interpellations,—*supra,* page 78; (f) provision of cause for the infidel's departure,—*supra,* page 61.

sect. In recent years arguments for and against the validity of such Baptism have been offered profusely and, therefore, the reader is respectfully requested to decide the problem in the light of his own deductions when he considers the decrees of the Roman Congregations and the theories of the several writers.[27] The consideration of our particular question is based on the premise that Baptism may become doubtful as to the *fact* of reception and that it may be resolved to the same state of doubt when its *validity* is attacked, although it is certain that the act was performed.

§1. *Doubtful Baptism of One Party*

For all practical purposes an Ordinary may apply the principle of Canon 1127 whenever he is in doubt as to the fact or validity of a Baptism received *by one party* to a marriage. At least to this limit may he extend the favor of the law.

In the legislation existing before 1918 a doubtful Baptism was presumed as valid *in ordine ad validitatem matrimonii*,[28] with the result that the Congregation of the Holy Office declared invalid several cases of marriage entered into between a doubtfully baptized non-Catholic and an infidel.[29] This solution offers no difficulty, for either the doubtful Baptism was valid and the marriage was null, or the Baptism was invalid and the Sovereign Pontiff implicitly included a dispensation

---

[27] Cf. *AER*, LXXIV (1926), 158-180; LXXV (1926), 136-151, 358-370; LXXVI (1927), 155-165, 496-504; LXXXIV (1931), 124-139, 282-295, 297-298; *Gregorianum*, VIII (1927), 41-54; Schenk, *Mixed Religion and Disparity of Cult*, pp. 119-147.

[28] S. C. S. Off., 17 Nov., 1830,—*Fontes*, n. 869; (Bulgariae), 5 July, 1853, ad 3,—*Fontes*, n. 925; cf. Schenk, *op. cit.*, p. 131, note 44.

[29] Quaeritur: "1. Matrimonium dubie baptizati cum non baptizata estne validum? 2. Si affirmative ad 1, poteritne pars dubie baptizata uti privilegio fidei post reiterationem baptismi, et viceversa poteritne pars non baptizata uti privilegio post baptismum, si pars dubie baptizata nolit converti aut pacifice cohabitare?" Resp.: "Ad 1: Matrimonium habendum esse uti invalidum ob impedimentum cultus disparitatis. Ad 2: Provisum in primo." —S. C. S. Off., 7 July, 1880, quoted in Wernz-Vidal, *Jus Canon.*, V, n. 631, note 61. Quaeritur: "Ad 1: Matrimonium dubie baptizati cum non baptizata estne validum?" Resp.: "Ad 1: Matrimonium esse habendum uti invalidum ob impedimentum cultus disparitatis."—S. C. S. Off., (Iaponiae), 14 July, 1880, ad 1,—*Fontes*, n. 1065.

from the interpellations (in as far as they were necessary) when he decreed the parties at liberty to marry again.[30] Hence, if an Ordinary is confronted today with a marriage case contracted before 1918 between an infidel and a doubtfully baptized non-Catholic, upon conversion of one party he may declare that union invalid because of the presumptive impediment of Disparity of Cult. And the possibility that the doubtful Baptism *may be* invalid is taken care of by the principle in force before the Code and recently stated anew in Canon 1127.

Although Arendt gives this very solution,[31] he derives his conclusions when speaking of the power of Canon 1127 to dissolve such a union. Evidently[32] treating of a marriage contracted after the Code between an infidel and a doubtfully baptized non-Catholic, he claims that union is invalid because of Disparity of Cult. Such a conclusion, however, is absolutely at variance with Canon 1070, §1, which now restricts this impediment to marriage contracted between a *Catholic* and an infidel.

Now, to discuss the power of Canon 1127 over a marriage entered into since Pentecost of 1918 between a non-Catholic doubtfully baptized and a person certainly unbaptized. Canon 1070, §1 considers such a union valid, for Disparity of Cult no longer affects non-Catholics when contracting marriage among themselves. Canon 1127, however, permits an Ordinary to consider that doubtful Baptism as invalid and, hence, he may allow the use of the Pauline Privilege with the condi-

---

[30] Arendt, "Nota Circa Canonem 1127," *Eph. Th. Lov.*, I (1924), 182; Creusen, "Baptême Douteaux et Mariage Indissoluble," *NRT*, LII (1925), 231.

[31] "Inquisitione rite praemissa dubium subsistere potest utrum *alterutri* coniugum baptisma reapse fuerit collatum: quandoquidem, baptismo existente, matrimonium fuisset nullum ex capite disparitatis cultus, ipso vero non existente, matrimonium in infidelitate legitimum et quamvis consummatum, a pontifice in favorem fidei possit dissolvi, locus est vel interpellationis dispensationi cum applicatione privilegii Paulini, vel usui pontificiae potestatis, qui implicite significatur formula qua simpliciter conceditur coniugi baptizato *documentum libertatis.*"—"Nota Circa Canonem 1127," *Eph. Th. Lov.*, I (1924), 182, n. 29.

[32] It is *possible* that Arendt really had in mind a marriage of this kind contracted *before* the Code, although the context of his article argues otherwise.

tional provision that Canon 1127 itself dissolves the marriage in the event that the doubtful Baptism is objectively valid. In other words, if the Baptism in question is *truly* invalid, the Pauline Privilege will dissolve the bond when the convert enters a new union; if the Baptism is *really and objectively* valid, the exercise of Pontifical power implicitly contained in Canon 1127 will immediately dissolve the marriage. In this way both horns of the dilemma are taken care of and any subsequent healing of the marriage is obviated. But in allowing the application of the Pauline Privilege in this fashion it is to be noted that all the other conditions of the Privilege must be verified; for example, the departure of the infidel should be ascertained and the interpellations made.

If anyone believes that sufficient intrinsic probability cannot be gleaned from the application of Canon 1127 as stated above, so as to permit the use of the Pauline Privilege when the validity of Baptism received by one party is doubtful, then he may summon to his aid the extrinsic certainty provided by the authority of the authors quoted above.[33] If writers of such prominent repute are willing to provide this sanction there should be no hesitation on the part of Ordinaries, whose place it is to apply the principle under these circumstances. Names like Vidal, Cappello, Creusen, Farrugia, Vermeersch and Vromant carry more than enough weight in the field of Canon Law to beget a working certainty for the application of Canon 1127 when doubt arises over the validity of one party's Baptism.

It may be objected that not all authors who have written since the Code include this species of doubt. Quite true, but it may be answered with equal force that neither do they *exclude* it. To our knowledge there are only two writers who specifically deny the use of Canon 1127 when the doubt hinges upon the validity of Baptism received by one party in an heretical sect, Augustine and Arendt.[34]

---

[33] Cf. *supra*, page 117, note 25; *AER*, LXXI (1924), 51, 404-406; LXXII (1925), 301-303, 623-628; *NRT*, L (1923), 230, 238-239; *HPR*, XXVI (1926), 189.

[34] Ayrinhac, "Pauline Privilege and Doubtful Baptism," *AER*, LXXIII (1925), 69-72, admits that the Privilege may be applied under these circumstances, and this on the strength of extrinsic probability. However, he

Augustine fails to support his exclusion of this one particular doubt with any reasons and, furthermore, from his statements immediately preceding it appears that he wrote this part of his Commentary before the promulgation of the Code and before the interpretation of the law had had an opportunity to become crystallized. For in the edition at hand, (Fourth Revised Edition, 1929), he still speaks of the Faculties given by the Congregation of the Propaganda, Faculties which were withdrawn from American Ordinaries in 1919.[35]

A longer summary concerning this doubt is proffered by Arendt,[36] in which he places and solves two cases. When speaking of a doubt touching upon the *validity* of Baptism conferred in an heretical sect, the author proposes that a marriage might be contracted before 1918 between an infidel and a person doubtfully baptized in a non-Catholic denomination, or after 1918 between contractants in the same conditions. In the first case the doubtful Baptism would be considered as valid *in ordine ad validitatem matrimonii* and, therefore, the marriage would be considered invalid. Both parties would be freed to contract again because non-Catholics were bound to the impediment of Disparity of Cult before the Code. It is in his solution to the second case that Arendt would exclude the Pauline Privilege as a dissolving factor, for upon the conversion of one party to the Faith and his conditional Baptism, the author would sever this marriage *only* by the intervention of the Sovereign Pontiff's power over a non-ratified legitimate union. There is no doubt but that the learned professor's solution provides one method of dissolving this union, but is

attacks the arguments generally brought forward to substantiate intrinsic probability and as a practical conclusion he would refer every case to Rome until an official decision is handed down.

[35] "The question may be asked: What about the faculties of our bishops who enjoyed the right of dispensing with gentiles (see Form I, art. II)? The answer, we believe, should be as follows: . . . 3. In *ordinary cases*, which do not fall under the three constitutions, bishops must proceed according to the Code. Therefore: (a) The marriage must have been contracted by both parties whilst they were certainly unbaptized: a dubious Baptism would not permit the application of the privilege."—Augustine, *A Commentary*, V, 368; cf. *AER*, LXXI (1924), 49.

[36] "Nota Circa Canonem 1127," *Eph. Th. Lov.*, I (1924), 182-183.

it necessary to call into action the greater agent of dissolution (Pontifical power) when a lesser (the Pauline Privilege) is at hand and might suffice? For by virtue of Canon 1127 an Ordinary may permit the use of the Privilege, after which a second union would dissolve the first bond if the Baptism is actually invalid. But the objection may then be raised: suppose that the Baptism is truly valid? In that event the first marriage is valid and the Pauline Privilege would be of no avail since one of the parties is baptized. But if the Church allowed the use of the Privilege under these conditions and by virtue of Canon 1127, she would be giving her sanction to a second invalid and adulterous union—a conclusion which cannot even be contemplated. This objection, however, may be obviated when it is stated that there seems to be sufficient grounds for holding that in virtue of Canon 1127 the Church implicitly grants a dissolution of the bond by Pontifical power if the Baptism is objectively valid. Therefore, in permitting the use of the Pauline Privilege an Ordinary includes the *conditional* provision that this power of the Pope as contained in Canon 1127 will immediately sever the union only if the Baptism in doubt is really valid.

In an effort to strengthen the proof for intrinsic probability of the use of Canon 1127 when one Baptism is doubtful, Vermeersch and Vromant argue as follows: If a doubtfully baptized non-Catholic contracts an uncertain marriage with an infidel, Canon 1070, §2 states the rule that the validity of the marriage must be upheld in accordance with Canon 1014. But the presumption of Canon 1014 in turn expressly yields to the presumption of Canon 1127 when the case concerns the validity of the marriage, of which point Canon 1014 treats; therefore, the marriage in question may be declared invalid because it is to the advantage of the Faith and the convert.[37] It is not easy to comprehend the exact force of this argument when applied in defense of our original premise, and it is even more difficult to understand its validity. For Canon 1070, §1 restricts the impediment of Disparity of Cult to a marriage

[37] Vermeersch, "Interpretatio Canonis 1127," *Periodica,* X (1922), (27); Vromant, *Comment. Facult. Apost.,* n. 85.

contracted between an infidel and a person baptized in the Catholic Church or converted to it from heresy or schism. Canon 1070, §2 is *purely complementary* to §1 of the same Canon and refers only to a doubt of Baptism received by either party to the union, one of whom *must be a Catholic.*[38] Hence, were the presumption of §2 to be applied to the non-Catholic Baptism of our stated case (as these authors have done), the impediment of Disparity of Cult would be resurrected for non-Catholics; a conclusion which cannot be admitted. Furthermore, Canon 1014 treats purely of a doubt concerning the *validity* of a marriage and, therefore, it cannot be applied in the case under discussion since the marriage is valid whether the contractants (both non-Catholics) are baptized or not. There is no element of doubt attached to the validity of this union on the score of Baptism.

A. Doubtful Baptism in the Catholic Church

What is to be said if the doubt concerns the validity of Baptism conferred *in the Catholic Church?* To posit a possible case: an infidel is married with a dispensation from the impediment of Disparity of Cult to a person whose baptism in the Catholic Church is doubtful as to fact or validity. When this putative Catholic is rebaptized conditionally it is certain that such a marriage could not be dissolved by virtue of the Pauline Privilege, and it has been stated above that it is contrary to the *practice* of the Church to intervene by way of Apostolic power.[39] Before and after the Code a doubtful Baptism is to be construed as valid when it affects the validity

---

[38] "Since the ambit of the impediment is defined in canon 1070, §1, and since the entire canon deals with the impediment of Disparity of Cult, the extension and restriction of canon 1070, §1 must be kept in mind when determining the provisions of canon 1070, §2. The marriages of baptized non-Catholics (who have never been converted to the Catholic Church) with the unbaptized are not included in the terms of canon 1070, §2. Only those marriages are comprehended, therefore, in which at least one of the parties at the time of the contracting of the marriage was bound by the impediment of Disparity of Cult *as it is defined in the Code.*"—Schenk, *Mixed Religion and Disparity of Cult*, p. 140.

[39] Canon 1120, §2; cf. *supra*, page 55; De Becker, *De Spons. et* p. 434, note 2; De Smet, *De Spons. et Matrim.*, n. 355.

of a marriage; especially the doubtful Baptism of a Catholic, since Catholics and those contracting with them are bound by the *favor matrimonii* rather than by the *favor fidei.*[40]

Concluding the statement of this problem, then, it is maintained that a doubtfully baptized heretic may have his marriage with an infidel dissolved by the Pauline Privilege in favor of the faith. And by the same means that union may be broken for the infidel party in as much as it opens for him the way to Baptism.[41]

§2. *Doubtful Baptism of Both Parties*

Within recent years the theory has been proposed by a few writers [42] that a marriage in which both parties are doubtfully baptized in a non-Catholic sect may be dissolved in favor of the faith by the application of Canon 1127. Such matrimonial cases may arise frequently in Protestant countries, and they may even become multiple when nursed by the laxity of civil divorce laws and the suspicion which is attached to the validity of Baptism as conferred in not a few non-Catholic denominations. The circumstances of the case may be better envisioned by stating a practical example: Two doubtfully baptized non-Catholics are married; civil divorce follows, and later on one spouse has entered a new contract. When the

---

[40] Canon 1014; Creusen, "Privilège Paulinien et Mixtes Mariages," *NRT*, L (1923), 88-95; Vromant, *Comment. Facult. Apost.*, n. 85; Wernz-Vidal, *Jus Canon.*, V. n. 44; Cappello, *De Sacram.*, III, nn. 51-53. Arendt, "Nota Circa Canonem 1127," *Eph Th. Lov.*, I (1924), 183, n. 30, excludes the use of the Pauline Privilege under these circumstances but suggests that if the infidel departs and the Catholic is conditionally baptized, the latter may beseech Rome for a dissolution from the bond of a marriage merely legitimate and not sacramentally ratified.

[41] Vermeersch, "Interpretatio Canonis 1127," *Periodica*, X (1922), (27).

[42] Cerato, *Matrim.*, n. 127; Donovan, "A New Marriage Case," *AER*, LXX (1924), 59-64; "Doubtful Baptisms and Pauline Privilege," *AER*, LXXI (1924), 48-53; "Doubtful Baptisms Again," *AER*, LXXII (1925), 622-628; Schaepman, in *Nederlandsche Katholieke Stemmen*, (1924), 308; (1925), 53. Vermeersch, "Interpretatio Canonis 1127," *Periodica*, X (1922), (27), held this same view, which he later corrected and denied in, "De Usu Privilegii Fidei in Re Dubia," *Periodica*, XIII (1924), (212).

other is converted and baptized conditionally in the Catholic Church, may the Holy See authorize him to marry a Catholic either by presuming the nullity of the two doubtful Baptisms, (thus permitting the application of the Pauline Privilege), or by dissolving the first marriage bond by Pontifical power, (since its sacramental character is doubtful)?

Without entering the forum of controversy [43] and lacking every intention of defining or suggesting the limits of the Holy See's power, it is our contention that an answer to the above case should be given in the negative as long as there is a possible and probable doubt remaining in favor of the double Baptism. For if moral certitude is not had that one of the two Baptisms is null and void, the Holy See does not permit and seems to lack the authority to permit a second marriage. This conclusion shall be substantiated by decisions of the Roman Curia, by the most common teaching of canonists, and by the use of theological principles.

A. Decisions of the Holy See

In a case proposed to the Holy Office before the Code, the problem concerned the doubtful validity of the Baptisms received by *both* parties. One partner refused to live peacefully with the other, who had been received into the Church. Now, it was asked, because of very grave doubt concerning his previous Baptism, may that convert be considered as equivalent to a convert from infidelity and by the application of the Pauline Privilege be permitted to enter a second union? To this question the Supreme Congregation answered, "*NEGATIVE.*" [44]

Authorities tell us that an analogous case has been submitted

---

[43] For a discussion of objections and answers the reader is referred to the *Nouvelle Revue Théologique*, LII (1925), 238-241, and the *American Ecclesiastical Review*, LXX (1924), 59-66; LXXII (1925), 622-628; LXXIII (1925), 62-72, 191-195.

[44] "Utrum pars conversa propter gravissimum dubium de baptismo in haeresi recepto aequiparari possit parti ab infidelitate conversae, et propter Paulinum privilegium ad alias nuptias transire?" S. C. respondit: "Negative."—S. C. S. Off., instr. (ad Vic. Ap. Oceaniae Central.), 18 Dec., 1872, ad 2,—*Fontes*, n. 1024. To our knowledge this is the only decision on a similar question given before 1918.

to the same Tribunal since 1918, and in honoring the negative opinion of two consultors the decision stated: "*Non constare de nullitate matrimonii nec esse locum usui privilegii Paulini.*" [45] This particular decision would not settle the question conclusively, but when taken in conjunction with the instruction of 1872 and the authority of the Holy Office in such matters, an Ordinary may not be permitted to interpret Canon 1127 more broadly.[46]

If doubt of both Baptisms arose after a marriage was contracted before 1918, the presumption in force would have concluded to the validity of both Baptisms and, therefore, to the sacramental character of the union. After 1918 a marriage contracted between two non-Catholics would be valid whether the Baptism received by one or both parties was certain or doubtful; for they are no longer bound by the impediment of Disparity of Cult when contracting among themselves.

B. Common Teaching of Canonists

To our knowledge no canonist who wrote before the promulgation of the Code expressed the opinion that a marriage of two doubtfully baptized persons could be dissolved in favor of the faith. And among the authors who have offered commentaries on the Code or its several parts, only three [47] specifically state that such unions are subject to dissolution by the application of Canon 1127. Proponents of this view have adduced the authority of Blat,[48] but this writer does not say

---

[45] Cf. Schaepman, in *Nederlandsche Kath. Stemmen,* (1925), 57, quoted by Creusen, "Baptême Douteaux et Mariage Indissoluble," *NRT,* LII (1925), 231; Vromant, *Comment. Facult. Apost.,* n. 86; Vermeersch, "De Usu Privilegii Fidei in Re Dubia," *Periodica,* XIII (1924), (212); Hilling, "Die Anwendung des Privilegium Paulinum," *AkKR,* CVII (1927), 183-186.

[46] Cf. Creusen, "Baptême Douteaux et Mariage Indissoluble," *NRT,* LII (1925), 231. Dr. Donovan admits this restriction in a practical case. Cf. *AER,* LXXII (1925), 622; LXXIII (1925), 191.

[47] Cerato, *Matrim.,* n. 127; Donovan, "A New Marriage Case," *AER,* LXX (1924), 59-64; "Doubtful Baptisms and Pauline Privilege," *AER,* LXXI (1924), 48-53; "Doubtful Baptisms Again," *AER,* LXXII (1925), 622-628; Schaepman, in *Nederlandsche Kath. Stemmen,* (1924), 308; (1925), 53.

[48] *Comment.,* III, pars I, n. 538.

that Canon 1127 applies to the marriage of *two* doubtfully baptized parties, and none of the Roman decisions which he quotes favors this case. Vermeersch at one time was in full agreement with this theory,[49] but completely retracted after reconsideration.[50] Every other author who has come to our attention expressly and in no uncertain terms states that Canon 1127 may be applied only when the doubt concerns the validity of Baptism received *by one party*.[51]

The common teaching of authors, therefore, is seen as opposed to the application of Canon 1127 in a matrimonial case when a doubt touches the validity of the Baptisms received by *both* parties.

C. *Theological Principles*

If a marriage has been contracted between two persons whose Baptisms conferred in an heretical sect are doubtful, that marriage is at least a legitimate union if the Baptisms were invalid. By such a marriage the parties become heirs to a right which neither can renounce, and which may be suppressed for a serious motive only by an authority constituted by a divine positive law. However, if those Baptisms were in reality valid, that union would be adorned with a sacramental character; and if consummated, no human authority whatever could dissolve the bond.[52] In favor of the common good the legislator may establish presumptions which dispense from the necessity of proving certain facts or rights, but in doing so he must be sure that such presumptions do not even materially expose him to the danger

---

[49] "Interpretatio Canonis 1127," *Periodica*, X (1922), (27).

[50] "De Usu Privilegii Fidei in Re Dubia," *Periodica*, XIII (1924), (212).

[51] Cf. Cappello, *De Sacram.*, *III*, n. 788; Farrugia, *De Matrim.*, n. 326; Wernz-Vidal, *Jus Canon.*, V, n. 631; Vromant, *Comment. Facult. Apost.*, n. 86; Vermeersch, "De Usu Privilegii Paulini in Re Dubia," *Periodica*, XIII (1924), (212); Vermeersch-Creusen, *Epitome*, II, n. 437; Creusen, "Privilège Paulinien et Mixtes Mariages," *NRT*, L (1923), 94; "Baptême Douteaux et Mariage Indissoluble," *NRT*, LII (1925), 239; Arendt, "Nota Circa Canonem 1127," *Eph. Th. Lov.*, I (1924), 180-181, nn. 21-24; De Smet, *De Spons. et Matrim.*, n. 355; Prümmer, in *AER*, LXXIII (1925), 62-64; Ayrinhac, "Pauline Privilege and Doubtful Baptism," *AER*, LXXIII (1925), 65-72.

[52] Canon 1118; Cf. *supra*, page XIV.

of violating the divine law or an inprescriptible right. To just such danger would the Sovereign Pontiff subject himself were he to dispense in the given case, for dissolution of a marriage both ratified and consummated is absolutely contrary to divine law.[53]

This solution is corroborated by the Holy See's manner of action in analogous cases, for it requires moral certitude that the bond of one marriage does not exist before a second union is permitted.[54] Likewise, marriage is never allowed if a doubt persists whether or no the contractants are related within any degree of the direct line of consanguinity, or within the first degree of the collateral line.[55]

Again, a right that is probable and in possession is to be respected. For marriage is a contract, and when entered into between doubtfully baptized persons its probable sacramental dignity provides a strong motive for seeking moral certitude of its validity. Hence, when there is question of dissolution, a contract made in good faith, probably valid, and as a result of which the parties are in possession of a right, should give way only to a certain right.[56]

Lastly, if one of the Baptisms *was valid,* any application of the Pauline Privilege would be of no avail. And if *both* were valid, the intervention of Pontifical power would be without effect. Therefore, any authorization to enter a new union would be in effect a permission to contract an invalid and adulterous marriage.

---

[53] Cf. Vromant, *Comment. Facult. Apost.*, n. 86; Creusen, "Baptême Douteaux et Mariage Indissoluble," *NRT*, LII (1925), 236; Arendt, "Nota Circa Canonem 1127," *Eph. Th. Lov.*, I (1924), 180, nn. 21-24; Vermeersch, "De Usu Privilegii Paulini in Re Dubia," *Periodica*, XIII (1924), (212); Hilling, "Die Anwendung des Privilegium Paulinum," *AkKR*, CVII (1927), 185.

[54] "Quamvis prius matrimonium sit irritum aut solutum qualibet ex causa, non ideo licet aliud contrahere, antequam de prioris nullitate aut solutione legitime et certo constiterit."—Canon 1069, §2.

[55] "Nunquam matrimonium permittatur, si quod subsit dubium num partes sint consanguineae in aliquo gradu lineae rectae aut in primo gradu lineae collateralis."—Canon 1076, §3.

[56] Cf. S. C. S. Off., instr. (ad Ep. Nesquallien.), 24 Jan., 1877,—*Fontes*, n. 1050; Wernz-Vidal, *Jus Canon.*, V, n. 44; Cappello, *De Sacram.*, III, nn. 51-53; Creusen, "Baptême Douteaux et Mariage Indissoluble," *NRT*, LII (1925), 236.

In conclusion, it seems that a new marriage cannot be permitted to one converted from heresy when that person has contracted a union at a time when both he and his partner were regarded as baptized. This holds even if the doubt of Baptism is sufficiently founded to impose the Sacrament again in a conditional manner. However, if after an exhaustive investigation there is no positive and probable reason for thinking the Baptisms valid, either because of lack of intention on the part of the minister, substantial defect in administration or positive doctrine of a denomination against the Sacrament, the use of the Pauline Privilege is not to be excluded. Simple possibility and probability of an act are not identical; for the more the probability of an act is diminished, the more justification is had for the use of the Pauline Privilege or of Pontifical power in the interest of a higher stake. For the moral law is not ruled by possibilities and, therefore, it is lawful for a good reason to place an act, the opposition of which to the moral law is not absolutely excluded.[57] The solution of this problem is left to the judgment of the Ordinary; [58] but if the Baptisms are later proved valid, the second union is null and the party is still bound to his first wife.

---

[57] Creusen, "Baptême Douteaux et Mariage indissoluble," *NRT*, LII (1925), 237.

[58] Quaeritur: "An degentes in iis protestantium locis, ubi baptisma dubium est, tamquam infideles habendi sint, ita ut inter catholicos et eos disparitatis cultus impedimentum dirimens adesse censeatur?" Resp.: ad 1: "Quoad haereticos quorum sectae ritualia praescribunt collationem Baptismi absque necessario usu materiae et formae essentialis, debet examinari casus particularis." Ad 2: "Quoad alios qui iuxta eorum rituale baptizant valide, validum censendum est Baptisma. Quod si dubium persistat, etiam in primo casu, censendum est validum Baptisma in ordine ad validitatem matrimonii." Ad 3: "Si autem certo cognoscatur nullum baptisma ex consuetudine actuali illius sectae, nullum est matrimonium."—S. C. S. Off., 17 Nov., 1830,—*Fontes*, n. 869; "Si autem certe dignoscatur invalidum esse eorum baptisma ex consuetudine actuali eiusdem sectae, matrimonium inter eos non esse ratum, et ut infideles esse habendos."—S. C. S. Off., (Bulgariae), 5 July, 1853, ad 3,—*Fontes*, n. 925; Cf. Creusen, "Baptême Douteaux et Mariage Indissoluble," *NRT*, LII (1925), 237-238; Vermeersch-Creusen, *Epitome*, II, n. 437; Prümmer, in *AER*, LXXIII (1925), 64; Ayrinhac, "Pauline Privilege and Doubtful Baptism," *AER*, LXXIII (1925), 71; Krasa, "Privilegium Paulinum," *LQS*, LXXV (1922), 98; Ione, "Protestanten die nach Scheidung ihrer ersten Ehe Katholisch werden und weider heiraten wollen," *LQS*, LXXIX (1926), 572; Hilling, "Die Anwendung des Privilegium Paulinum," *AkKR*, CVII (1927), 186.

§3. *Summary*

It may not be amiss at this point to sketch briefly what has been said above and to offer a summary of concrete cases involving doubtful Baptism which may or may not be solved by an Ordinary in virtue of the Pauline Privilege. Therefore:

(1) A marriage contracted between two certainly unbaptized persons may be dissolved.

(2) A union entered into between a doubtfully baptized person and one certainly baptized may not be dissolved in this way.

(3) The matrimonial bond may be broken when contracted before or after 1918 between a person doubtfully baptized and one certainly not baptized, even when the doubt is sufficiently strong to warrant the reception of conditional Baptism.[59]

(4) A marriage may not be dissolved when entered into with a dispensation by an infidel and a person doubtfully baptized *in the Catholic Church.*

(5) Wedlock may not be severed when contracted by persons whose Baptisms are *both* doubtfully valid.

(6) Marriage between two doubtfully baptized parties may be dissolved when it becomes morally certain that the Baptisms were invalid. However, the greatest caution is urged under these circumstances.

---

[59] Needless to say, the Privilege may be applied to either party in this case and the marriage may be dissolved if it opens the way to Baptism for the infidel partner. Cf. Vermeersch, "Interpretatio Canonis 1127," *Periodica,* X (1922), (27); Wernz-Vidal, *Jus Canon.,* V, n. 631; Vromant, *Comment. Facult. Apost.,* nn. 83, 85.

CHAPTER VII

PRACTICAL APPENDIX

Before bringing this work to a conclusion it is well to state briefly those acts by which the competent authority permits the application of the Pauline Privilege and a second marriage. Apart from those sections regarding the competent tribunal and the proclamation of the banns, it is not our intention to become dogmatic; rather, the following suggestions are offered more with the hope that they may prove of some value to those who come into contact with such cases.

§1. *The Competent Tribunal*

When speaking of the tribunal competent to accept, hear and judge the merits of a case involving the Pauline Privilege, a distinction must be made between the power of the Ordinary and that of the Roman Curia. A case of the Privilege need not ordinarily become what is known in ecclesiastical procedure as a matrimonial cause. For the latter involves a strictly judicial trial, whereas the Privilege is merely the permission granted to a convert to contract a second marriage. Hence, when all the conditions necessary for its application are verified, the Ordinary or his delegate is competent to authorize a new union for a convert.[1]

However, when a true matrimonial action is instituted for any reason, the diocesan court is not capable of adjudication, but the case must be sent to Rome for a decision.[2] For in

[1] Cf. *supra*, page 92; Canon 1964 gives the rule that in cases where only one party is a Catholic, the competent judge of a matrimonial case is the Ordinary of the place where that Catholic has his domicile or quasi-domicile. By analogy it is inferred that in the Pauline Privilege the same Ordinary is to grant the permission for a new marriage.

[2] Canon 1962; cf. Arendt, "De Exclusiva S. Officii Competentia Circa Matrimonium Mixtum," *Jus Pont.*, VII (1927), 120-137; Cappello, *De Sacram.*, III, n. 870; Wernz-Vidal, *Jus Canon.*, V, n. 690; Roberti, "De Legitimitate ad Causam et Competentia in Matrimoniis Mixtis," *Apollinaris*, I (1928), 218-219, 303-305.

Canon 1962 the Holy See specifically excludes from the judicial province of the Ordinary all causes which directly or indirectly refer to the Pauline Privilege. This fact is supported by Canon 1964, which declares that in all other causes[3] the competent judge is one of several possible Ordinaries.

The Holy See exercises its judicial power over marriage through the agency of the Sacred Congregations and Tribunals deputized for this purpose. Among these the Congregation of the Holy Office alone is competent to decide matrimonial causes which entail the Pauline Privilege.[4]

Likewise, this Congregation must be addressed in seeking a dispensation from the interpellations, or a decision on any doubt which the Ordinary feels is beyond his powers of solution.[5]

§2. *Civil Divorce*

The application of the Pauline Privilege, whereby a convert is permitted to enter a second marriage, is in no way contingent upon the granting of a civil divorce for the first contract. Nevertheless, that civil process may not only be tolerated when a marriage has been or is to be canonically dissolved or declared invalid, but it is to be recommended for several reasons.[6] In

[3] In addition to the Pauline Privilege, Canon 1962 excepts matrimonial causes which affect royal personages or a non-consummated union.

[4] "Ipsa sola (i.e., Congregatio S. Officii) cognoscit ea quae, sive directe sive indirecte, in iure aut in facto, circa privilegium, uti aiunt, Paulinum et matrimonii impedimenta disparitatis cultus et mixtae religionis versantur; itemque ad eam spectat facultas dispensandi in hisce impedimentis. Quare quaelibet huiusmodi quaestio ad hanc Congregationem est deferenda, quae tamen potest, si ita censeat et casus ferat, quaestionem remittere ad aliam Congregationem vel ad Tribunal Sacrae Romanae Rotae."—Canon 247, §3; Cf. Canon 1962; Pius X, const. "*Sapienti consilio*," 29 June, 1908, ad §1, 1°,—*Fontes*, n. 682; *AAS*, XX (1928), 75.

[5] Particularly there may arise a *dubium iuris vel facti* concerning the validity of Baptism in connection with the Privilege. Cf. Cappello, *De Sacram.*, III, n. 781; Wernz-Vidal, *Jus Canon.*, V, n. 690.

[6] S. C. S. Off., instr. (ad Ep. Neo-Aurelianensis), 9 Sept., 1824,—Kenrick, *Theol. Moral.*, II, p. 306; De Smet, *De Spons. et Matrim.*, n. 391; Wernz-Vidal, *Jus Canon.*, V, n. 711; Cappello, *De Sacram.*, III, n. 838; Fahrner, *Geschichte des Unauflöslichkeitsprinzips*, p. 287, note 1; Braun, "Auflösung der von Ungläubigen abgeschlossenen Ehe," *AkKR*, XLVI (1881), 413-414; Feije, *De Imped. et Disp. Matrim.*, nn. 498, 583; Könings, *Theol. Moral.*, II, p. 239.

the majority of the United States of America there are laws governing divorce[7] which may subject contractants and the officiating minister to civil penalties if a second marriage is attempted before the State declares the first dissolved. Accidental questions of civil law, e.g., succession to an estate, alimony, must also be safeguarded, as well as the civil competence of the convert to marry anew. Hence, it is suggested that pastors and Ordinaries inform themselves of the convert's civil freedom before allowing or assisting at a second marriage.

§3. *Necessary Documents*

When a convert applies for permission to use the Pauline Privilege certain proofs or documents must be furnished before an Ordinary or his delegate may proceed to grant a decision. In order to give or deny permission with the utmost safety, the proper authority should be provided with the following documents as a minimum:

(1) Certificate of the first marriage, or a certified copy.

(2) Sworn statements testifying to the non-Baptism of both parties. In this respect the parties concerned should furnish affidavits that they have not been baptized since attaining the use of reason; near relatives and friends who are in a position to know certainly that neither party was baptized at any time should also provide affidavits to this effect. These requirements may vary according to peculiar circumstances, and if the Ordinary is fully satisfied as to the veracity of the parties themselves he may deem their personal oaths sufficient.

(3) Certificate of the convert's subsequent Catholic Baptism.

(4) Answers given by the party remaining in infidelity to the canonical interpellations; accompanied by the sworn testimony of witnesses if the interrogations were made privately. Or, in the absence of any response, there must be presented a Curial document stating that the interpellations have been made but no reply given.

(5) Certificate of civil divorce, or a certified copy.

[7] In those countries wherein the civil law does not admit of divorce, the convert should fulfill all those formalities which the law *does* require.

In as far as possible these depositions should be witnessed and sworn to before an *ecclesiastical notary* in preference to one constituted by civil law as competent to witness affidavits.

§4. *The Banns of Marriage*

It has happened not infrequently[8] that a convert, about to contract a new marriage with a Catholic by the application of the Pauline Privilege, has wrongfully obtained that permission from the Ordinary with the aid of dishonest witnesses and fraudulent documents. A convert may easily circumvent any line of questioning which a pastor may introduce during a course of instructions, and therefore, every avenue of investigation should be enrolled to discover the convert's former status. For example, a convert from infidelity produced every document prescribed by the ecclesiastical authorities, and in virtue of the Pauline Privilege he was allowed to enter a second marriage with a Catholic girl. A few weeks later it was discovered that his first wife was not only baptized but that she had never been interpellated, as the man claimed. Subsequent investigation disclosed the fact that *all* documents had been forged and the man had perjured himself in providing his personal testimony. Had the banns of marriage been proclaimed as the Code demands,[9] this convert might have been forestalled in his nefarious work and the ensuing tangle would have been obviated. The Code admits that for a legitimate reason the Ordinary may dispense from the publication of the banns, if he prudently judges that dispensation necessary.[10] But otherwise, with the exception of cases of mixed marriage, the Code demands the matrimonial proclamations.[11] Augustine argues that Canon 1022 does not specifically include *all* Catholic marriages, and, therefore, the banns may be omitted without dispensation when a convert is entering wedlock.

---

[8] Two of these cases have come to our attention within the current year (1931).

[9] "Publice a parocho denuntietur inter quosnam matrimonium sit contrahendum."—Canon 1022.

[10] Canon 1028.

[11] Canon 1026.

> Must or should the banns be published in case one party is *newly converted?* We think the answer should be as follows: Taking the text of Canon 1022 in the sense of a universal law, such marriages should be looked upon as Catholic marriages, and therefore the law would apply to them. However, the text does not say that *all* Catholic marriages *must* be called, and Canon 1028 allows the ordinaries to dispense for any lawful reason. Neither is the law a perfect one, since it has no penal sanction attached to it. The purpose of the law is to discover impediments. This aim could be obtained only in part, since the friends of the former non-Catholic would hardly attend the service. Besides, the publication of the banns is not intended to arouse curiosity or ridicule or surprise. Finally, the instruction will easily permit the pastor to find possible impediments. Hence, we believe the banns in the above-mentioned case may be omitted without a special dispensation.[12]

Turning Augustine's first argument around, the very fact that the Ordinary may dispense from the banns in particular cases supposes that *in all other* instances of marriage between Catholics the law binds, unless the Ordinary *does* dispense. Otherwise there could be singled out no definite line of demarcation and the application of Canon 1022 would become a purely arbitrary matter. Secondly, the statement that the friends of a former non-Catholic would hardly attend a Catholic service is purely gratuitous and presumes that the efficiency of the law is conditioned by personal friendship. On the other hand, it cannot be said with certainty that the convert's friends were *all* non-Catholics, nor may the possibility be precluded that the faithful may communicate the news of an approaching marriage to interested parties. Lastly, although the publication of the banns is not intended to excite curiosity or surprise, it may do so very advantageously if a partner to an infidel union discovers that her former spouse is contemplating a new marriage without any consideration for her rights. Any possible ridicule is merely a presumption which gives way to the common welfare

[12] Augustine, *Rights and Duties of Ordinaries*, p. 289.

when the publication of the banns advises the faithful that this is not another case of mixed marriage.[13]

§5. *Pertinent Formularies*

The following formularies[14] are offered with the hope that they may be of some practical assistance to those who are engaged with cases of the Pauline Privilege.

I

A letter of citation sent by the Ordinary or his delegate to the party remaining in infidelity, containing the substance of the interpellations and ordering the infidel to appear at a stated time and place for questioning as to his dispositions.

> By the commission and command of the Right Reverend N. N., Bishop of N. N., and at the request of N. N., a convert from infidelity; I, the undersigned, hereby require, ask and exhort N. N., the consort of the above mentioned N. N., to express and declare by word of mouth at *or* in . . . . . . (*indicate city and address*) within thirty days following the date of this summons, whether: (1) he *or* she wishes to embrace the Holy Catholic Faith and with a sincere heart receive Holy Baptism, as his *or* her consort has done; and if he *or* she is not willing to do this, whether: (2) he *or* she is willing and disposed to cohabit peacefully with N. N. (*name of convert*) without blaspheming the Creator, namely, that such cohabitation will not be a source of mortal sin for N. N. (*name of convert*). And if he *or* she refuse to be baptized and declares that he *or* she will not cohabit peacefully, the aforesaid N. N. (*name of convert*) will proceed to another matrimonial alliance with a Catholic person.
>
> (*Date and place*) (*Signed*) N. N.
> (*Curial Seal*) (*Delegate of Bishop*)
> (*Signed*) N. N.
> (*Chancellor*)

[13] *AER*, LXXIX (1928), 648. In as much as they are fully apt in the problem of banns following upon a permission to use the Pauline Privilege, the gist of the arguments stated above has been borrowed from Schenk, *Mixed Religion and Disparity of Cult*, pp. 282-283.

[14] Cf. Muñiz, *Procedimientos Eclesiásticos*, II, n. 508.

II

The official acts of each case may be made up and filed on record according to the following formularies. Exact addresses (with street and numbers) are always to be indicated.

(a)

The convert's petition addressed to the Ordinary asking that the infidel spouse be interpellated; this must be signed by the convert and the pastor of the convert.

Ad Reverendissimum Dominum N. N., Ordinarium Dioecesis N. N.
Reverendissime Excellentissime Domine:

N. N., (*tot*) annos nata, (*tali civitate, oppido, talis dioecesis, status, provinciae*) nunc (*tali paroecia, talis dioecesis*) domicilium habens, ea qua par est reverentia exponit: se ante baptismum contraxisse matrimonium iuxta mores regionis cum N. N., non-baptizato, qui (*tali loco*) nunc commoratur; nunc vero se optare ut supradictus N. N., non-baptizatus, secundum Ecclesiae leges interpelletur, in hunc finem, ut ipsa possit cum eodem N. N. denuo matrimonialiter cohabitare aut ad novas convolare nuptias. Hinc oratrix Reverendissimam Excellentiam Vestram humillime per me infrascriptum parochum rogat ut hac in causa canonicae fiant interpellationes ad normam canonis 1121.

(*Date and place*) (*Signed*) N. N.
(*Seal of Parish*) (*Parochus*)
(*Signed*) N. N.
(*Oratrix*)

(b)

A statement by the Ordinary or his delegate that in compliance with the request of the convert a summons is to be sent to the infidel, notifying him that he is to appear for the purpose of being interpellated; and that he may answer in writing in lieu of appearing personally.

Decretum Citationis

Visis precibus oratricis N. N. circa interpellationes instituendas, infrascriptus Ordinarius hisce praesentibus decernit N. N. citandum esse per litteras rite confectas, a delegato Rev. Dom. N. N., et Notario Ecclesiastico subsignatas et sigillo Curiae munitas, ut infra .... dies a die intimationis factae compareat ad audiendas interpellationes quae ipsi faciendae erunt ad normam canonis 1121. Si vero N. N. non comparuerit, interpellatio fiat in scriptis.

(*Date and place*) (*Signed*) N. N.
(*Curial Seal*) (*Ordinarius*)
(*Signed*) N. N.
(*Notarius*)

(c)

A statement by the Notary of the Curia to the effect that the infidel appeared and was interpellated; that the latter requested and received a grant of one month's time for reflection; that this period has now elapsed without any answer being given.

Notitia Interpellationis Factae

(*Tali loco, die, mense, anno*) coram Reverendo Domino N. N. huius Dioecesis comparuit N. N., (*tali civitate*) domicilium habens, qui ab eodem Rev. Dom. N. N. interrogatus asseruit se non esse baptizatum, et utique sese esse coniugatum cum N. N. Tunc Rev. Dom. N. N. ei intimavit ipsum interpellari, requirente eius uxore nunc in Ecclesia Catholica baptizata, ut responderet duabus hisce quaestionibus: Primo, an velit et ipse converti ac baptismum suscipere; Secundo, an saltem velit et dispositus sit cohabitare pacifice cum sua uxore N. N. sine contumelia Creatoris, quorum verborum sensum interpellans explanavit. Sed cum N. N. petierit aliquas inducias ad deliberandum, Rev. Dom. N. N. concessit terminum unius mensis intra quem interpellatus deberet respondere aut significare se esse impeditum quominus respondere posset, eique interpellato exposuit eius silentium termino inutiliter elapso tanquam responsum negativum praesumptum iri.

De quibus actis ego Notarius fidem facio et hoc

instrumentum redigo subsignatum a Rev. Dom. Delegato.

(*Date and place*) (*Signed*) N. N.
(*Curial Seal*) (*Delegatus*)
(*Signed*) N. N.
(*Notarius*)

(d)

A statement by the Notary of the Curia to the effect that the priest delegated to make the interpellations has made the following report: that the period granted to the infidel for the purpose of deliberation has elapsed without a reply from same; that he has been urged twice to forward an answer; that the interpellating official deems this silence equal to a negative answer; that the petitioner may apply the Pauline Privilege.

Notitia Temporis Inutiliter Elapsi, Interpellationis Bis Repetitae, Praesumptionis Responsi Negativi, et Decreti De Iure Oratricis Utendi Privilegio Paulino

(*Loco, die, mense, anno*) coram me infrascripto Notario huius Curiae Episcopalis, Reverendus Dominus N. N. dixit: Cum N[1]. N[1]. factae fuerint interpellationes praescriptae a canone 1121, sicut in actis constat, cumque interpellatus terminum unius mensis induciarum, ipso petente, concessarum praetermiserit quin responderet nec significaret se esse impeditum quominus responderet, et etiam alterum mensem quo durante, de mandato verbali Rev. Domini bis per litteras Curiae N. N. monitus est eius responsum desiderari; Rev. Dom. per praesentes declarat N. N. sufficienter interpellatum quoad matrimonium quod intendat contrahere eius uxor N. N. vi privilegii Paulini ad normam canonum 1120 et sequentium, atque silentium tanquam negativum responsum legitime esse praesumendum. Mandavit Rev. Dom. exemplar authenticum huius decreti tradendum esse coniugi baptizatae N. N. ut ipsi liceat uti iure suo.

Talia decrevit et subscribit Reverendus Dominus N. N., de quibus ego Notarius fidem facio.

(*Date and place*) (*Signed*) N. N.
(*Curial Seal*) (*Delegatus*)
(*Signed*) N. N.
(*Notarius*)

(e)

A statement by the Notary of the Curia to the effect that the interpellations have been sent to the infidel *in writing;* that no answer has been received within one month; that the Ordinary therefore decrees the convert free to enter a second marriage.

Notitia Interpellationis in Scriptis Factae

Ego infrascriptus Notarius Curiae Episcopalis (*talis civitatis*) fidem facio, hodierna die de mandato Reverendissimi Ordinarii huius dioecesis, per publicos tabellarios et cum syngrapha receptionis (*vel per manus talis personae*) N^{i}. N^{i}. (*tali civitate*) commoranti, commendatas litteras misi quae sic sonant: "Nos, N. N., Ordinarius Dioecesis N. N.—Per praesentes, postulante N. N., in Ecclesia Catholica baptizata, coniuge N^{is}. N^{is}., interpellamus praefatum N. N. ut intra terminum unius mensis computandi a die receptionis harum litterarum respondeat hisce interpellationibus: An N. N. velit et ipse converti atque in Ecclesia Catholica baptismum suscipere; an saltem velit et dispositus sit cohabitare pacifice cum sua coniuge N. N. sine contumelia Creatoris, ita, scilicet, ut talis cohabitatio non sit causa seu motivum peccati mortalis. Quo termino unius mensis elapso quin harum interrogationum responsio recipiatur, cum interpellatus N. N. valeat respondere, actorum testimonium proferetur eius coniugi N. N. ut huic liceat, si maluerit, convolare ad novas nuptias. Datum —, tali civitate, die, mense, anno, N. N., Ordinarius Dioecesis, locus sigilli,—De mandato Rev. Dom., N. N., Notarius."

Transumptum concordat cum documento originali quod praefato N. N. mitto.

(*Date and place*) (*Signed*) N. N.
(*Curial Seal*) (*Notarius*)

BIBLIOGRAPHY

Sources

Acta Apostolicae Sedis, Romae, 1909.

Acta Sanctae Sedis, 41 vols., Romae, 1865-1908.

Bucceroni, Januarius, *Enchiridion Morale,* 4 ed., Romae, 1905.

Canones et Decreta Concilii Tridentini, 19 ed., Taurini, 1913.

Codex Iuris Canonici Pii X Pontificis Maximi iussu digestus Benedicti Papae XV auctoritate promulgatus, Romae, 1918.

Codicis Iuris Canonici Fontes, cura Emi. Petri Card. Gasparri editi, 5 vols., Romae, 1926-1930.

Collectanea S. Congregationis de Propaganda Fide, 2 vols., Romae, 1907.

Concilii Plenarii Baltimorensis III (1884), Baltimorae, 1886.

Corpus Iuris Canonici, ed. Richter-Friedberg, 2 vols., Lipsiae, 1922.

Corpus Iuris Civilis: Institutiones, recognovit P. Krueger; *Digesta,* recognovit Th. Mommsen, retractavit P. Krueger, vol. I, Berolini, 1928; *Codex Justinianus,* recognovit et retractavit P. Krueger, vol. II, Berolini, 1929; *Novellae,* recognovit R. Schoell, opus Schoelli morte interceptum absolvit G. Kroll, vol. III, Berolini, 1928.

Corpus Scriptorum Ecclesiasticorum Latinorum, Vindobonae, 1866.

Decretales D. Gregorii Papae IX, una cum Glossis Restitutae, Romae, 1582.

Decretum Gratiani emendatum et notationibus illustratum, una cum Glossis, Gregorii XIII Pont. Max. iussu editum, 2 vols., Romae, 1582.

De Journel, M. J. Rouet, *Enchiridion Patristicum, Loci SS. Patrum, Doctorum, Scriptorum Ecclesiasticorum quos in usum Scholarum collegit,* 4 & 5 ed., Friburgi Brisgoviae, 1922.

Denziger, H.–Bannwart, C., *Enchiridion Symbolorum Definitionum et Declarationum de Rebus Fidei et Morum*, 14 & 15 ed., Friburgi Brisgoviae, 1922.

Hardouin, J., *Conciliorum Collectio Regia Maxima*, 12 vols., Parisiis, 1715.

Jaffe, Philippus, *Regesta Pontificum Romanorum*, 2 ed., 2 vols., Lipsiae, 1881.

Mansi, Joannes, *Sacrorum Conciliorum Nova et Amplissima Collectio*, 53 vols., Paris-Arnhem-Leipzig, 1901-1927.

Monita ad Missionarios Provinciae Nankinensis, Zi-ka-wey, 1899.

Theodosiani Libri XVI cum Constitutionibus Sirmondianis, ed. Th. Mommsen, Berolini, 1905.

Thesaurus Resolutionum Sacrae Congregationis Concilii, 167 vols., Romae, 1718-1908.

AUTHORS

Abbas Antiquus, *In Libros Decretalium aurei Commentarii*, Venetiis, 1588.

Ayrinhac, H. A., *General Legislation in the New Code of Canon Law*, New York, 1923.

———, *Marriage Legislation in the New Code of Canon Law*, New York, 1918.

[Bachofen], Charles Augustine, *A Commentary on the New Code of Canon Law*, 4 ed., 8 vols., St. Louis, 1918-1929.

———, *Rights and Duties of Ordinaries according to the Code and Apostolic Faculties*, St. Louis, 1924.

Ballerini, Antonius, *S. Ambrosii Opera Omnia*, 6 vols., Milan, 1875.

Ballerini, A.–Palmieri, D., *Opus Theologicum Morale*, 3 ed., 7 vols., Prati, 1898-1901.

Beda Venerabilis, *Opera Quae Supersunt Omnia*, edidit J. A. Giles, Londoni, 1843.

Benedictus XIV, *De Synodo Dioecesana*, 2 vols., Romae, 1806.

Berardi, Carolus, *Gratiani Canones Genuini ab Apocryphis Discreti, Corrupti ad emendationem Codicum Fidem Exacti, Difficiliores Commoda interpretatione illustrati*, 4 vols., Venetiis, 1777.

Bernardini a Piconio, *Opera Omnia,* Tomus IV, Parisiis, 1872.

Bernardus Papiensis, *Summa Decretalium,* ed. Th. Laspeyres, Ratisbonae, 1860.

Billot, Ludovicus, *De Ecclesiae Sacramentis Commentarius in Tertiam Partem S. Thomae,* 2 ed., 2 vols., Romae, 1897.

Billuart, Carolus, *Cursus Theologiae iuxta Mentem Divi Thomae,* 20 vols., Parisiis, 1827-1831.

Blat, Albertus, *Commentarium Textus Codicis Iuris Canonici,* 6 vols., vol. III, *De Sacramentis,* Romae, 1921-1927.

Brunnemann, Joannes, *Commentarius in Codicem Justinianeum,* 2 vols., Coloniae Allobrogum, 1771.

Buckland, W. W., *A Text-book of Roman Law,* Cambridge, 1921.

Cajetan, Thomas de Vio, *Epistolae Pauli et aliorum Apostolorum ad graecam veritatem castigatae,* Venetiis, 1531.

Calmet, Augustinus, *Commentarius Literalis in Omnes Libros Veteris et Novi Testamenti,* ed. Latina a J. D. Mansi, 8 vols., Venetiis, 1754-1756.

Cappello, Felix M., *Tractatus Canonico-Moralis De Sacramentis,* vol. III, *De Matrimonio,* 2 ed., Romae, 1927.

Catholic Encyclopedia, 15 vols., New York, 1907-1912.

Cerato, Prosdocimus, *Matrimonium a Codice I. C. Integre Desumptum,* 4 ed., Patavii, 1927.

Chelodi, Joannes, *Ius Matrimoniale iuxta Codicem Iuris Canonici,* 3 ed., Tridenti, 1921.

Cogliolo, Pietro, *Manuale delle Fonti del Diritto Romano,* 2 ed., Torino, 1911.

Corluy, Joseph, *Spicilegium,* Tomus II, Gandavi, 1884.

Cornelius a Lapide, *Commentarius in Omnes Divi Pauli Epistolas,* 2 ed., Jerome Albritius, Venetiis, 1717.

Cornely, Rudolphus, *Commentarius in S. Pauli Apostoli Epistolas (Cursus Scripturae Sacrae)*, Tomus II, *Prior Epistola ad Corinthios,* Parisiis, 1890.

Cosci, Christopher, *De Separatione Tori Conjugalis tam nullo existente seu Soluto quam salvo Vinculo Matrimonii eiusque Effectibus,* 4 ed., Florentiae, 1856.

D'Annibale, Josephus, *Summula Theologiae Moralis,* 3 ed., 3 vols., 1892.

De Angelis, Philippus, *Praelectiones Iuris Canonici, ad Methodum Decretalium Gregorii IX Exactae*, 6 vols., Romae, 1880.

De Becker, Julius, *De Sponsalibus et Matrimonio Praelectiones Canonicae*, Bruxellis, 1896.

De Coninck, Aegidius, *De Sacramentis et Censuris*, 2 ed., 2 vols., Antverpiae, 1619.

De Justis, Vincentius, *De Dispensationibus Matrimonialibus Tractatus in tres libros digestus*, Lucae, 1726.

De Labriolle, Pierre, *The History and Literature of Christianity from Tertullian to Boethius*, translation by H. Wilson, New York, 1925.

De Smet, Aloysius, *Tractatus Theologico-Canonicus de Sponsalibus et Matrimonio*, 4 ed., Brugis, 1927.

Durandus a Sancto Porciano, *In Petri Lombardi Sententias Theologicas Commentariorum libri IV*, Venetiis, 1586.

Edersheim, Alfred, *Sketches of Jewish Life in the Days of Christ*, Boston, 1874.

Esmein, A., *Le Mariage en Droit Canonique*, 2 vols., Paris, 1891.

Estius, Gulielmus, *In Quatuor Libros Sententiarum Commentaria*, 4 vols., Parisiis, 1680.

Fahrner, Ignaz, *Geschichte des Unauflöslichkeitsprinzips und der vollkommenen Scheidung der Ehe im kanonischen Recht.*, Freiburg im Breisgau, 1903.

Farrugia, P. Nicolaus, *De Matrimonio et Causis Matrimonialibus, tractatus canonico-moralis iuxta Codicem Iuris Canonici*, Romae, 1924.

Feije, Henricus, *De Impedimentis et Dispensationibus Matrimonialibus*, 3 ed., Lovanii, 1885.

Fletcher, Margaret, *Christian Feminism, A Charter of Rights and Duties*, London, 1915.

Frassen, Claudius, *Scotus Academicus seu Universa Doctoris Subtilis Theologica Dogmatica*, 12 vols., Romae, 1723.

Funk, Francis Xavier, *A Manual of Church History*, translated from the German by P. Perciballi, edited by W. H. Kent, 2 vols., London, 1914.

Gasparri, Petrus, *Tractatus Canonicus de Matrimonio*, 3 ed., 2 vols., Parisiis, 1904.

Gigot, Francis E., *Christ's Teaching Concerning Divorce in the New Testament*, New York, 1912.

Giraldi, Ubaldus, *Expositio Iuris Pontificii*, nova Romana editio, Romae, 1829-1830.

Gothofredus, Dionysius, *Corpus Iuris Civilis Romani, in quo Institutiones, Digesta ad Codicem Florentinum Emendata, Codex Item et Novellae, cum Notis Integris*, 9 ed., 2 vols., Coloniae Munatianae, 1781.

Gothofredus, Jacobus, *Codex Theodosianus cum Perpetuis Commentariis*, 6 vols., Lipsiae, 1736.

Grandclaude, E., *Jus Canonicum iuxta Ordinem Decretalium*, 3 vols., Parisiis, 1882.

Hildenbrand, Carl, *Untersuchungen über die germanischen Pönitentialbücher*, Würzburg, 1851.

Hostiensis (Henricus de Segusio), *Commentaria in V Libros Decretalium*, 3 vols., Venetiis, 1581.

Howard, George Elliot, *The History of Matrimonial Institutions*, 3 vols., Chicago, 1904.

Hurter, H., *Theologiae Dogmaticae*, 6 ed., 3 vols., Oeniponte, 1889.

Iglesias, *Brevis Commentarius in Facultates quas S. C. de Prop. Fide dare solet Missionariis*, Taurini-Romae, 1924.

Jemolo, Arthur, "Il Privilegio Paolino dal principio del secolo XI agli albori del XV, *Studi Sassaresi*, II (1923), 243-335.

Kenrick, Francis P., *Theologia Moralis*, 2 vols., Mechliniae, 1861.

Könings, Antonius, *Theologia Moralis*, 7 ed., 2 vols., Neo-Eboraci, 1889.

Könings, A.–Putzer, J., *Commentarium in Facultates Apostolicas*, 3 ed., Ilchestriae, 1893.

Lancelotti, Giovanni, *Institutiones Iuris Canonici*, Lugduni, 1579.

Leage, R. W., *Roman Private Law*, London, 1924.

Leibell, J. F., *Readings in Ethics*, Chicago, 1926.

Lemhkuhl, Augustinus, *Theologia Moralis,* 3 ed., 2 vols., Friburgi Brisgoviae, 1886.

Le Plat, J., *Monumenta ad historiam Concilii Tridentini,* 7 vols., Lovanii, 1781.

MacRory, Joseph, *The Epistles of St. Paul to the Corinthians,* St. Louis, 1915.

Mansella, Joseph, *De Impedimentis Matrimonium Dirimentibus ac de Processu Iudiciali in Causis Matrimonialibus,* Romae, 1881.

McHugh, John–Callan, Charles, *Catechism of the Council of Trent for Parish Priests,* New York, 1923.

M'Clymont, J. A., *The New Testament and Its Writers,* New York, 1893.

Meyer, H. A. W., *A Commentary on the New Testament,* Edinburgh, 1883.

Michel, *Questions Pratiques sur le Mariage dans les Missions,* Maison-Carrèe, 1903.

Mielziner, A., *The Jewish Law of Marriage and Divorce,* New York, 1901.

Migne, Jacques Paul, *Patrologiae Cursus Completus, Series Graeca,* 161 vols., Parisiis, 1858-1864.

———, *Patrologiae Cursus Completus, Series Latina,* 221 vols., Parisiis, 1844-1855.

Muñiz, T., *Procedimientos Eclesiásticos,* 2 ed., 3 vols., Barcelona, 1928.

Nampon, A., *Catholic Doctrine as Defined by the Council of Trent,* translated from the French, Philadelphia, 1869.

Nicolaus de Tudeschis (Panormitanus), *Omnia Quae Extant Commentaria,* 8 vols., Venetiis, 1578.

Noldin, H., *De Principiis Theologiae Moralis, Scholarum Usui accommodavit, recognovit et emendavit A. Schmitt,* 20 ed., 3 vols., Oeniponte, 1929.

———, *De Iure Matrimoniali iuxta Codicem Iuris Canonici, Scholarum Usui Accommodavit,* Lincii, 1919.

Ojetti, Benedictus, *Synopsis Rerum Moralium et Juris Pontificii,* 3 ed., 4 vols., Romae, 1911.

Palmieri, Dominicus, *Tractatus de Matrimonio Christiano,* Romae, 1880.

Paucapalea, *Die Summa des Paucapalea über das Decretum Gratiani*, edited by J. F. Schulte, Giessen, 1890.

Perrone, Joannes, *De Matrimonio Christiano*, 3 vols., Leodii, 1861.

———, *Praelectiones Theologicae*, Tomus VIII, 2 ed., Romae, 1844.

Pesch, Christianus, *Tractatus Dogmatici*, 9 vols., Friburgi Brisgoviae, 1897.

Petrovits, Joseph J. C., *The New Church Law on Matrimony*, 2 ed., Philadelphia, 1926.

Petrus Lombardus, *Petri Lombardi Libri IV Sententiarum*, studio et cura PP. Collegii S. Bonaventurae in lucem editi, 2 ed., 2 vols., Ad Claras Aquas, 1916.

Pichler, Vitus, *Epitome Iuris Canonici*, 2 vols., Venetiis, 1755.

Pignatelli, Jacobus, *Consultationes Canonicae*, 11 vols., Coloniae Allobrogum, 1700.

Pirhing, Ernricus, *Jus Canonicum Nova Methodo Explicatum*, 2 vols., Dilingae, 1678.

Pontius, Basilius, *De Sacramento Matrimonii Tractatus cum Appendice de Matrimonio Catholici cum haeretico*, 2 ed., Bruxellis, 1627.

Prümmer, Dominicus, *Manuale Theologiae Moralis*, 2 & 3 ed., 3 vols., Friburgi Brisgoviae, 1923.

Raymundus de Peneforte, *Summa*, Veronae, 1744.

Reiffenstuel, Anacletus, *Jus Canonicum Universum*, 4 vols., Romae, 1838.

Richard, C. L., *Collectio Variorum dissertationum Casum Apostoli*, Leodii, 1779.

Roberti, Franciscus, *De Processibus*, 2 vols., Romae, 1926.

Robertus Flamesburiensis, *Summa de Matrimonio et usuris ex Roberti Poenitentiali*, edited by J. F. Schulte, Gissae, 1868.

Rolandus Bandinellus (Alexander III), *Die Summa Magistri Rolandi nachmals Papstes Alexander III*, edited by F. Thaner, Innsbruck, 1874.

Roskovany, Augustinus, *De Indissolubilitate Matrimonii*, Tomus II, Augustae Vindelicorum, 1840.

Rosset, M., *De Sacramento Matrimonii*, 6 vols., Parisiis, 1895-1896.

Rufinus, Magister, *Die Summa Decretorum des Magister Rufinus*, edited by H. Singer, Paderborn, 1902.

Rupprecht, Theodorus, *Notae Historicae in Universum Ius Canonicum*, Venetiis, 1764.

Sanchez, Thomas, *De Sancto Matrimonii Sacramento Disputationum, Tomi Tres*, Lugduni, 1669.

Santi, Franciscus, *Praelectiones Iuris Canonici*, 5 vols., Ratisbonae, 1884.

Sarpi, Paul, *Histoire du Concile de Trent*, translated from the Italian by Mothe-Josseval, Amsterdam, 1783.

Scavini, Petrus, *Theologia Moralis Universa ad Mentem S. Alphonsi M. de Ligorio*, 9 ed., 4 vols., Mediolani, 1869.

Schanz, Martin, *Geschichte der Römischen Litteratur bis zum Gesetzgebungswerk des Kaisers Justinian*, Tomus II, München, 1892.

Schenk, Francis J., *The Matrimonial Impediments of Mixed Religion and Disparity of Cult*, Washington, 1929.

Scherer, Rudolf Ritter von, *Handbuch des Kirchenrechts*, 2 vols., Graz, 1886-1898.

Schmalzgrueber, Franciscus, *Jus Ecclesiasticum Universum*, 12 vols., Romae, 1844.

Schulte, J. F., von, *Die Geschichte der Quellen und Literatur des Canonischen Rechts von Gratian bis Papst Gregor IX*, 3 vols., Stuttgart, 1875-1880.

———, *Lehrbuch des Katholischen Kirchenrechts*, Giessen, 1873.

———, *Die Glosse zum Dekret Gratian's von ihren Anflängen bis auf die jüngsten Ausgaben*, 4 ed., Vienna, 1872.

Sherman, C. P., *Roman Law in the Modern World*, 3 vols., New York, 1924.

Sirmond, Jacques, *Concilia antiqua Galliae cum Epistolis pontificum, principum constitutionibus et aliis Gallicanae eccl. monumentis*, 3 vols., Parisiis, 1629.

Smisniewicz, Leon, *Die Lehre von den Ehehindernissen bei Petrus Lombardus und bei seinen Kommentatoren: Albert d. Gr., Thomas v. Aquin, J. Bonaventura und J. D.*

Scotus, den Hauptvertretern der Hochscholastik, dargestellt nach Massgabe der vierfachen Kausalität der Ehe, Posen, 1917.

Sohm, Rudolph–Ledlie, J. C., *The Institutes, A Text-book of the History and System of Roman Private Law,* London, 1907.

Soto, Dominicus, *In Quartum* (quem vocant) *Sententiarum,* Tomi I, II, Venetiis, 1575.

Souter, Alexander, *A Study of Ambrosiaster,* Cambridge, 1905.

Sylvius, Franciscus, *Commentarius in Tertiam Partem S. Thomae Aquinatis et in ejusdem supplementum,* 2 ed., Duaci, 1622.

Tancredus, *Tancredi Summa de Matrimonio,* edited by A. Wunderlich, Gottingae, 1841.

Theodore of Canterbury, *Poenitentiales Theodori,* edited by Carl Hildenbrand, Würzburg, 1851.

Thomas Aquinas, *Summa Theologica,* 2 Roman edition, Romae, 1894.

———, *Commentaria in Omnes D. Pauli Apostoli Epistolas,* nova editio, Tomus I, Parisiis, 1870.

Tirini, Jacobus, *Commentarius in Universam S. Scripturam,* 5 vols., Taurini, 1882-1884.

Tixeront, J., *A Hand-book of Patrology,* translated from the 4. French edition, St. Louis, 1923.

Tournely, Honoratus, *Praelectiones Theologicae de Sacramento Matrimonii,* Tomus IX, Parisiis, 1765.

Van Steenkiste, J. A., *Commentarius in Omnes S. Pauli Epistolas,* 4 ed., Tomus I, Brugis, 1886.

Vecchiotti, S. M., *Tractatus Canonicus de Matrimonio,* Taurini, 1868.

Vermeersch, Arthurus, *Commentaria de Formulis Facultatum S. C. de Prop. Fide,* Brugis, 1922.

———, *De Casu Apostoli seu De Fidei Privilegio,* Brugis, 1911.

Vermeersch, A.–Creusen, J., *Epitome Iuris Canonici,* 3 ed., 3 vols., Mechliniae-Romae, 1927.

Vlaming, Th. M., *Praelectiones Iuris Matrimonii,* 3 ed., 2 vols., Bussum in Hollandia, 1921.

Vromant, G., *Facultates Apostolicae quas S. C. de Prop. Fide delegare solet Ordinariis Missionum, Commentaria in Formulam Tertiam*, Louvain, 1926.

Waterworth, J., *The Canons and Decrees of the Sacred and Oecumenical Council of Trent, with Essays on the External and Internal History of the Council*, London, 1848.

Wernz, Franciscus X., *Jus Decretalium*, 2 ed., 6 vols., Prati, 1912.

Wernz, F. X.–Vidal, Petrus, *Jus Canonicum ad Codicis Normam Exactum*, 3 vols., vol. V, *Ius Matrimoniale*, Romae, 1923-1928.

Westermarck, Edward, *The History of Human Marriage*, 5 ed., 3 vols., 1922.

Winslow, Francis Joseph, *Vicars and Prefects Apostolic*, Washington, 1924.

Wirceburgensis, *Theologia Dogmatica*, Tomus X, *De Sacramento Matrimonii*, 3 ed., 10 vols., Parisiis, 1880.

Zitelli, Zephyrinus, *De Dispensationibus Matrimonialibus recentissimas sac. urbis congreg. resolutiones Commentarii*, Romae, 1887.

PERIODICALS

American Ecclesiastical Review, The, Philadelphia, 1889-

L'Ami du Clergè, Langres.

Analecta Ecclesiastica, Romae, 1893-1911.

Apollinaris, Commentarium Iuridico-Canonicum, Romae, 1928-

Archiv für katholisches Kirchenrecht, Mainz, 1857-

Ephemerides Theologicae Lovanienses, Lovanii, 1924-

Gregorianum, Romae, 1920-

Homiletic and Pastoral Review, The, New York, 1900-

Jus Pontificium, Romae, 1921-

Nederlandsche katholieke Stemmen, Brugis, 1900-

Nouvelle Revue Théologique, Tournai, 1869-

Periodica de re canonica et morali utili praesertim Religiosis et Missionariis, Brugis, 1905-

Studi Sassaresi, Series Seconda, Vol. II, Sassari, 1923.

Theologisch-praktische Quartalschrift, Linz, 1832-

Zeitschrift für katholische Theologie, Innsbruck, 1877-

Universitas Catholica Americae

WASHINGTONII, D. C.

FACULTAS IURIS CANONICI

1931

No. 68

DEUS LUX MEA

TITULI

QUOS

AD DOCTORATUS GRADUM

IN

UTROQUE IURE

APUD UNIVERSITATEM CATHOLICAM AMERICAE

CONSEQUENDUM

PUBLICE PROPUGNABIT

DONALDUS JOSEPHUS GREGORY

SACERDOS ARCHIDIOECESIS SANCTI PAULI

IURIS UTRIUSQUE LICENTIATUS

HORA IX A. M. DIE XXVII MAII A. D. MCMXXXI

TITULI

DE IURE CANONICO

I. De Dissertatione.
II. De Historia Iuris Canonici.
III. Canones 1–7 De Ambitu Codicis.
IV. Canones 8–24 De Legibus Ecclesiasticis.
V. Canones 25–30 De Consuetudine.
VI. Canones 31–35 De Temporis Supputatione.
VII. Canones 36–62 De Rescriptis.
VIII. Canones 63–79 De Privilegiis.
IX. Canones 80–86 De Dispensationibus.
X. Canones 87–107 De Personis in Genere.
XI. Canones 108–110 De Clericis in Genere.
XII. Canones 111–117 De Clericorum Adscriptione Alicui Dioecesi.
XIII. Canones 118–123 De Iuribus et Privilegiis Clericorum.
XIV. Canones 124–144 De Obligationibus Clericorum.
XV. Canones 145–195 De Officiis Ecclesiasticis.
XVI. Canones 196–210 De Potestate Ordinaria et Delegata.
XVII. Canones 211–214 De Reductione Clericorum ad Statum Laicalem.
XVIII. Canones 487–498 De Notione Religionis, et de Erectione et Suppressione Religionis, Provinciae, Domus.
XIX. Canones 499–517 De Superioribus et de Capitulis.
XX. Canones 518–530 De Confessariis et Cappellanis.
XXI. Canones 531–537 De Bonis Temporalibus Eorumque Administratione.

XXII. Canones 539–541 De Postulatu.
XXIII. Canones 542–552 De Novitiatu et de Requisitis ad Eius Admissionem.
XXIV. Canones 553–571 De Novitiorum Institutione.
XXV. Canones 572–586 De Professione Religiosa.
XXVI. Canones 587–591 De Ratione Studiorum in Religionibus Clericalibus.
XXVII. Canones 592–612 De Obligationibus Religiosorum.
XXVIII. Canones 613–625 De Privilegiis Religiosorum.
XXIX. Canones 637–645 De Egressu e Religione.
XXX. Canones 646–672 De Dimissione Religiosorum.
XXXI. Canones 673–681 De Societatibus sive Virorum sive Mulierum in Communi Viventium sine Votis.
XXXII. Canones 1012–1018 De Matrimonio in Genere.
XXXIII. Canones 1019–1034 De Iis Quae Matrimonii Celebrationi Praemitti Debent.
XXXIV. Canones 1035–1057 De Impedimentis in Genere.
XXXV. Canones 1058–1066 De Impedimentis Impedientibus.
XXXVI. Canones 1067–1080 De Impedimentis Dirimentibus.
XXXVII. Canones 1081–1093 De Consensu Matrimoniali.
XXXVIII. Canones 1094–1103 De Forma Celebrationis Matrimonii.
XXXIX. Canones 1104–1107 De Matrimonio Conscientiae.
XL. Canones 1108–1109 De Tempore et Loco Celebrationis Matrimonii.
XLI. Canones 1110–1117 De Matrimonii Effectibus.
XLII. Canones 1118–1132 De Separatione Coniugum.
XLIII. Canones 1133–1141 De Matrimonii Convalidatione.
XLIV. Canones 1552–1568 De Notione Iudicii et Foro Competenti.

XLV. Canones 1569–1607 De Variis Tribunalium Gradibus et Speciebus.
XLVI. Canones 1608–1645 De Disciplina in Tribunalibus Servanda.
XLVII. Canones 1646–1666 De Partibus in Causa.
XLVIII. Canones 1667–1705 De Actionibus et Exceptionibus.
XLIX. Canones 1706–1725 De Causae Introductione.
L. Canones 1742–1746 De Interrogationibus Partibus in Iudicio Faciendis.
LI. Canones 1747–1749 De Probationibus in Genere.
LII. Canones 1754–1791 De Testibus et Attestationibus.
LIII. Canones 1792–1805 De Peritis.
LIV. Canones 1812–1824 De Probatione per Instrumenta.
LV. Canones 1868–1877 De Sententia.
LVI. Canones 1960–1992 De Causis Matrimonialibus.
LVII. Canones 2142–2194 De Modo Procedendi in Nonnullis Expediendis Negotiis vel Sanctionibus Poenalibus Applicandis.
LVIII. Canones 2195–2199 De Natura Delicti Eiusque Divisione.
LIX. Canones 2199–2211 De Imputabilitate Delicti, de Causis Illam Aggravantibus vel Minuentibus et de Iuridicis Delicti Effectibus.
LX. Canones 2212–2213 De Conatu Delicti.
LXI. Canones 2214–2240 De Poenis in Genere.
LXII. Canones 2241–2285 De Poenis Medicinalibus seu de Censuris.
LXIII. Canones 2286–2305 De Poenis Vindicativis.
LXIV. Canones 2306–2311 De Remediis Poenalibus.
LXV. Canones 2312–2313 De Poenitentiis.

DE IURE ROMANO

LXVI. De Fontibus Iuris Romani.
LXVII. De Periodis Iuris Romani.

LXVIII. De Evolutione Iuris Romani.
LXIX. De Codificatione Justinianea.
LXX. De Interpolationibus.
LXXI. De Criteriis Interpolationes Cognoscendi.
LXXII. De Variis Interpretationis Scholis.
LXXIII. De Persona.
LXXIV. De Statu Libertatis.
LXXV. De Personis in Mancipii Causa.
LXXVI. De Legibus *Aelia Sentia, Fufia Caninia, Junia Norbana.*
LXXVII. De Statu Civitatis.
LXXVIII. De Capitis Diminutione.
LXXIX. De Statu Familiae.
LXXX. De Patria Potestate.
LXXXI. De Adoptione et Adrogatione.
LXXXII. De Iustis Nuptiis.
LXXXIII. De Tutela.
LXXXIV. De Cura.
LXXXV. De Rerum Acquisitionis Modis.
LXXXVI. De Iure Dominii.
LXXXVII. De Iure Possessionis.
LXXXVIII. De Iure in Re Aliena.
LXXXIX. De Successione Universali.
XC. De Obligationibus in Genere.
XCI. De Obligationibus Extra Contractuales.
XCII. De Furtu.
XCIII. De Damno Iniuria Dato.
XCIV. De Iniuria.
XCV. De Lege Aquilia.
XCVI. De Lege Publica Romana.
XCVII. De Fontibus Legum Constitutionalium.
XCVIII. De Regno.
XCIX. De Republica.
C. De Imperio.

VIDIT FACULTAS:

VALENTINUS T. SCHAAF, O.F.M., S.T.B., J.C.D., *Vice-Decanus.*

LUDOVICUS H. MOTRY, S.T.D., J.C.D., *a Secretis.*

FRANCISCUS J. LARDONE, S.T.D., J.U.D.

VIDIT RECTOR MAGNIFICUS UNIVERSITATIS:

JACOBUS HUGO RYAN, Ph.D., S.T.D., LL.D., Litt.D.

BIOGRAPHICAL NOTE

Donald Joseph Gregory was born in Chicago, Illinois, on July 11, 1903. He attended the parochial school of St. Mel and his preparatory training was received at Quigley Preparatory Seminary (Chicago) and St. Mary's College (Kansas). His philosophical and theological studies were made at the St. Paul Seminary (St. Paul), and upon their completion he received the degree of Bachelor of Sacred Theology from the Catholic University of America. He was ordained to the Holy Priesthood on June 10, 1928. In September of the same year he was sent by Archbishop Austin Dowling to the Catholic University to pursue a graduate course of studies in Canon Law.

CATHOLIC UNIVERSITY OF AMERICA

CANON LAW STUDIES

1. FRERIKS, REV. CELESTINE A., C.PP.S., J.C.D., Religious Congregations in Their External Relations, 121 pp., 1916.
2. GALLIHER, REV. DANIEL M., O.P., J.C.D., Canonical Elections, 117 pp., 1917.
3. BORKOWSKI, REV. AURELIUS L., O.F.M., J.C.D., De Confraternitatibus Ecclesiasticis, 136 pp. 1918.
4. CASTILLO, REV. CAYO, J.C.D., Disertacion Historico-canonica sobre la Potestad del Cabildo en Sede Vacante o Impedida del Vicario Capitular, 99 pp., 1919 (1918).
5. KUBELBECK, REV. WILLIAM J., S.T.B., J.C.D., The Sacred Penitentiaria and Its Relations to Faculties of Ordinaries and Priests, 129 pp., 1918.
6. PETROVITS, REV. JOSEPH J. C., S.T.D., J.C.D., The New Church Law on Matrimony, X-461 pp., 1919.
7. HICKEY, REV. JOHN J., S.T.B., J.C.D., Irregularities and Simple Impediments in the New Code of Canon Law, 100 pp., 1920.
8. KLEKOTKA, REV. PETER J., S.T.B., J.C.D., Diocesan Consultors, 179 pp., 1920.
9. WANNENMACHER, REV. FRANCIS, J.C.D., The Evidence in Ecclesiastical Procedure Affecting the Marriage Bond, 1920. (Not Printed.)
10. GOLDEN, REV. HENRY FRANCIS, J.C.D., Parochial Benefices in the New Code, IV-119 pp., 1921. (Printed 1925.)
11. KOUDELKA, REV. CHARLES J., J.C.D., Pastors, Their Rights and Duties According to the New Code of Canon Law, 211 pp., 1921.
12. MELO, REV. ANTONIUS, O.F.M., J.C.D., De Exemptione Regularium, X-188 pp., 1921.

13. SCHAAF, REV. VALENTINE THEODORE, O.F.M., S.T.B., J.C.D., The Cloister, X-180 pp., 1921.
14. BURKE, REV. THOMAS JOSEPH, S.T.B., J.C.D., Competence in Ecclesiastical Tribunals, IV-117 pp., 1922.
15. LEECH, REV. GEORGE LEO, J.C.D., A Comparative Study of the Constitution "Apostolicae Sedis" and the "Codex Juris Canonici," 179 pp., 1922.
16. MOTRY, REV. HUBERT LOUIS, S.T.D., J.C.D., Diocesan Faculties according to the Code of Canon Law, II-167 pp., 1922.
17. MURPHY, REV. GEORGE LAWRENCE, J.C.D., Delinquencies and Penalties in the Administration and the Reception of the Sacraments, IV-121 pp., 1923.
18. O'REILLY, REV. JOHN ANTHONY, S.T.B., J.C.D., Ecclesiastical Sepulture in the New Code of Canon Law, II-129 pp., 1923.
19. MICHALICKA, REV. WENCESLAS CYRILL, O.S.B., J.C.D., Judicial Procedure in Dismissal of Clerical Exempt Religious, 107 pp., 1923.
20. DARGIN, REV. EDWARD VINCENT, S.T.B., J.C.D., Reserved Cases According to the Code of Canon Law, IV-103 pp., 1924.
21. GODFREY, REV. JOHN A., S.T.B., J.C.D., The Right of Patronage According to the Code of Canon Law, 153 pp., 1924.
22. HAGEDORN, REV. FRANCIS EDWARD, J.C.D., General Legislation on Indulgences, II-154 pp., 1924.
23. KING, REV. JAMES IGNATIUS, J.C.D., The Administration of the Sacraments to Dying Non-Catholics, V-141 pp., 1924.
24. WINSLOW, REV. FRANCIS JOSEPH, A.F.M., J.C.D., Vicars and Prefects Apostolic, IV-149 pp., 1924.
25. CORREA, REV. JOSE SERVELION, S.T.L., J.C.D., La Potestad Legislativa de la Iglesia Catolica, IV-127 pp., 1925.
26. DUGAN, REV. HENRY FRANCIS, M.A., J. C.D., The Judiciary Department of the Diocesan Curia, 87 pp., 1925.

27. KELLER, REV. CHARLES FREDERICK, S.T.D., J.C.D., Mass Stipends, 167 pp., 1925.
28. PASCHANG, REV. JOHN LINUS, J.C.D., The Sacramentals According to the Code of Canon Law, 129 pp., 1925.
29. PIONTEK, REV. CYRILLUS, O.F.M., S.T.B., J.C.D., De Indulto Exclaustrationis necnon Saecularizationis, XIII-289 pp., 1925.
30. KEARNEY, REV. RICHARD JOSEPH, S.T.B., J.C.D., Sponsors at Baptism According to the Code of Canon Law, IV-127 pp., 1925.
31. BARTLETT, REV. CHESTER JOSEPH, A.M., LL.B., J.C.D., The Tenure of Parochial Property in the United States of America, V-108 pp., 1926.
32. KILKER, REV. ADRIAN JEROME, J.C.D., Extreme Unction, V-425 pp., 1926.
33. MCCORMICK, REV. ROBERT EMMETT, J.C.D., Confessors of Religious, VIII-266 pp., 1926.
34. MILLER, REV. NEWTON THOMAS, J.C.D., Founded Masses According to the Code of Canon Law, VII-93 pp., 1926.
35. ROELKER, REV. EDWARD G., S.T.D., J.C.D., Principles of Privilege According to the Code of Canon Law, XI-166 pp., 1926.
36. BAKALARCZYK, REV. RICHARDUS, M.I.C., J.U.D., De Novitiatu, VIII-208 pp., 1927.
37. PIZZUTI, REV. LAWRENCE, O.F.M., J.U.L., De Parochis Religiosis, 1927. (Not Printed.)
38. BLILEY, REV. NICHOLAS MARTIN, O.S.B., J.C.D., Altars According to the Code of Canon Law, XIX-132 pp., 1927.
39. BROWN, BRENDAN FRANCIS, A.B. LL.M. J.U.D., The Canonical Juristic Personality with Special Reference to its Status in the United States of America, V-212 pp., 1927.
40. CAVANAUGH, REV. WILLIAM THOMAS, C.P., J.U.D., The Reservation of the Blessed Sacrament, VIII-101 pp., 1927.

41. DOHENY, REV. WILLIAM J., C.S.C., A.B., J.U.D., Church Property: Modes of Acquisition, X-118 pp., 1927.
42. FELDHAUS, REV. ALOYSIUS H., C.PP.S., J.C.D., Oratories, IX-141 pp., 1927.
43. KELLY, REV. JAMES PATRICK, A.B., J.C.D., The Jurisdiction of the Simple Confessor, X-208 pp., 1927.
44. NEUBERGER, REV. NICHOLAS J., J.C.D., Canon 6 or the Relation of the Codex Juris Canonici to the Preceding Legislation, V-95 pp., 1927.
45. O'KEEFFE, REV. GERALD MICHAEL, J.C.D., Matrimonial Dispensations, Powers of Bishops, Priests, and Confessors, VIII-232 pp., 1927.
46. QUIGLEY, REV. JOSEPH, A.M., A.B., J.C.D., Condemned Societies, 139 pp., 1927.
47. ZAPLOTNIK, REV. IOANNES LEO, J.C.D., D. Vicariis Foraneis, X-142, 1927.
48. DUSKIE, REV. JOHN ALOYSIUS, A.B., J.C.D., The Canonical Status of the Orientals in the United States, VIII-196 pp., 1928.
49. HYLAND, REV. FRANCIS EDWARD, J.C.D., Excommunication, Its Nature, Historical Development and Effects, VIII-181 pp., 1928.
50. REINMANN, REV. GERALD JOSEPH, O.M.C., J.C.D., The Third Order Secular of Saint Francis, 201 pp., 1928.
51. SCHENK, REV. FRANCIS J., J.C.D., The Matrimonial Impediments of Mixed Religion and Disparity of Cult. XVI-318 pp., 1929.
52. COADY, REV. JOHN JOSEPH, S.T.D., J.U.D., A.M., The Appointment of Pastors, VIII-150 pp., 1929.
53. KAY, REV. THOMAS HENRY, J.C.D., Competence in Matrimonial Procedure, VIII-164 pp., 1929.
54. TURNER, REV. SIDNEY JOSEPH, C.P., J.U.D., The Vow of Poverty, XLIX-217 pp., 1929.
55. KEARNEY, REV. RAYMOND A., A.B., S.T.D., J.C.D., The Principles of Delegation, VII-149 pp., 1929.

56. CONRAN, REV. EDWARD JAMES, A.B., J.C.D., The Interdict, V-163 pp., 1930.
57. O'NEILL, REV. WILLIAM H., J.C.D., Papal Rescripts of Favor, VII-219 pp., 1930.
58. BASTNAGEL, REV. CLEMENT VINCENT, J.U.D., The Appointment of Parochial Adjutants and Assistants, XV-262 pp., 1930.
59. FERRY, REV. WILLIAM A., A.B., J.C.D., Stole Fees, X-108 pp., 1930.
60. COSTELLO, REV. JOHN MICHAEL, A.B., J.C.D., Domicile and Quasi-Domicile, VII-201 pp., 1930.
61. KREMER, REV. MICHAEL NICHOLAS, A.B., S.T.B., J.C.D., Church Support in the United States, VI-137 pp., 1930.
62. ANGULO, REV. LUIS, C.M., J.C.L., Legislación de la Iglesia Católica sobre la intención en la aplicación de la Misa, 1931.
63. FREY, REV. WOLFGANG, O.S.B., A.B., J.C.L., The Act of Religious Profession, 1931.
64. ROBERTS, REV. JAMES BRENDAN, A.B., J.C.L., The Banns of Marriage, 1931.
65. RYDER, REV. RAYMOND ALOYSIUS, A.B., J.C.L., Simony, 1931.
66. CAMPAGNA, REV. MICHAEL ANGELO, Ph.B., J.U.L., Il Vicario Generale del Vescovo, 1931.
67. COX, REV. JOSEPH GODFREY, A.B., J.C.L., The Administration of Seminaries, 1931.
68. GREGORY, REV. DONALD JOSEPH, S.T.B., J.U.L., The Pauline Privilege, 1931.
69. DONOHUE, REV. JOHN FRANCIS, A.M., J.C.L., The Impediment of Crime, 1931.
70. DOOLEY, REV. EUGENE A., O.M.I., J.C.L., Church Law on Sacred Relics, 1931.

www.ingramcontent.com/pod-product-compliance
Lightning Source LLC
LaVergne TN
LVHW050231080826
844660LV00012B/512

* 9 7 8 0 8 1 3 2 2 2 5 7 8 *